T0368137

Ian Steedman
Paul Sweezy
Erik Olin Wright
Geoff Hodgson
Pradeep Bandyopadhyay
Makoto Itoh
Michel De Vroey
G.A. Cohen
Susan Himmelweit
Simon Mohun
Anwar Shaikh

Verso

The Value Controversy

**British Library
Cataloguing in Publication Data**

Steedman, Ian
  The value controversy
    1. Value   2. Marxian economics
    I. Title   II. Sweezy, Paul
    335.4'12   HB203

    ISBN: 978-0-86091-738-0

© Verso Editions and NLB, 1981,
  for the collection

Verso Editions and NLB
15 Greek Street, London W1

Photoset in Monophoto Times New Roman by
Servis Filmsetting Ltd, Manchester

Printed and bound by
Billing and Sons Ltd, Worcester

Contents

Editorial Note

One of the fruits of the revival of socialist economic theory over the past decade has been a wide-ranging debate about the validity of Karl Marx's labour theory of value. At the heart of the discussion stands the theoretical work of Piero Sraffa, in particular his *Production of Commodities by Means of Commodities*, and the conclusions drawn from it by such economists as Ian Steedman in his *Marx After Sraffa* (1977). Initially confined to a relatively narrow grouping of specialists, the controversy about value theory has since spread to wider circles of the left. But although general awareness that the stakes of the dispute are of concern to all socialists is now extensive, understanding of the issues involved has remained more restricted than need be. This volume is intended to present a comprehensive yet accessible overview of the discussion to date.

The idea of the collection arose out of a conference held in London in November 1978 under the joint auspices of the *New Left Review*, the *Cambridge Journal of Economics*, and the Conference of Socialist Economists, which publishes the journal *Capital and Class*. Several of the essays printed here are expanded versions of papers presented to that conference; others were produced in response to conference papers; finally, several were written independently of the conference and its sequels.

Although every effort has been made to render the present volume representative of all major points of view and reflective of all the central issues involved, there is no suggestion that this debate is in any way completed. On the contrary, the controversy is continuing, the many participants striving to further clarify both their positions and the scope of the discussion and its implications for Marxism. In that sense, this volume is itself a contribution to an ongoing debate.

VERSO – NLB

7

8

Bibliographical Note

'Ricardo, Marx, Sraffa', by Ian Steedman, is an expanded version of an article first published in the *New Statesman*, 5 January 1979.

'Marxian Value Theory and Crises', by Paul Sweezy, is a somewhat expanded and edited version of a paper presented to the November 1978 London conference on value theory. It was first published in *Monthly Review*, July–August 1979.

'The Value Controversy and Social Research', by Erik Olin Wright, based on a presentation to the London conference, was first published in *New Left Review*, 116, July–August 1979.

'Value, Production, and Exchange', by Michel De Vroey, was first published as 'A Restatement of the Marxian Labour Theory of Value', Working Paper no. 8005, Université Catholique de Louvain, 1980.

'The Labour Theory of Value and the Concept of Exploitation', by G.A. Cohen, first appeared in *Philosophy & Public Affairs*, 8, no. 4, summer 1979, © Princeton University Press. Reprinted by permission of Princeton University Press.

'Real Abstractions and Anomalous Assumptions', by Susan Himmelweit and Simon Mohun, appeared in an earlier version in *Capital and Class*, 6, autumn 1978.

'Labour and Profits', by Geoff Hodgson; 'In Defence of a Post-Sraffian Approach', by Pradeep Bandyopadhyay; 'Reconsiderations', by Erik Olin Wright; 'Joint Production: The Issues After Steedman', by Makoto Itoh and 'The Poverty of Algebra', by Anwar Shaikh, appear here for the first time.

Biographical Note

Ian Steedman, author of *Marx After Sraffa*, is Professor of Economics at Manchester University.

Paul Sweezy, author of *The Theory of Capitalist Development* and co-author of *Monopoly Capital*, is an editor of *Monthly Review*.

Erik Olin Wright, author of *Class, Crisis and the State*, is Associate Professor of Sociology at the University of Wisconsin.

Geoff Hodgson, author of *Socialism and Parliamentary Democracy, Capitalism, Value and Exploitation*, and *Labour at the Crossroads*, is Principal Lecturer in economics at Newcastle upon Tyne Polytechnic.

Pradeep Bandyopadhyay is Associate Professor of Sociology at Trent University, Ontario, Canada.

Makoto Itoh, author of *Value and Crisis*, teaches economics at the University of Tokyo.

Michel De Vroey is at the Institut des Sciences Economiques, Université Catholique de Louvain, Belgium.

G.A. Cohen, author of *Karl Marx's Theory of History: A Defence*, is Reader in Philosophy, University College, London.

Susan Himmelweit teaches economics at the Open University.

Simon Mohun teaches economics at Queen Mary College, University of London.

Anwar Shaikh is Associate Professor of Economics at the New School for Social Research, New York.

Ricardo, Marx, Sraffa

Ian Steedman

All serious political thought, of whatever hue, is based, whether more or less explicitly, on theoretical foundations, of which theories of political economy always constitute an important part. Moreover, some attitude—positive or negative, overt or latent—towards Marx's political economy always has a place in any political view to the left of centre. This essay therefore sets out, very briefly, some recent arguments which demonstrate that certain central aspects of Marx's political economy are entirely *independent* of any 'labour theory of value'. Since the ineradicable difficulties involved in labour theories of value have always, and quite reasonably, been regarded as barriers to the serious consideration of Marx's political economy, it will be clear that this demonstration is of considerable significance.

Some Marxist economists will, of course, be reluctant to concede the irrelevance of the 'labour theory of value', but it is now generally recognized that the demonstration of that irrelevance is logically impeccable (some remaining doubts about the *significance* of the argument will be mentioned below). I shall set out the more important of the 'non-labour theory of value' propositions, then briefly consider certain questions about the proposed approach, and, finally, hint at some wider implications.

Brief Historical Note

The force of the argument presented below will be appreciated more fully if certain historical points are borne in mind. The criticisms of Marx's political economy which have been most influential are perhaps those of the Austrian economist E. von Böhm-Bawerk. (Although those of the English economist P.H. Wicksteed, who converted Bernard Shaw to 'Jevonian' economics, played an important role in Fabian thought.) The criticisms of both Böhm-Bawerk and Wicksteed were launched from the standpoint of an economic theory fundamentally different from that of Marx (and from that of the physiocrats, Adam Smith, and Ricardo, upon whose works Marx drew). Marx, like his classical predecessors, conceived the economic process as involving the creation of a *surplus* product, over and above the needs of input replacement and workers' consumption, that was appropriated as profit, interest, and rent. Böhm-Bawerk and Wicksteed, by contrast, conceived that process as involving production through the mutual co-operation of various 'factors', there being *no* element of asymmetry as between labour and the other 'factors'. Criticism of Marx's entire analysis thus became strongly associated both with the rejection of the 'labour theory of value' and with the adoption of this alternative view of the economic process.

Yet, although less widely noticed, criticism of Marx's arguments was also made by authors who did not seek completely to overturn the surplus-appropriation view of the economic process. Thus the Russian economist V.K. Dmitriev, in 1898, and the Polish statistician-economist L. von Bortkiewicz, in 1906–7, whilst working within the surplus approach, showed how Marx's analysis of profits and prices was flawed and indicated how it might be corrected without abandoning that general approach. The contributions of both Dmitriev and Bortkiewicz were nevertheless ignored for many years, despite Paul Sweezy's valiant attempt, in his *Theory of Capitalist Development* (1942), to gain serious attention for the work of Bortkiewicz.

In 1960 Piero Sraffa published his *Production of Commodities by Means of Commodities*, the explicit purpose of which was to lay the foundation for an internal-logical critique of all those economic theories that presupposed the existence of a 'factor of production', capital, conceived as a given aggregate value.

It was soon realized that Sraffa's work was not only successful in its explicit purpose but also provided a basis for a definitive demonstration that the theoretical analysis of wages, profits, and prices, within a surplus approach, was entirely independent of any 'labour theory of value' and, indeed, that any labour theory is necessarily a barrier to the development of a surplus-based theory. Consequently, the frequent identification of opposition to a 'labour theory of value' with opposition to a 'surplus-appropriation' theory of the economic process—an identification that grew quite naturally out of the work of Böhm-Bawerk and Wicksteed—can now be clearly seen to be mistaken. Rejection of any kind of 'labour theory of value' can, following the work of Dmitriev, Bortkiewicz, and Sraffa, be rooted firmly *within the surplus approach itself.*

The Surplus Approach After Sraffa

Before setting out what I take to be the modern surplus approach and the associated rejection of the 'labour theory of value', I should perhaps declare my interest: I have been involved to a significant extent in defending and expounding such views, principally in my book, *Marx After Sraffa* (New Left Books, 1977). I should thus make it clear both that I am not a neutral observer of the recent debates and that the results presented below are in no sense my results.

Amongst non-economists, it is often assumed that a 'labour theory of value' amounts to the proposition that 'under normal capitalist conditions, the relative prices of commodities will tend to equal the relative quantities of labour-time required for the production of those commodities'. It must therefore be said at once both that under that interpretation no labour theory of value would merit ten seconds' consideration and that no serious economist has ever entertained such a theory. Neither Adam Smith, nor Ricardo, nor Marx asserted that commodities would tend to exchange in proportion to their labour contents, under developed capitalist conditions; indeed, each of them expressly denied it. In particular, Marx went out of his way, in *Capital* Volume 3, part II, to explain just *why* commodities would not exchange in such proportions. It so happens that Marx's explanation was faulty, but what is significant, at this point, is that he sought to provide that explanation. If a 'labour theory of value' is not to be dismissed out of hand, it must amount, not to the proposition stated above, but rather to the proposition that 'the rate of profit and normal prices, under capitalist conditions, can be *explained in terms of* labour quantities'. It was this latter (much less restrictive) proposition that Marx maintained. We must now consider how Marx's argument went astray.

In the course of the argument already referred to (*Capital* Volume 3, part II), Marx asserted that, if wages were advanced along with non-wage capital, then the rate of profit, r, would be determined by

$$r = \left(\frac{S}{C+V}\right),$$ where S, C, and V denote the aggregate amounts of

labour required—directly and indirectly—to produce, respectively, the bundle of commodities going to the capitalists, the bundle needed to replace used-up means of production, and the bundle comprising workers' wages. (The phrase 'labour required directly and indirectly' may be explained by example: the labour required—directly and indirectly—to produce a car comprises not only the labour of car workers but also that of the workers who produce the steel, rubber, glass, etc. used in car production, and that of workers who produce the pig-iron, coal, chemicals, etc., used in making that steel, rubber, glass, and so on, and on, and on. . . .) He then used this expression for the rate of profit, to show, as was mentioned above, that commodity prices will not be proportional, except by a fluke, to the quantities of labour required for their production. But if prices are

not proportional to labour contents then the ratio $\left(\frac{S}{C+V}\right)$, in which

both the surplus product and the total capital advanced are 'valued' in terms of labour contents, will not be equal—flukes apart—to the ratio of surplus product to total capital advanced, where both are 'valued' in terms of prices. This latter ratio is, however, precisely what

is *meant* by the rate of profit. Thus $\left(\frac{S}{C+V}\right)$ is *not* the rate of profit,

contrary to Marx's assertion; Marx's argument concerning the rate of profit and normal prices is *internally inconsistent*.

From a formal standpoint, Marx's error lay in trying to determine first the rate of profit and then the normal prices of commodities (or 'prices of production' as Marx called them); the fact is that the profit rate and prices of production have to be treated *simultaneously* within the theory. Suppose then, that, in the spirit of the surplus approach, we take as given—for the immediate purpose of examining profits and prices and not, of course, as given in any more fundamental sense—the *physical* quantities of outputs and inputs, including labour-time, in each industry and the bundle of commodities constituting real wages. Starting from these physical data we may show three things (see, for example, *Marx After Sraffa*, chapters 3 and 4). *First*, those data suffice to determine, proximately, the rate of profit and the prices of production. *Second*, the rate of profit does not, in fact, depend on all those data, but only on real wages and the direct and indirect conditions of production of those wage goods. The production conditions of commodities which neither enter the real-wage bundle directly, nor are used in producing commodities which do so enter, have *no* influence on the rate of profit. *Third*, no quantities of embodied labour play any necessary role in the determination of either the rate of profit or prices of production: embodied-labour quantities are entirely redundant, even within a surplus-based theory. That this is so is easy to see without entering into the technical details of the argument. The quantities of labour embodied in—or required, directly and indirectly, to produce—a commodity are determined precisely by the physical quantities we took as data. But those same data suffice to determine the rate of profit and prices of production: hence embodied-labour quantities are necessarily redundant.

Indeed, such labour quantities are found to be not merely redundant but either ill-defined or endowed with peculiar properties (such as being negative!) when we move on to discuss the 'choice' between alternative production methods, which capitalists are forced to make under the pressures of competition, the analysis of fixed-capital equipment, and the phenomenon—of great importance in oil refining, the chemical industry, and so on—of productive processes yielding several different products simultaneously. All these important complexities of contemporary capitalist economies can be dealt with, in so far as they affect the determination of the rate of profit and production prices, within the physical-quantities version of the surplus approach. But ill-defined or negative embodied-labour quantities can obviously contribute nothing to the analysis. (Although it would be quite inappropriate to enter here into the rather technical arguments involved, it must be noted that such oddities as negative quantities of embodied labour can certainly be avoided by adopting *new*, linear programming, definitions of such quantities; what is important for our present purpose is that those newly defined quantities still play no role in explaining the rate of profit and prices of production.)

Further on Marxist Political Economy

Once it has been established that a surplus approach to profits and prices has absolutely no need of any 'labour theory of value', it is natural to ask whether the 'physical quantities' version of that approach can make any contribution to questions which have exercised writers in the Marxist tradition. Four issues will be briefly taken up here: heterogeneity of labour, the 'labour process', 'the falling tendency of the rate of profit', and 'exploitation'.

Marxist theory, working in terms of quantities of direct and indirect labour, has always been plagued by the questions: How are different types of labour, for example skilled and unskilled labour, to be treated? Can they be 'reduced' one to another and then added together? The physical-quantities version of the surplus analysis simply makes such questions redundant. It can be shown that each type of labour-time can be treated as such—there being no need to effect any kind of 'reduction'—without causing any significantly greater difficulty in the theory of the rate of profit and prices of production. Again, whilst the physical-quantities approach does not, *per se*, capture all that Marxist economists refer to when they discuss the labour process (far from it), it would appear to provide a clear framework that can be used to *discipline* such discussion and to express at least some of its results. The physical approach cannot, of course, contribute a great deal to the Marxist discussion of the 'tendency of the rate of profit to fall', since it has been recognized for a long time that Marx's own discussion was really completely inconclusive. He picked out, quite reasonably, one factor tending to pull the profit rate down and, following J.S. Mill, a number tending to push it up, but he gave *no* non-arbitrary basis for referring to the former as *the tendency* and to the latter as merely *counteracting influences*; the labels could just as (un-) reasonably have been reversed. If this unproductive discussion is to be continued, however, at least it should be recognized that $\left(\dfrac{S}{C+V}\right)$ is not the rate of profit and that the latter depends on only some conditions of production.

   Marxist discussion has always laid great stress on 'exploitation', where that term is not given its everyday, multidimensional meaning (bringing in wages, conditions, the harshness of labour discipline, and so on) but rather a narrow, technical meaning. In this latter meaning it refers to the fact that workers perform more labour than would be required merely to produce their real wages (and replace the produced means of production thereby used up). The difference, or 'surplus labour', produces the commodities going (net) to the capitalists (and replaces the corresponding means of production). Now, the physical-quantities version of the surplus approach naturally does not deny the existence of such 'surplus labour'; indeed it would seem to provide the indispensable basis for clear thinking about the amount of 'surplus labour'. It does, however, make very clear the fact that the existence of (narrowly defined) exploitation and the existence of profit are no more than two sides of the same coin; they are simply 'labour' and 'monetary' expressions of the physical surplus. But Marxist writers only too often suggest that by relating profit to (narrowly defined) exploitation they have *explained* the existence of profit. They have not; they have simply noticed both ways of expressing the existence of the surplus product! To explain the existence of profit is just *the same thing* as to explain (narrowly defined) exploitation. The task is thus to explain why real wages and conditions of production bear—and persist in bearing—such a relation to one another that surplus product, profit, and (narrowly defined) exploitation continue to exist. Many theories unattractive to Marxists have, of course, been put forward in explanation of that persistent relation, in terms, for example, of 'capital scarcity', 'time preference', and so on. If Marxists are to present a superior theory they must, as a precondition, stop imagining that the existence of (narrowly defined) exploitation *explains* the existence of profit. It does not.

Qualifications and Doubts

I now consider three questions that may reasonably be asked about the physical-quantities version of the surplus approach to economic theory and about the associated rejection of the 'labour theory of value', even though there is not space for fully adequate replies to those questions.

It may be asked, first, 'How can one be satisfied with a theory that takes so much—alternative possible production methods and real wages – as given?' The answer is, quite simply, that one cannot and should not be. The physical-surplus analysis of the rate of profit and prices of production is intended to be no more than one—important—part of an adequate theory of the working of capitalist economies. That it is not sufficient does not alter the fact that it is important.

A second doubt, often expressed by Marxists, may be phrased as follows: 'In referring repeatedly to quantities of embodied labour, and never to "values", you unwittingly betray the fact that you have shown the irrelevance of *Ricardo's* labour theory of value but not of *Marx's*. Marx meant far more by the term "value" than just the labour required, directly and indirectly, to produce a commodity, and thus his theory is unscathed by your criticisms.' To review this objection fully would take, at least, an entire essay; only two points can be noted here. First, it is certainly true that in Marx's writings the term 'value' often conveys *more than* 'the quantity of embodied labour'. Second, it is just as certainly true that Marx often uses the term with just this simple meaning and that if, with the intention of 'saving' Marx's theory of value, Marxists break all connection between Marx's 'values' and amounts of embodied labour, then they will find great difficulty in interpreting many of Marx's perfectly sensible statements and in retaining any significant meaning to Marx's theory of value. Defenders of Marx's value theory have yet to show that there exists a middle way between, on the one hand, exposing it to the criticism set out above, and, on the other, draining it of all genuine content.

A third possible question, which is sometimes related to the immediately preceding one, is whether the physical-surplus analysis can contribute to our understanding of the complexities of money, fluctuations in effective demand, the analysis of long-term changes, and so on. One must not expect one element of an analysis to deal with everything! Yet nor should one conclude too quickly that the analysis of the rate of profit and its proximate determinants is irrelevant to an understanding of major long-term changes in the capitalist economy, for instance the effects of a major technical advance, such as the introduction of microprocessors. The patient analysis of the likely effects of such an advance on wages, profits, and relative prices cannot, if one is serious, be waived.

Wider Implications

The fact that the surplus approach of the classical economists and Marx can be freed from dependence on any 'labour theory of value' naturally has no immediate and narrowly party-political significance; yet it does have certain wider implications for all those to the left of centre. On the one hand, it means that rhetoric appealing to the 'labour theory of value' can no longer be excused—if it ever could— by suggesting that the only alternatives to such a theory necessarily involve acceptance of the ideas of 'capital's (marginal) contribution' and so on. In particular, the suggestion that (narrowly defined) exploitation is the *explanation* of profit must be abandoned and proper theories of the persistence of the surplus must be advanced. On the other hand, the clear separation of the surplus-appropriation theory from any 'labour theory of value' should *encourage* all those who are simultaneously attracted by the former but sceptical about the latter. Rather than feeling inhibited by the labour-theory albatross about their necks, they should unequivocally cast it aside and concentrate on developing a coherent theory of capitalist development, drawing on—amongst other sources—the surplus analysis of production and distribution and the theory of effective demand.

Marxian Value Theory and Crises

Paul Sweezy

I

There is, in my opinion, no direct connection between value theory and crises, nor between the kind of price theory some wish to substitute for value theory and crises. Crises (in the broad sense that Marxists ordinarily use the term) are enormously complicted phenomena, and they differ from one another so much that no general theory, and still less no simple theory, can hope to provide more than the beginning of a serious analysis of any given crisis situation. Nevertheless, I think it is true that crises cannot be understood properly unless they are envisaged as integral to an overall conception of the nature and functioning of the capitalist accumulation process, and I for one find the theory of value to be the only basis on which such a conception can be built.

Perhaps I should say that I find it the only basis presently available on which such a conception can be built. I am aware that those, like Ian Steedman, who want to throw out the theory of value altogether but who nevertheless concede that it provided the approach that enabled Marx to arrive at his understanding of the accumulation process still do not think that value theory is in any way essential to this achievement. You can, they say, substitute price theory à la Sraffa without precluding any further inquiries along Marxian lines you may care to undertake. To quote Steedman (the concluding sentence in his recent book *Marx After Sraffa*): 'It can scarcely be overemphasized that the project of providing a materialist account of capitalist societies is dependent on Marx's value magnitude analysis *only* in the negative sense that continued adherence to the latter is a major fetter on the development of the former.'[1]

It has occurred to me that by speaking of Marx's 'value *magnitude* analysis', Steedman may be implying that there is another kind of value analysis, a *qualitative* value analysis, concerned with social relations rather than economic magnitudes, which helps instead of hindering 'the project of providing a materialist account of capitalist societies'. If so, I entirely agree with him. Only I happen to believe that the marriage of the qualitative and quantitative analyses was one of Marx's greatest achievements and that separating them runs the danger, as in the case of separating Siamese twins, of killing them both.

In many years of writing and teaching (which also ought not be separated), I have found this position difficult, and all too often impossible, to explain. Those brought up in capitalist society are as a rule totally accustomed to the increasingly elaborate division of labour which it fosters and which is reflected in a corresponding division of knowledge and the professional specializations that deal in knowledge. Against this background, it is only natural to take for granted that theoretical systems can be taken to pieces, with some parts being retained and others rejected, more or less as diners confronted with a smorgasbord take the dishes that appeal to them and bypass the others. Anyone who thinks in this way has little hesitation in disassembling Marx's analysis of capitalism and holding on to or discarding constituent components according to his or her particular tastes. It doesn't occur to such a person that the theoretical system may be more like a machine or an organism that needs all of its parts to function.[2]

---

[1] I should add that I doubt that Sraffa would endorse this view. Steedman himself points out that 'Sraffa's *Production of Commodities by Means of Commodities* presents *no* criticisms of Marx': it was, in other words, what its subtitle proclaims 'A Prelude to a Critique of Economic Theory'—economic theory of course meaning neo-classical orthodoxy. And Joan Robinson, who is as down on value theory as Steedman and puts her own interpretation on Sraffa's work, warns against attributing her view to Sraffa: 'Piero', she says, 'has always stuck close to pure unadulterated Marx and regards my amendments with suspicion.' 'The Labor Theory of Value', *Monthly Review*, December 1977, p. 56n.

[2] To avoid misunderstanding: this obviously does not imply the impossibility of improving either the parts or the way they function as a whole, nor does it deny that there may be parts which are dispensable, like the vermiform appendix in the human body.

But analogies can be more than suggestive. Let me try to make my point more directly. Roughly the first two parts of the first volume of *Capital* plus most of the first three chapters of the third part (amounting in all to about one-quarter of the volume as a whole) are predominantly qualitative in the sense indicated, i.e., they focus on identifying and clarifying the basic relations of commodity-producing societies in general and capitalism in particular. Thereafter—and this holds in the main for the second and third volumes as well—there is a heavier emphasis on quantifying these relationships, or rather the economic variables and their interconnections which express these relationships. Throughout, reasoning is in terms of value theory, and there is no effort to make an explicit distinction between the qualitative and quantitative dimensions of value. For Marx, the quantitative is saturated with the qualitative, and the qualitative is expressed through the quantitative.

The beauty of this approach, as I see it, is that it enables us to achieve a clear and coherent vision of capitalism *as a historical process*. The early history of capitalism is seen not (or not only) as a chaos of rapine and violence but as the process through which the distinctively capitalist mode of production came into the world, with the capital/labour relation replacing the lord/serf relation as the central relation of exploitation in a new form of class society. Every class society is characterized by the necessary/surplus labour dichotomy, hence by an implicit rate of exploitation, but only in capitalism does this take the value form, with the rate of exploitation expressing itself as a rate of surplus-value. This, and *not* the rate of profit (as Steedman *et al.* seem to believe), is the crucial variable which enables Marx to get a firm handle on the history of capitalism. By dividing surplus-value into absolute surplus-value and relative surplus-value (neither of which would make sense without the concept of a *rate* of surplus-value), Marx was able to lay bare the anatomy of the class struggles which were endemic to capitalism from its earliest beginnings. This task was carried through in the third and fourth parts of the first volume of *Capital*, and especially in the incomparable chapter 15, 'Machinery and Large-Scale Industry'.[3]

[3] How solidly Marx established the framework for his analysis is shown by the way Harry Braverman could use it without essential modification more than a hundred years later, in *Labor and Monopoly Capital*, to bring the story up to date.

From there, using the results already achieved, Marx went on to analyse the accumulation process, showing among other things: (1) how the mechanism for adjusting the rate of wages to the value of labour-power is radically different from that which adjusts the price of any other commodity to its value, with the reserve army of labour (or relative surplus population) playing the key role of 'pivot upon which the law of demand and supply of labour works';[4] (2) how the normal outcome of capitalist accumulation must be a polarization between riches and poverty; (3) why the form of the accumulation process must be one of cyclical ups and downs rather than a linear progression; and (4) the manner in which competition of capitals must lead, via concentration and centralization, to its own negation in monopoly.

Have I made my point now, i.e. that it was through marrying qualitative with quantitative value theory that Marx was able to illuminate the history of capitalism in a way that no theorist before or after him has been able to hold a candle to? If not, perhaps it will help to quote Schumpeter, who was a severe critic of Marx but at the same time understood what Marx was trying to do better than most self-styled Marxists. The following passage from Schumpeter's *Capitalism, Socialism and Democracy* (p. 44), if I interpret it correctly, says about Marx's achievement pretty much what I have been trying to express, but does so in very different language:

'There is . . . one thing of fundamental importance for the methodology of economics which he [Marx] actually achieved.

---

[4] This mechanism, not to mention its enormous implications for the functioning of capitalism, necessarily escapes the attention of those who, like Steedman, confine their attention to economies which are 'fully developed, capitalist commodity economies, in which *all* [emphasis added] production activities are organized and controlled by capitalists (or their agents).' (*Marx After Sraffa*, p. 16.) This just happens *not* to be true of capitalism in the real world, where production of by far the most important single commodity, labour-power, is *not* organized or controlled by capitalists. Much that is most distinctive and valuable in Marx's analysis of capitalism stems from the fact that he never for one moment lost sight of this crucial difference between labour-power and other commodities. Let me add, though this is not the place to elaborate on the matter, that if account is taken of this special characteristic of labour-power, it involves a total misconception of Marx's theory to write, as Steedman does: 'Wages are treated in this work, as they were by Marx, as being exogenously determined . . . in a given economy in a given period.' (Ibid., p. 20.) It could be argued, to my mind unpersuasively, that Marx treated *the value of labour-power* as exogenously determined, but never wages.

24

Economists have always either themselves done work in economic history or else used the historical work of others. But the facts of economic history were assigned to a separate compartment. They entered theory, if at all, merely in the role of illustrations, or possibly of verifications of results. They mixed with it only mechanically. Now Marx's mixture is a chemical one; that is to say, he introduced them into the very argument that produces the results. He was the first economist of top rank to see and to teach systematically how economic theory may be turned into historical analysis and how the historical narrative may be turned into *histoire raisonnée*.'

Schumpeter could hardly have been expected to agree that value theory was the key to Marx's success in this enterprise, but it is difficult to see how he or anyone else could deny that it guided Marx every step of the way. And it would be equally difficult to make out a case that any theorist since Marx, dispensing with the theory of value, has had a success comparable to his.[5] Nor do I think it at all likely that anyone following the advice of Ian Steedman, Joan Robinson, and others to chuck the theory of value in favour of a Sraffa-type theory of prices will make any significant contribution to the solution of Marx's 'problematic'.

Here we meet what I suppose would be the ultimate objection of these critics of value theory. Economic magnitudes in the real world, as Marx was of course well aware, are expressed in terms of prices of production, not values. From a Marxist standpoint, this, in and of itself, is not a weakness or flaw in the theory—rather the contrary. Reality is made up of appearance *and* essence. Prices of production belong to the realm of appearance, values to the realm of essence. Unless we can move back and forth between them as needed, we can never achieve more than a quite superficial understanding of capitalism. *But*, say the critics, you *cannot* move back and forth

[5] Schumpeter himself might be put forward as a candidate for the honour, and his own conception of the scope of his theoretical endeavour would at least give the nomination a certain plausibility. But as I have argued elsewhere (*Modern Capitalism and Other Essays*, pp. 140–41), history has not dealt kindly with Schumpeter's theory of capitalist development in the more than half a century since it was first formulated; and of course, as far as Marxists are concerned, the absence of any theory of class antagonism or class struggle from Schumpeter's version of *histoire raisonée* renders it largely irrelevant. On this, see my note 'Schumpeter's Theory of Innovation', in *The Present as History*, pp. 274–82.

between the two realms except under very special assumptions; and if these assumptions are dropped, seriously misleading distortions result.

This at any rate is the way I interpret Steedman's argument which is summed up in a diagram on p. 48 of *Marx After Sraffa*. The diagram has a box on its left-hand side labelled 'Physical production and wage data'. From this an arrow, (a), in the northeasterly direction connects to a box labelled 'All value quantities'; another arrow, (b), in the southeasterly direction connects to another box labelled "Profits and prices".[6] Between the value box and the price box there is a dotted and interrupted arrow, (c). Steedman comments: 'The dashed and "blocked off" arrow (c) represents the fact that one cannot, in general, explain prices and profits from value quantities as set out in the general value schema. . . . We thus have to picture our theoretical structure as having a "fork-like" character, with a value prong, arrow (a), and a "profit-price" prong, arrow (b). *There is*, in general, *no way from one prong to the other.*' (p. 49.) This, unless I have misunderstood Steedman, is his entire reason for wanting to jettison what he calls value magnitude analysis.

My answer is essentially simple, though it could undoubtedly be elaborated at considerable length. Despite what Steedman says, there *are* general ways of getting from the value prong to the price-profit prong. This of course is what is known in the Marxist literature as the transformation problem. As is by now well known, the way proposed by Marx himself is faulty (Steedman spends more space on this than he needs to, in view of the large amount that has been written on the subject in recent years). But there are other ways which are logically impeccable. One is the Bortkiewicz solution, of which there are a number of variants and refinements; and another is what may be called the iterative solution, presented most fully by Anwar Shaikh.[7] It is true that in general a logically satisfactory solution to the

---

[6] By 'prices' Steedman means what Marx called 'prices of production'; neither is concerned with market prices.

[7] 'Marx's Theory of Value and the "Transformation Problem"', in Jesse Schwartz (ed.), *The Subtle Anatomy of Capitalism*, Santa Monica, California, 1977. For the record I should like to state that an arithmetical version of the iterative solution was put forward in an unpublished manuscript many years ago by my late friend Harmon Alexander, who at the time was a screen writer and only later, in his fifties, acquired a formal training in economics.

26

transformation problem yields results different in certain respects from those of Marx's faulty method. Total price does not equal total value, and the rate of profit in the price scheme is not equal to the rate of profit in the value scheme. But these are changes of dimension only, not of substance; and there is no reason to suppose that analysing the accumulation process on the basis of values yields results which need to be altered in any significant way by shifting to prices.

Aha, you may say, if this is true, then why do we need the value analysis at all? Reality presents itself in terms of prices. If it can also be analysed in terms of prices, why bother with those alleged value 'essences' and the whole rigmarole of transforming them into prices? But wait a minute! I did *not* say that reality could be analysed in terms of prices: I said that the results of the analysis would not be significantly altered by shifting to prices. I do not believe that the analysis could (or would) have been made in terms of prices. And the reason is that the key concept and variable in the analysis, the centre of gravity which holds everything else in place, is the rate of surplus-value, *and it is precisely the rate of surplus-value which disappears, vanishes without a trace, from an analysis made in terms of prices.*[8]

I would like to stress here, though it is not possible to develop the point within the limits of this paper, that in comparison with the rate of surplus-value the rate of profit is both a secondary concept and one which, taken by itself, tends strongly to foster fetishistic thinking. The notion that the rate of profit is somehow, and unlike the rate of surplus-value, an 'operational' concept in terms of which capitalists make decisions is without foundation. Capitalists do not know what the overall rate of profit is, and each one makes decisions on the basis of his own rate of profit, which is rarely and then only by accident equal to the overall rate. (This is of course even more true when we abandon the competitive assumptions which make the overall rate the norm around which individual rates tend to fluctuate.) And the

[8] I did not understand this when I was writing *The Theory of Capitalist Development* some four decades ago. As a result the fifth and sixth sections of the chapter on the transformation problem (entitled respectively 'The Significance of Price Calculation' and 'Why Not Start with Price Calculation?'), while not wrong, do not reach the heart of the matter, which is the crucial role of the rate of surplus-value in the entire Marxian theory of capitalism.

fact that the rate of profit states a relationship between profit and total capital rather than between profit and variable capital all too easily—as shown by the entire history of bourgeois economic thought—gives rise to the theory of the productivity of capital, an example *par excellence* of fetishistic thought.

II

Crises must of course by analysed within the framework of a theory of the accumulation process, and in this restricted sense value theory is essential to the analysis of crises. An understanding of the accumulation process tells us why crises are possible and even inevitable. But a great deal more is involved, and if we are to understand particular crises we have to take account of much which does not figure in value theory. Here I want to focus on two factors which I believe play a specially important role in the crises which characterize the present phase of capitalist development, including the one which the capitalist world is currently undergoing. These are (1) monopoly (using the term to include oligopoly), and (2) finance (money and debt). I shall limit myself to the briefest possible outline.

As pointed out above, the competition of capitals leads, via the twin phenomena of concentration and centralization (both inseparable aspects of the accumulation process), to the replacement of free competition by various forms of monopoly. This in turn means that the mechanism whereby an average rate of profit is formed ceases to operate in the assumed way, and without an average rate of profit there is no longer any reason to assume an orderly correspondence between values and prices of production. It we start from a situation (competitive capitalism) in which economic reality presents itself in terms of prices of production, we now have a situation (monopoly capitalism) in which this role is played by monopoly prices. These are transformed prices of production in exactly the same sense that prices of production are transformed values.[9] There is, however, this

---

[9] It follows, of course, that monopoly prices are *also* transformed values. Hence analysing monopoly prices does not imply repudiating the theory of value (as some critics of Paul Baran's and my *Monopoly Capital* have alleged). But, as argued in

28

difference, that there are no general rules for relating monopoly prices to prices of production, as there were for relating prices of production to values. About all we can say is that monopoly prices in various industries tend to be higher than prices of production in proportion to the difficulties new capitals have in entering those industries. And of course a corresponding hierarchy of profit rates will emerge, highest in the industries most difficult to enter, lowest in those where entry is free (as is assumed to be the case under competitive capitalism). An average rate of profit still exists in a mathematical sense, but it is not one which tends to impose itself on individual capitals, and it does not govern the distribution of surplus-value throughout the system as the average rate of profit does under competitive conditions.

I have long been arguing, beginning with *The Theory of Capitalist Development* (1942) and on various occasions since,[10] that the transition from competitive to monopoly capitalism has a profound effect on the accumulation process. The redistribution of surplus-value in favour of large monopolistic units of capital and to the disadvantage of small competitive units greatly enhances the system's accumulation potential. At the same time, however, attractive outlets for capital investment are curtailed. To put it another way, the big monopolies tend to be very profitable and hence able to accumulate rapidly; but at the same time they are afraid of spoiling their own markets by over-investing, so they go slow in expanding their productive capacity. To protect their monopolistic positions they erect what barriers they can against outsiders invading their markets (one of the most effective ways is to maintain a considerable margin of unused capacity which can be quickly activated in retaliation against unwanted newcomers). Such typical monopolistic behaviour adds up to a recipe for much slower growth than the economy would be capable of, and slow growth relative to the economy's potential is

Monopoly Capital and also below, shifting from value to monopoly price does have important consequences for the accumulation process, which is not true of shifting from value to price of production.

[10] See, for example, *The Theory of Capitalist Development*, chapter XV; *Modern Capitalism and Other Essays* (1972), pp. 39–42; 'Some Problems in the Theory of Capital Accumulation', *Monthly Review*, May 1974, pp. 40–42.

another name for stagnation, precisely the situation in which the global capitalist system now finds itself.

The implication of this line of reasoning is that in a developed monopoly capitalist economy (and especially one in which the process of monopolization is continuing or even accelerating, as it has been in the United States and Western Europe throughout the present century), stagnation—slow growth, heavy unemployment, much idle productive capacity—must be regarded as the norm, not the exception. Hence what needs to be explained is *not* stagnation but extended periods of buoyancy and rapid expansion such as we in the West have been living through since the Second World War.

This is the problem which Paul Baran and I posed and attempted to explore in *Monopoly Capital.* Clearly it requires that attention be directed not only to the internal logic of the accumulation process—which cannot but be abstract in the sense of dealing with no more than a small number of variables—but also to the overall historical environment within which the accumulation process unfolds. In interpreting the development of us capitalism over the past century, Baran and I attributed decisive importance to 'epoch-making innovations' (the railroad and the automobile) on the one hand and major wars and their aftermaths on the other. The great railroad boom of the second half of the nineteenth century, we argued, came to an abrupt end with the panic of 1907. Incipient stagnation then characterized the period until 1914, when the First World War took over, followed by its aftermath boom and the automobile-led prosperity of the 1920s. Stagnation, unmitigated by further shocks or stimuli, set in with the cyclical downswing of 1929–33 and lasted throughout the decade of the 1930s. This was interrupted by the Second World War, which was duly followed by a reconversion and reconstruction boom.

After that, however, and largely as a consequence of the vast changes in the structure and organization of world capitalism brought about by the war, the historical determinants of the course taken by the accumulation process were transformed in important respects. There was never any doubt that the internal logic of the monopoly capitalist system was functioning in what had long since become the normal fashion, but the environment within which this logic worked its way was new and enormously complicated. Baran and I did not attempt to analyse this new pattern of interaction in any detail, and the few comments we devoted to it (*Monopoly Capital*, pp. 244–8) were unsystematic and impressionistic.[11]

It is, of course, not my intention to try to repair this omission here. I want only to mention what we can now see in retrospect were some of the major factors, and to stress one: the huge growth of debt, which I think has been unduly neglected; which is just at this time precipitating what I have elsewhere called a 'crisis within the crisis';[12] and which needs to be integrated into the theory of the accumulation process in a way which, so far as I am aware, has not yet even been attempted.

By far the most important postwar development was the imposition of American hegemony on the capitalist world: for the first time since the decline of British hegemony in the late nineteenth century, the international capitalist system came under the dominant leadership of a single great power. This had, among other things, the following consequences: 1. The establishment of a new international monetary system based on the gold-linked dollar, which now served as standard of value, reserve currency, and international means of payment. 2. The extensive dismantlement of the trading and currency blocs which had grown up in the interwar period, with a resultant vast growth of world markets, including the capital market and (to a lesser but still important extent) the market for labour-power. 3. The buildup in the United States of a military machine of historically unprecedented proportions, which had the dual function of policing the world capitalist system and facing up to the military power of the 'socialist' bloc under the hegemony (until the Sino–Soviet split) of the USSR. In discharging its global responsibilities the United States was forced to fight two major regional wars—in Korea and Vietnam— and many lesser armed confrontations.

In this new historical environment capitalism experienced a secular boom comparable to, and in many respects exceeding, anything in its earlier history. The accumulation of capital on a world scale was

[11] This was at least partly because *Monopoly Capital* was conceived and largely written in the early stages of the postwar prosperity, and, as we noted, 'it is still not possible to say when the whole movement will lose its momentum' (p. 245). In the event, the momentum was sustained for more than a decade after this was written.

[12] *Monthly Review*, December 1978.

released from paralysing restrictions which had grown up during and as a result of the Great Depression of the 1930s. The United States, benefiting from its hegemonic position and with its economy continually stimulated by enormous military budgets, acted as a dynamo standing at the centre of the system as a whole and driving it inexorably onward and upward. As always happens in such a period, but now more than ever, capitalists became infected with a spirit of optimism, which was reinforced and provided with a seemingly scientific foundation by various brands of 'new economics' purporting to prove that panics and depressions were a thing of the past and that ahead lay endless expansion punctuated only by minor setbacks and recessions. In this heady atmosphere, there seemed to be no limit to the amount of capital investment that could be profitably undertaken, the only question being whether the payoff would begin next year or a few years later. Under these conditions, the exigencies of competition dictated action now, and the combined action of all the competitors created mutual markets for their products which appeared to be self-sustaining and hence to guarantee against the old disease of over-production.

What was really happening, of course, was what had happened innumerable times in the past: behind the illusion of self-sustaining growth was the process of building up excess capacity. What brought the true situation to light was the cyclical downturn of 1974, exacerbated and made more traumatic by the shock of vastly increased oil prices following the Yom Kippur war of 1973. Suddenly the economic climate changed: excess capacity showed up in industry after industry—steel, automobiles, ship-building, textiles, heavy chemicals, and many more; capital accumulation faltered; unemployment grew beyond anything known in the postwar period; the rate of growth of industrial production fell below the postwar average and remained there even during the ensuing cyclical upswing. A new period of stagnation, reminiscent of the 1930s, had apparently arrived.

There was, however, one highly significant exception to this pattern, the United States itself. There the cyclical upswing began early in 1975. By the end of 1976 the growth rate of industrial production was back up to the postwar average, and it has remained above the average ever since. At the same time, the unemployment rate, which had reached 8.5 per cent of the labour force in 1975, has steadily declined to 6 per cent at the time of writing (November 1978).[13]

Why this exception? The answer is clear: the expansion of the US economy has been fuelled by a veritable explosion of public and private debt. To quote the most prestigious journal of American business and finance: 'Since late 1975 the US has created a new debt economy, a credit explosion so wild and so eccentric that it dwarfs even the borrowing binge of the early 1970s.' (*Business Week*, October 16, 1978.) The crux of this phenomenon has been the growth of consumer debt which both causes and reflects the leading role of consumption in the current recovery (contrary to the usual pattern of investment-led recovery). Also important has been the persistence of federal government deficits (almost $50 thousand million in 1978) into the fourth year of a cyclical recovery, a quite unprecedented occurrence.

But it is not only at the national level that the financial sector has played a crucial part in the recent behaviour of the capitalist system. Thanks to its hegemonic role, the United States was able to supply the liquidity requirements of a rapidly expanding world capitalist economy through running a persistent deficit in its balance of payments. The dollars thus injected into the central banks and monetary systems of other countries served for more than a decade to lubricate the global mechanisms of trade and finance, while conferring on the United States itself a seemingly limitless power to command the resources and control the destinies of the subordinate units in the world system. This continuing deficit in the US balance of payments was also the main source of what came to be known as Eurodollars, a form of transnational money not under the control of any central bank or governmental authority. Eurodollars in turn became the basis of a credit expansion which added many billions to the pool of dollars outside the United States. It is symptomatic of the uncontrolled (and unprecedented) nature of this phenomenon that

[13] It should be obvious that this performance of the US economy, so much stronger than that of the other advanced capitalist countries, has acted to keep the latter from faltering even more dramatically than has been the case. Without a relatively vigorous US recovery, the world capitalist system would have been in considerably worse shape than it actually is.

no one knows how large this pool is, though it certainly runs into hundreds of billions and some estimates have been as high as $600 thousand million.

Borrowers from this vast pool of money have included not only corporations and financial institutions but also governments all over the world. To quote the *Business Week* report cited above: 'It is that massive flow of funds from the international market that is enabling nations to keep rolling over old debt and taking on new debt nearly without limit. In just four years, the industrialized countries of the world have doubled their Euromarket debt, the less developed countries that do not export oil have tripled their Euromarket debt, and now even many of the OPEC nations themselves are borrowing on so vast a scale that they will owe nearly $10 billion by the end of this year, compared with a mere $990 million in 1974.'

This enormous expansion of debt, on both the national and international levels, has of course had the effect of cushioning the impact of the sharp downturn of 1974: without it there can be little doubt that the end of the secular postwar boom would have been the beginning of a depression at least comparable to that of the early 1930s.

Stressing the role of debt expansion in the recovery from the recession of 1974–5 is necessary, but it could also be misleading if it were taken to imply that we are dealing here with a factor which has become important to the functioning of capitalism only in recent years. The truth is, as Marx himself observed many times and in many contexts, that debt (or credit, which is the same thing looked at from the other side) has been crucial to capitalism since earliest times. The growth of long-distance trade is scarcely imaginable without a developed credit system; the public debt acted as a lever of primitive accumulation and has always been a keystone of every modern banking system; all the great speculative manias that have punctuated the history of capitalism, from the South Sea Bubble through the Crédit Mobilier to the great Wall Street stock-market boom-and-crash of the 1920s, have been exercises in the use and misuse of credit; one can even argue, as Samir Amin has recently done, that the functioning of a fully developed, highly complicated capitalist production/circulation process—such as Marx sought to portray in the expanded reproduction schemes of volume 2 of *Capital*—would be impossible in the absence of credit.[14] And yet it would be hard to deny that something quantitatively and qualitatively new has been added in the latest period, beginning with the establishment of US hegemony at the end of the Second World War and growing steadily in importance ever since.

- This is obviously not the occasion to try to elucidate a subject which is as complex as it is important. I will only mention some of the main elements which would have to be taken into account and accorded their due weight: (1) The development, pioneered by the United States, and greatly facilitated by improved communications and information-processing technologies, of a comprehensive and flexible network of financial institutions geared to serving the needs of giant corporations and the governments which support and defend them. (2) The multi-nationalization of banking, following in the wake of the multi-nationalization of industrial and commercial capital. (3) The adoption by capitalist states, directly and through their central banks, of fiscal and monetary policies aimed at preventing the recurrence of serious depressions, such as that of the 1930s, which are perceived by all ruling bourgeoisies as a potentially mortal threat to the continued existence of capitalism. Fiscal and monetary policies of this kind began to be consciously formulated in the 1930s and became normal and accepted functions of the capitalist state after the Second World War. Originally conceived as anti-cyclical (e.g., government deficits in the down phase of the cycle would be matched by surpluses in the upswing), these policies were gradually extended to encompass anti-stagnationist goals, in other words, to exercise an uninterrupted expansionary pressure on overall demand for goods and services. In the United States, which has been the leader in developing these policies (just as it has been in fashioning the new financial institutions to implement them), government deficits had become perennial before the end of the 1960s; and the explosion of private debt, a major consequence of expansionary fiscal and monetary policies, likewise began long before the recession of 1974–5.

One might suppose, following the logic of Keynesian theory, that persistent expansionary fiscal and monetary policies of this kind

[14] Samir Amin, *The Law of Value and Historical Materialism*, New York 1978, p. 22.

could at least overcome the tendency to stagnation. But, paradoxical as it may seem, this has not been the case. The underlying reason is that the economies of the advanced capitalist countries, which constitute the core of the global capitalist system, are by now so dominated by giant monopolistic corporations able to control their price and output policies in the interest of maximizing profits that a very large part of the impact of expansionary fiscal and monetary policies takes the form of inflation rather than increases in real output. Furthermore, inflation, once it has reached a certain intensity in terms of magnitude and duration, tends to perpetuate itself through its effects on costs (including the cost of living, which is a major determinant of wages) and on expectations.

None of this is to argue that the explosion of debt—which we can now see is but one manifestation of a very complex set of financial and political mechanisms—has no counter-cyclical and/or counter-stagnationist effects. Without it capitalism would probably long since have sunk into a state of near collapse. But sooner or later—and perhaps sooner rather than later—it may turn out that the cure creates problems no less serious than the disease. Already the chemical mixture of growing monopolization, exploding debt, and endemic inflation has given rise to a situation of great and growing instability and tension, reflected particularly in increasingly erratic movements in world financial and foreign-exchange markets. Only time will tell what the future holds in store, but even now it seems safe to say that the crisis of world capitalism is only in its early stages and that many shocks and surprises still await us.

The Value Controversy and Social Research

Erik Olin Wright

Debates on the labour theory of value are usually waged at the most abstract levels of theoretical discourse.* Frequently these debates are preoccupied with questions of the appropriate methodological stance toward social analysis, epistemological disputes about what it means to 'explain' a social process, and mathematical arguments about the merits of competing ways of formally deriving certain categories from others. Rarely are the issues posed in terms of their implications for the concrete investigations of social life in which social scientists would engage. This will be the central theme of this essay: the implications of the labour theory of value and its critiques for empirical investigation. In order to keep the discussion as focused as possible, I will organize the analysis primarily around one central aspect of the labour theory of value—its account of the determination of profits in capitalist societies.[1] In some ways this is not the

* I would like to thank Anwar Shaikh, Andrew Levine, Sam Bowles, and Michael Burawoy for extremely helpful criticisms and suggestions on earlier drafts of this paper. Anwar Shaikh in particular helped to clarify and elaborate many of the underlying arguments. I would also like to thank the participants in the Class Analysis and Historical Change Program seminar in the Sociology Department, the University of Wisconsin, for providing a forum to explore these ideas and to force me to make explicit and comprehensible the issues involved.

[1] The analysis will focus on the determination of the *magnitude* of profits rather than the *rate* of profits. This choice was made mainly for convenience in the exposition of certain arguments, since the use of a ratio (the rate of profit) makes the analysis somewhat more complex. None of the logic of what follows hinges on this choice, however, and with appropriate modifications the argument could be restated in terms of profit rates. (It is assumed throughout the discussion that money profits have been appropriately scaled in terms of constant money units, so that none of the arguments are affected by arbitrary changes in the numeraire.)

most basic issue within the debates over the labour theory of value, since analysis of the determinants of profits presupposes the debates over the relationship of embodied labour times (values) to prices of commodities. Nevertheless, since the analysis of profits plays such a central role in Marxist theory as a whole, and since it has particularly important immediate empirical implications, we will centre our discussion on this particular issue.

One of the difficulties in embarking on an assessment of the empirical implications of theoretical alternatives is that, typically, each of the alternative positions characterizes the debate itself in different ways. The preliminary task of this paper, therefore, will be to translate each of the positions in the debates on the labour theory of value onto a common conceptual terrain, so that it will be possible to assess their empirical implications in terms of a common framework. Such an act of translation cannot be 'innocent', to use a favourite expression of Louis Althusser, but to a greater or lesser extent must presuppose one of the theoretical stances in the debate. In this essay, the evaluation and elaboration of each of the positions will be from the vantage point of the Marxist labour theory of value itself.

In the following section, I shall present a brief exposition of three perspectives on the determination of profits: a 'causal-agnostic' account as developed in the work of Anthony Cutler, Barry Hindess, Paul Hirst, and Athar Hussain;[2] the 'Sraffian' account as elaborated in the work of Ian Steedman;[3] and a reconstructed version of the traditional Marxist account based on the labour theory of value. In each case I shall present a substantive model of determination of profits rather than try to elaborate all the technical details of the theoretical position. Following this exposition, we will consider the implications of each model for the kinds of questions one would ask in an empirical study. This analysis will then be illustrated by a discussion of the relationship of recent research on the nature of the labour process to the labour theory of value.

The analysis that follows should be seen more as attempting to redefine in certain critical ways the terms of the debate rather than

---

[2] Anthony Cutler, Barry Hindess, Paul Hirst, and Athar Hussain, *Marx's 'Capital' and Capitalism Today*, vols. I and II, London 1977, 1978.
[3] Ian Steedman, *Marx After Sraffa*, London, NLB, 1977.

definitively resolving all of the points in dispute.[4] In a sense, therefore, I am trying to pose an alternative agenda of theoretical (and empirical) research, and in so doing to establish more systematically the conditions for the adequacy (or inadequacy) of the labour theory of value. In various places I will point out where unresolved questions remain which need to be addressed.

With these limitations in mind, let us now turn to the exposition of alternative accounts.

1. Alternative Accounts of Profit Determination

Although, in terms of historical development, the Marxist model of determination of profits is the earliest of the three we will consider, presentation of the different positions is made easier by discussing first the conceptually simplest model, the causal-agnostic account of profits, and then turning to the Sraffian and Marxist perspectives.

The Causal-Agnostic Account

In order for profits to be produced in a capitalist society, many necessary conditions must occur. Capitalists must organize their investments and financial transactions, means of production must be

---

[4] In particular, I will not attempt to deal with the knotty problem of joint production (i.e. the problem of how to calculate labour values in situations in which two commodities are simultaneously produced by a single labouring activity). Since joint production has been an important part of the recent Sraffian critique of the labour theory of value, the objection could thus be raised that avoiding this problem undermines my entire argument. While I acknowledge this limitation in my analysis, it is important to note that in spite of the mathematical elegance of the Sraffian strategy for calculating prices and profits under conditions of joint production, it is not so clear that this can be considered a real *theory* of joint production. If a theory is meant to identify the real mechanisms by which certain outcomes are produced, then it must do more than provide a satisfactory method of calculating those outcomes (although calculation is important as well). The structure of calculation must itself reflect or appropriate the structure of the process which it is trying to explain. The Sraffian strategy used to calculate a consistent set of prices under conditions of joint production does not even claim to be an account of the real mechanisms that generate those prices in capitalist production. Thus, while the Sraffians may have a valid critique of simple Marxist approaches to calculating prices and profits under conditions of joint production, I do not feel that there is yet a developed substantive theory of joint production inconsistent with the labour theory of value.

combined with labour within the production process, the weather and geological conditions must fall within certain definable limits, and so on. All of these are *necessary* conditions in the specific sense that if they vary outside certain limits, no profits will be possible. If the weather produces horrendous flooding, or if geological conditions produce massive earthquakes, for example, profits will not be produced. A similar argument can be made about capitalists' actions, technological processes, labour, and many other factors. Of course, not all necessary conditions can be thought of as real determinants of profits. Without oxygen on the planet, for example, profits would be impossible, and thus the existence of oxygen is a necessary condition for profits to occur. Only those necessary conditions which have 'pertinent effects', that is, whose range of variation in the world generates real effects on profits, can be considered theoretically relevant necessary conditions. Given that all such pertinent necessary conditions have real effects, so the causal-agnostic argument runs, it is arbitrary to raise any of them to the privileged status of the 'essential' cause of profits, or as Marxists typically put it, the 'origin' of profits.

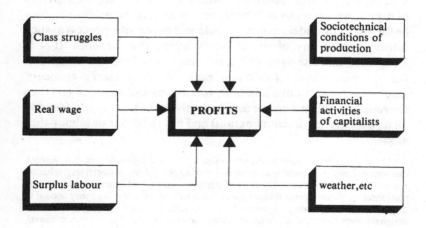

FIGURE 1
**The Causal-Agnostic Account of the
Determination of Profits**

This basic argument can be schematically represented as in figure 1. Profits are pictured as the outcome of a plurality of causes. Some may be more important than others in the sense that their typical range of variation produces greater variation in profits, but since they are all pertinent necessary conditions for profits, none of them can be given privileged status.

This position has been argued at length by Cutler et al.[5] They insist that it is theoretically arbitrary to see any determinant of profits as the 'origin' of profits: 'If one does not seek a single, general determinant of profits—rejecting both Marxist and Orthodox general accounts of their origin and accepting that the profits capitalist enterprises actually make have no single "origin" (that they cannot be ascribed to any one category of agents or factors in the production process, and are the product of many determinations)—then there is no *a priori* reason to conceive exchange in this way' (i.e., conceiving exchange as an equation of equal quantities of labour).[6] This is not to suggest that the amount of surplus labour performed within production has no effects on profits, but simply that surplus labour has no privileged status in the analysis of profits. Since surplus labour is always performed in conjunction with specific technologies, activities of capitalists, divisions of labour, and other factors, profits can only be theoretically understood as an outcome of the total process as such rather than of any of the elements within that process: 'If it is recognized that the agency of transformation of the *raw* material is the complex *process* (including each of its necessary elements, machines, the collective labourer, techniques and knowledges) then the resulting product can be ascribed only to the process itself (and to all its effectiveness in combination) and not to labour or labour-time alone.'[7]

[5] Cutler et al. do not refer to their position as a 'causal-agnostic' position. Rather, they simply define it negatively as the rejection of all general causal doctrines: 'What we are challenging is not merely the economic monist causality of Marxism, but the very pertinence of all such general categories of causality and the privilege they accord to certain orders of causes as against others' (p. 128). It would seem appropriate to designate their position a 'causal-pluralist' account of profits, but since causal-pluralism would itself count as a 'general doctrine' of causation (i.e., the doctrine that there are never privileged determinants), it is more appropriate to designate their position as simply an agnostic one.

[6] Cutler et al., Marx's 'Capital' and Capitalism Today, I, p. 19.

[7] Ibid., p. 44.

It is not clear from this analysis whether *all* pertinent necessary conditions for profits are treated as conceptually equal determinants, or whether the authors restrict the analysis to the necessary conditions within production. There is no discussion of whether or not, for example, meteorological conditions or political institutions should be included in the analysis of the process through which profits are determined. It is also not entirely clear from their discussion whether they believe that it is impossible, in principle, to provide any theoretical ordering of the multiple, pertinent, necessary conditions of profits. In any event, in the analysis of the book, the authors refrain from imposing any such order on the various causes of profits. It is for this reason that their account of profits can be called a 'causal-agnostic' account.

The Sraffian Account

Unlike the causal-agnostic stance toward the determination of profits, theorists using the Sraffian perspective argue that the various causes which influence profits can be theoretically ordered in a systematic manner. In particular, proponents of this view argue that profits can be considered a direct consequence of two factors: the socio-technical conditions of production and the real wage paid to workers.[8] Other causes of profits have their effects only by virtue of their influence on these two factors. This account is schematically represented in figure 2.

The Sraffian argument is based on a mathematical analysis of the necessary conditions for formally calculating profits from a set of

---

[8] Throughout this discussion I will use the expression 'socio-technical conditions' of production rather than simply 'technical' or 'physical' conditions. This is simply to emphasize that technical conditions can never be understood simply as physical input-output relations, but always have a social content. Above all, the length of the working day and the intensity of labouring activity within production are all 'physical' properties of the production process from the point of view of a technical input-output analysis, even though these are in good part stamped directly by social relations. Even in the case of machines, the social content of the technical input may be just as 'real' and significant as the narrowly technical content. Some theorists in the Sraffian tradition do in fact treat socio-technical conditions as mere physical coefficients of production. Ian Steedman, the main theorist we will consider, is careful to avoid this technological reduction, and explicitly acknowledges that physical conditions of production have a social content.

42

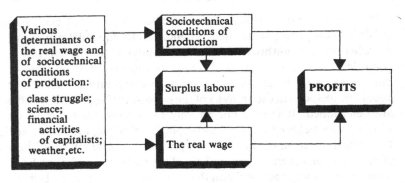

FIGURE 2
The Sraffian Account of the Determination of Profits

initial conditions. Steedman and others have argued, using the work of Piero Sraffa as the point of departure, that it is possible to calculate a unique profit rate simply by knowing the real wage rate and the socio-technical conditions of production. The categories of the labour theory of value, they argue, do not enter into this calculation at all. Indeed, in order to define value magnitudes themselves, it is first necessary to specify the socio-technical conditions of production. Thus, at best, analysing value categories is a redundant step, an unnecessary detour from the systematic analysis of the two determinants of profit.[9]

[9] Steedman also argues that under certain circumstances (i.e., joint production and fixed capital) the attempt to calculate profits from values is not only unnecessary, but can give an incorrect answer. After demonstrating that values can give incorrect calculations of the profit rate, however, he then goes on to show that if values themselves are calculated in a somewhat more complex manner, as suggested by M. Morishima, a correct calculation of the rate of profit again becomes possible. The heart of his critique, therefore, is that values are irrelevant for the calculation of profits.

The objection has been raised by both Marxists and non-Marxists that Morishima's strategy for calculating labour times is such a departure from Marx's own method that the proofs based on this method have absolutely nothing to do with the labour theory of value. The heart of this objection is that whereas in Marx's analysis labour values are always additive—that is, the labour value in two commodities is always the sum of the labour values in each—in Morishima's approach labour values may be non-additive. The question then becomes whether within Marxist theory, non-additive values make any sense at all. This seems to me to be an issue which requires much deeper investigation before it can be definitely answered. In any event, as stated earlier, I will not attempt to deal with the problem of joint production here.

The logic of this analysis rests on two premises. First, a mathematical calculation has the status of a proof about a process of causation. A mathematical derivation is viewed as a kind of thought-experiment, which replicates, in thought, a set of real conditions that cannot be observed in a pure state in a social world. If the assumptions used to frame this derivation are reasonable, then a redundant step in the calculation is viewed as a redundant step in the real world's causal process. Second, this formal argument is bolstered by a behavioural argument about the nature of the choices and decisions of the actors within the process being studied. Since the actors themselves make choices based on the real wage and on the technical conditions of production, and since these conditions are sufficient to provide a derivation of the magnitude of profits, the mathematical argument can be interpreted as linking the behaviours of real people to the structural outcome (profits).

It is important to note that this perspective on profit determination does not argue that the socio-technical conditions of production and the real wage rate alone provide a full theory of profits, but only that they are the proximate causes of profits. Class struggle, for example, can still play a pivotal role in the dynamics of profit determination, in the form of struggles over both the technical conditions of production and the real wage. An example of the former would be struggle within production over the introduction of new machines; struggles within the labour market, of course, shape the real wage.

The critical point of the model is not to collapse the theory of profits into a simple two-factor account, but rather to argue that other causes have their effects on profits by virtue of their effects on real wages and technical conditions. Thus, class struggles which have no effects on either of these factors could not have effects on aggregate profits.

Marxist Accounts

Traditional Marxist accounts share with Sraffian accounts a commitment to organizing the multiple determinants of profits into an ordered structure of determination. But they differ in assigning a privileged status to surplus labour (in the form of surplus-value)[10]

[10] For convenience in this discussion I will not constantly refer to 'surplus labour in the form of surplus-value', but simply to 'surplus-value'. Surplus labour is ap-

within the structural model of determination: in Marxist theory, real wages and technical conditions ⨍ production have their effects on profits by virtue of their effects on the creation of surplus-value. Other causes of variation in profits may be two steps removed from the final outcome. The weather, for example, may influence profits by virtue of its influence on socio-technical conditions and real wages; these, in turn, influence profits by virtue of their effects on surplus-value. This basic model is illustrated in figure 3.

In this account, changes in the mix of commodities in the real wage or changes in the socio-technical conditions of production that have no consequences for the amount of surplus-value could have no effects on the total amount of profit. Only insofar as they influence surplus-value can they affect aggregate profits. It is by virtue of this strategic location within the process of profit-determination that Marxists have referred to surplus-value as the 'origin' of profits.

The various critical discussions of the labour theory of value based on the work of Sraffa and others have demonstrated that, stated in this simple way, the model in figure 3 is simply incorrect. It can be shown, for example, that where there are choices of techniques of production, it is possible to increase (or decrease) the total magnitude of profits even if there are no changes in the amount of total surplus-value produced. At least at first glance, this would seem to invalidate the model of determination in figure 3 in favour of that presented in figure 2.

In fact, it is possible to recast slightly the model of determination in the traditional Marxist theory so as to preserve the central point of the theory and yet accommodate these objections. In order to do this, however, it is necessary to move beyond the simple notion of homogeneous determination expressed in the models so far, and replace it with a more complex notion of causation, one in which

---

propriated by dominant classes in all class societies, but it only takes the form of surplus-value in capitalist ones. It should be noted that even in capitalist society some surplus labour is performed which is not represented as surplus-value (e.g. by wage-earners in state bureaucracies, in which no commodities are produced but surplus labour may still be performed). It is only that surplus labour which is performed in productive sectors of the economy and thus embodied in commodities as surplus-value that constitutes the basis of profits within Marxist theory. For simplicity, therefore, I will generally refer directly to surplus-value in this exposition.

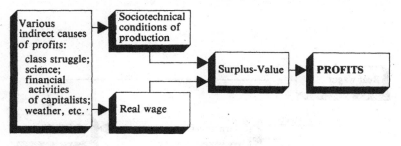

FIGURE 3
**The Marxist Account of the Determination of Profits,
Simple Version**

there are different kinds of causal relations between elements in a theory. These different kinds of causation I have referred to elsewhere as 'modes of determination'.[11]

For our immediate purposes, two modes of determination are particularly important:

1. *Structural limitation*, in which one structure or element systematically sets limits of possible variation on another structure or element. Within those limits, there is a variety of possible outcomes, but the limits themselves are determinate.

2. *Selection* of specific outcomes from a range of structurally limited possibilities. In a sense, this is a mode of determination which establishes limits within limits. Depending upon the specific process being investigated, there could be several nested layers of such selection processes.

The model of determination in figure 3 can now be recast in terms of modes of determination. A first approximation of this more complex model appears in figure 4. To keep this initial elaboration simple, I have limited the model to four elements: the real wage, the socio-technical conditions of production, surplus-value, and profits. The socio-technical conditions of production establish the basic limits

---

[11] See Erik Olin Wright, *Class, Crisis and the State*, London, NLB 1978, chapter 1 for an extended discussion of modes of determination.

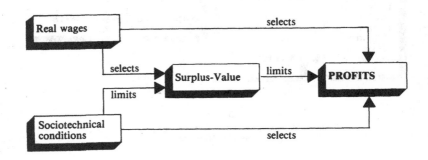

FIGURE 4

**Modes of Determination in the Marxist Account of Profits,
First Approximation**

on the creation of surplus-value. Since total labour performed in production is one aspect of the socio-technical conditions of production, these conditions clearly specify the maximum possible amount of surplus-value (i.e., the maximum when the real wage is zero). Within these limits, the real wage specifies exactly what proportion of the total labour performed within production will be 'surplus' value, and thus real wages act as a selection determinant of surplus-value within the limits established by the technical conditions of production.

The interesting part of the model involves the mutual interdependence between surplus-value, real wages, technical conditions, and profits. As pictured in figure 4, surplus-value establishes the fundamental limits on the range of possible profits. With a given quantity of surplus-value, there is an absolute ceiling on the possible quantity of profits. When surplus-value is zero, no profits at all are possible; as surplus-value increases, the possible maximum profit also increases monotonically.[12] Within these limits, however, both the socio-

---

[12] Steedman cites Morishima's analysis in support of the proposition that 'the profit rate and growth rate are positive if and only if surplus labour, as newly defined by

technical conditions of production and the real wage have a selection effect on profits. This means that if we were to hold constant the amount of surplus labour performed (i.e. the amount of surplus-value), and were to vary the techniques of production or the real wage (with the constraint that such variation would not affect the amount of surplus labour), we could in fact alter total profits, *but only within the determinate limits.*[13] Surplus-value, then, would remain the 'origin' of profits, not in the sense that it is the *only* determinant of profits, but in the sense that the effectivity of all other determinants of profits occurs either by virtue of their effects on surplus-value or within limits established by surplus-value.

Figure 5 illustrates the outcome of this limiting process (the shape of the limits is arbitrary in this diagram). For any given amount of surplus labour performed in production, there is an upper and lower bound on the amount of profits produced. The amount of surplus-value, then, constitutes the explanation of those levels of profits that are impossible; the socio-technical conditions of production and the real wage explain—'predict'—which of the many possible levels of profits actually occurs.

This interpretation of surplus-value as setting the limits on possible profits may not, initially, seem very intuitive. How can it be, in the real world (as opposed to in the mathematics), that the amount of surplus-value places bounds on possible profits? One possible way of looking at this is to see the range of possible profits within those bounds as a consequence of the social process by which values (labour times) are transformed into prices. It has often been remarked that under conditions where there is the same 'organic composition of capital' in all economic sectors (i.e., where the

---

Morishima, is positive' (p. 204). Positive surplus labour, therefore, generates positive profits. Since any productive technology has a finite maximum possible profit for given levels of inputs, therefore for a given level of surplus labour (surplus-value) the maximum profit will be positive and finite. This implies that as surplus labour is increased, maximum possible profits also increase.

[13] This argument does not concern the problem of how capitalists actually make their choices among techniques. Capitalists certainly do not in any sense 'hold constant' the amount of surplus labour. The argument here is about a structural constraint on the possible effects of various choices which capitalists make, regardless of how they actually make their decisions. That is, the maximum possible profit which a capitalist can obtain by trying to change techniques of production is limited by the amount of surplus labour generated in production.

48

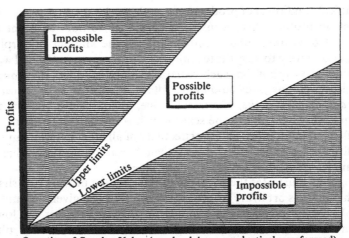

Quantity of Surplus-Value (surplus labour productively performed)

FIGURE 5
Surplus-Value and Possible vs. Impossible Profits

Note: The shape of the limits in this figure must be seen as rather speculative. They have been drawn as straight lines for simplicity, rather than because of a formal theory which indicates that this is indeed the shape of the limits. Anwar Shaikh is currently working on a formal derivation of the shape of these limits.

Shaikh has suggested in a personal communication that the angle between these two lines is determined by two factors: (1) The degree of homogeneity of organic compositions of capital across sectors. In situations where the organic compositions of capital are identical across sectors, the angle becomes zero and the limits collapse into a single straight line. As the organic compositions become more heterogeneous, the angle becomes wider. In a modern economy in which all sectors are highly interconnected, it is extremely unlikely that this heterogeneity of organic compositions of capital is very large. (2) The rate of accumulation (as a proportion of total possible accumulation). For a given structure of socio-technical conditions of production (i.e. a given distribution of organic compositions of capital across sectors of production), the angle between the limits will vary with the rate of accumulation. When all surplus-value is accumulated, regardless of the heterogeneity of organic compositions of capital, the angle will also be zero. The maximum angle, then, occurs when the rate of accumulation is zero, i.e. when all surplus-value is taken out of the cycle of production. (A proposition closely related to this one is proven in Anwar Shaikh, *Theories of Value and Theories of Distribution*, PhD dissertation, Columbia University, 1973.)

If these propositions are correct, then to the extent that the organic compositions of capital in highly integrated economies tend to be relatively homogeneous across sectors and the rate of accumulation tends to be close to the maximum, the limits on possible profits will be fairly narrow. A full defence and specification of these propositions in terms of a theory of limits on profits remains to be elaborated.

technical conditions of production are the same, expressed in labour-value terms), prices will be directly proportional to values and thus the upper and lower bound on profits will coincide. Under these conditions, figure 4 is reduced to figure 3, and the profit/surplus-labour relationship in figure 5 collapses into a single line.

Under normal conditions, of course, the organic compositions of capital are not the same in all sectors, and thus there will be a systematic pattern of deviations of prices from values. In sectors with high organic compositions of capital (e.g., petrochemicals), prices will be above values; in sectors with low organic compositions (e.g., textiles), prices will be below values. Since there is no necessary reason for positive deviations and negative deviations to exactly balance out in the aggregate (even in an 'equilibrium' situation), the quantity of actual aggregate social profits will depend upon the specific distributions of such deviations. In these terms, the upper and lower bounds in figure 5 can be viewed as defining the maximum possible positive and negative aggregate deviations of prices from values that can be generated through the process by which value magnitudes are transformed into actual prices. In this way of posing the question, the transformation 'problem' is understood as a transformation 'process', a real process that occurs in the world and has real effects on the actual levels of profits. The total amount of surplus labour performed defines the limits of what can be converted into profits through this transformation process; the actual distribution of organic compositions of capital in the economy determines the actual profits which will be obtainable within these limits.[14]

Two major objections could be raised to the model of determination in figure 4: (1) since surplus-value is itself determined by the socio-technical conditions and the real wage, it plays no autonomous role in the process and is thus still 'redundant'; (2) it is arbitrary to claim that surplus-value establishes the basic limits on the outcome, since if any 'factor of production' is held constant, there will be an upper limit to profits. The first objection basically misses the point of the model. The argument is not that surplus-value is an autonomous

---

[14] It should be noted that this issue has nothing to do with the problem of 'realization' of surplus-value, i.e., of actually selling the commodities which embody that surplus-value.

cause of profits or a primal cause, an 'unmoved mover' in the profit determination process. On the contrary, it is precisely because surplus-value is an endogenous factor within that process that it can be viewed as a privileged determinant. This point is much simpler if we look at figure 3, the model of determination which would hold if organic compositions of capital were the same in all sectors of the economy. In this model, surplus-value is still seen as entirely a consequence of the socio-technical conditions of production and the real wage. But here we can see that these two factors have their effects on profits only by virtue of their effects on surplus-value. You could change the real wage and technical conditions as much as you like, but if those changes did not affect the quantity of surplus-value, then the amount of profits would remain unchanged. Surplus-value, therefore, is the fundamental source of profits in figure 3, in the sense that changes in surplus-value are the necessary *and* sufficient conditions for changes in profits.

The fact that the model becomes more complex in figure 4 does not change this basic relationship. Changes in surplus-value are no longer sufficient conditions for changes in actual profits, but they remain necessary and sufficient conditions for changes in the *limits* on possible profits.

The second objection raises a different sort of problem. Certainly, given the actual availability of resources, if a particular input to production becomes severely restricted, then the maximum amount of profits that is possible in practice could be less than the maximum specified in figure 5. Shortages of specific resources can therefore impose narrower real limits than the amount of surplus labour performed in production. Furthermore, absence of or restriction on a source of raw materials could make it impossible to increase actual productive labour and hence surplus-value and profit. These observations may give rise to the argument that, from the point of view of the formal *calculation* of limits, it is arbitrary to base those limits in labour rather than in any other factor of production. In practical terms, non-labour limits may have a more constraining effect on profits than labour limits (e.g., in an energy crisis).

Ultimately, to answer this objection we must move beyond the simple model represented in figure 4. The reason for selecting surplus-value as the pivotal limiting process is not because in every situation surplus-value defines the actual limits to profits. It could well be that in some circumstances shortages of raw materials or energy or some other factor of production put a ceiling on profits that is more restrictive than the surplus-value limits. Rather, the central reason for selecting surplus-value as the key limiting process is because it enables us to construct a theory of the social determination of profits, in particular a theory of the systematic linkage between class structure, class struggle, and profits.

To understand the rationale behind this claim, we need briefly to examine the concept of classes in Marxist theory and see how the specific theory of profits plays a role in the general theory of classes. For our present purposes the key point is that classes are defined above all by positions within production relations, not by their positions within market relations or other aspects of social relations. The decisive aspect of those production relations centres on the ability of one class to force another class—the direct producers—to perform labour beyond what is needed for the reproduction of the direct producers themselves, and to appropriate the products of that 'surplus labour'. In all class modes of production, the dominant class is defined by those positions which appropriate surplus labour, the subordinate class by those positions which have their surplus labour appropriated.[15]

Different modes of production differ in the precise mechanisms through which this surplus labour is produced and appropriated. In feudalism, as has often been pointed out, the mechanisms of appropriation are transparent: the feudal peasant is directly forced to perform surplus labour for the feudal lord in the form of labour dues. How, then, does it come to pass in capitalist society, where workers are not forced to perform labour dues, that the capitalist class manages to appropriate the labour of workers? The labour theory of

---

[15] It is impossible here to present a sustained justification for defining classes in terms of social relations of production, and in particular in terms of the social relations of domination over labour and surplus labour. This definition is not simply posed as an analytical convention on the part of the theorist, but rather as a way of understanding the real dynamics of social struggle and social change. For a more elaborate defence of the underlying logic of this conception of class, see Erik Olin Wright, *Class Structure and Income Determination*, New York 1979, chapters 1 and 2, and 'Varieties of Marxist Conceptions of Class Structure', discussion paper, Institute for Research on Poverty, University of Wisconsin, Madison, 1978.

value in general, and the theory of surplus-value in particular, provide a framework for understanding this relationship, i.e., how it happens that capitalist profits—the monetized value of the surplus product—embody the mechanism through which capitalists appropriate surplus labour from workers. The focus on surplus labour as the underlying process which establishes limits on profits, therefore, is itself derived from the class analysis of exploitation in general and of the specific forms of such exploitation in capitalism.

There is, therefore, an element of truth in the charge that the choice of surplus-value as a limiting condition is 'arbitrary'. It is arbitrary with respect to the specific problem of *calculating* profits, and if this was the only reason for a theory of profit determination, then indeed there would be no grounds for choosing surplus-value over any other factor as a limiting condition (furthermore, one would want in principle to refuse any a priori claim about limiting conditions and would simply observe empirically which factor-scarcities tended to impinge most consistently on profits). But the choice is far from arbitrary with respect to a broader theoretical project— understanding classes and class struggle in terms of social relations of production, and linking such class struggles to the specific analysis of capitalist mechanisms of appropriating surplus labour through surplus-value and profits. It is because we are interested in understanding class relations and class struggle that we seek a model of determination of profits that allows us to link classes to profits, not because we have an autonomous interest in profits as such, independently of their social determinants and consequences. In these terms, the specific way in which one formalizes the model for the calculation of profits is conceptually subordinated to the qualitative theory of social relations within which profits acquire their social content.[16] The theory of profit determination is an element in the theory of classes rather than vice versa.

[16] This answer to the objection that the focus on surplus labour as a limiting process is arbitrary comes perilously close to a Weberian methodological stance on theory construction, namely that the categories we choose are strictly subordinated to the subjective preferences of the analyst. Because Marxists are subjectively committed to a certain set of values and thus have an interest in studying exploitation, an ideal-type model revolving around surplus labour is appropriate. In fact, the argument does not rest simply on the value preferences of the theorist, but on the realist claim that classes

Figure 4 does not, by itself, illustrate this broader theoretical structure. In the first place, class struggle does not explicitly appear in the model, and it must be formally reincorporated for this model to serve as a guide for research. Secondly, the model as it stands is rather undialectical, in the sense that the determinations all run in one direction and there is no mechanism internal to the model for restructuring the elements in the model themselves. A Marxist theory of profits must not simply be an account of the 'variables' which determine profits, but of the total social process within which profit determination represents one particular aspect.

In order to make the model more dialectical in this sense, we need to introduce one additional mode of determination: *transformation*. This is a mode of determination in which the practices of individuals and classes act to restructure (transform) elements within a social process. The very concept of 'practice' within Marxist theory must be understood in terms of transformation as a relation of determination: practices are activities through which nature, social relations, and experiences are transformed. Like 'selection', transformation relations occur within structurally defined limits; not every transformation is possible at any given moment in the history of a social structure. Transformations differ from selections in involving the conscious activities of classes and individuals rather than simply the relations between structural elements. [17]

With this understanding of transformation, we can now further extend the model of determination to include class struggle and class structure. This model is presented in figure 6. Within this model, forms of class struggle act as transformation determinants of real wages within limits established by the underlying socio-technical conditions of production. Given those technical constraints, only certain transformations of real wages are possible. Similarly, class

and class struggle, defined in terms of production relations, are the decisive social forces which shape social change. Classes are real, not simply analytical conventions. Surplus labour also establishes real limits on possible profits, not simply analytical limits (although actual profits may generally fall well within those limits). The model of profit determination in figure 4, therefore, provides a way of linking these two categories within a theory of profit determination.

[17] For a more extended discussion of transformation as a mode of determination, see Wright, *Class, Crisis and the State*, pp. 21–3.

54

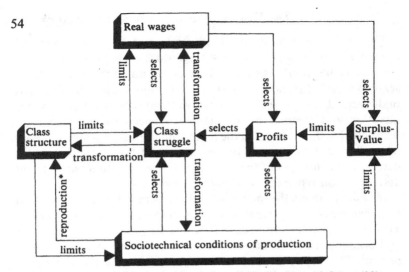

*For a discussion of reproduction as a mode of determination, see Wright, *Class, Crisis and the State*, pp. 18-21.

FIGURE 6

**Modes of Determination in the Marxist Account of Profits,
Complex Approximation**

struggles transform the technical conditions of production themselves, in particular in the form of struggles over the labour process and
technological change. And, of course, class struggle transforms class
structure. Class struggle, in turn, is structurally limited by class
structure and is influenced by the level of profits in a selection
relationship: when profits are low, the capitalist class will attempt to
engage in class practices which lower the real wage and transform the
technical conditions of production in ways which increase surplus
value; when profit rates are high, the working class will be able more
effectively to struggle for increases in real wages and to resist
proletarianization within the labour process. In this sense, profits act
as a selective mechanism on class struggle, particularly on economic
forms of class struggle. Real wages and the socio-technical conditions
of production also act as selection determinants of class struggle,
within limits imposed by class structures.

One particular aspect of this model is especially worth noting.
Class struggles do not directly affect surplus-value and exploitation,
but operate through effects on the socio-technical conditions of
production (in particular on the total amount of labour performed,

i.e., the length and the intensity of the working day) and on the real wage of workers. This is one of the distinctive features of capitalism. In pre-capitalist modes of production class struggles were directly struggles over surplus labour, i.e., over that portion of total social labour which was appropriated by the dominant class. This was particularly true when such appropriation took the form of forced labour. In capitalism, precisely because the performance of surplus labour is disguised through the exchange process and the organization of production as a capitalist labour process, class struggles are never over surplus labour as such.

If the model in figure 6 is correct, however, it is still the case that class struggles have their most decisive impact on profits *by virtue of their effects on surplus-value.* As we shall see later on in this paper, this has very important implications for the kinds of empirical research agenda which this model generates.

The model as it stands is underdeveloped in a number of respects. First of all, there are critical elements which are totally absent from the model: the state, forms of class organization, ideology, etc. Particularly in assessing the relationship between class structure and class struggle these additional elements play a central role.[18] Secondly, there are a number of connections between the elements in the model which have not been specified. For example, profits probably have a selective effect on technical conditions of production even apart from their impact via class struggle, since a given level of profits makes possible certain kinds of innovations and not others. The connections appearing in the model, therefore, do not exhaust the possible linkages between elements. Finally, the model itself does not put any concrete content on the various relations of determination, though it does indicate their general character. There is no indication, for example, of how narrow or broad the limits of profits imposed by surplus-value actually are. There is no specification of the actual range of possible real wages imposed by the socio-technical conditions of production, nor of the range of forms of class struggle imposed by the underlying class structure. In order to add such concrete content it is necessary to transpose the model from the high level of abstraction at which we have discussed it so far and use it in

---

[18] See Wright, *Class, Crisis and the State*, pp. 97–110.

56

the investigation of specific class structures, socio-technical conditions of production, forms of struggle, etc. In these terms, the model should be seen as a road map for a research agenda rather than as a summary of the results of an investigation.

2. Theoretical Assessment

From the vantage point of the Marxist labour theory of value, both the causal-agnostic model and the Sraffian model of profit determination are partially correct but incomplete. They are correct in that, in different ways and at *different levels of abstraction*, they do in fact specify real relations, real effects. They are incomplete in that they inadequately theorize the conditions under which they in fact represent the real process of profit determination.

In the case of the causal-agnostic account, the model can be viewed as a collapsed *description* of all the processes which have determinate effects on profits. Figure 1 is a causal account at the lowest level of abstraction, a level in which it is impossible to order causes within any kind of systematic structure of determination. All one can do is give an account of the various 'factors' which have effects.

The Sraffian account of profits is a considerable advance beyond this simple, descriptive model. It can be interpreted as specifying the determination of the level of profits at a middle level of abstraction. Given the basic limits on profits imposed by the underlying structure of class relations and balance of class forces, reflected in the level of surplus labour, the Sraffian model provides an account of the selection determinants of profits. If one's interest in studying profits is limited to calculating profits, then this level of abstraction is as far as one needs to go. As in any causal process, a complete prediction of the outcome is possible simply on the basis of the analysis of all of the selection processes.[19]

[19] A simple way of illustrating this argument is by comparing pluralist theory with the Marxist analysis of the capitalist state. The pluralist theory of electoral politics may be able quite accurately to predict the outcomes of specific elections, the kinds of coalitions which form in the US Congress around competing 'interest groups', and the likelihood for given pieces of legislation passing. Pluralism as a theory of politics (at least in its sophisticated versions) may in fact provide a rich account of the selection

A complete social explanation of the outcome, however, requires an understanding of the social determinants of structural limitation, and this requires moving to a higher level of abstraction. This is precisely what the Marxist model of profit determination attempts to do in the analysis of the relationship of surplus labour to profits. This analysis goes beyond the Sraffian account in two critical aspects. First, it specifies the structural limits within which the Sraffian selection processes have their effects. Whereas the Sraffian account accurately calculates the level of specific profits, the Marxist account explains the social possibility of those profits. Second, the Marxist account embeds its analysis of the determination of profits in a larger theory of social relations and determinations, a theory in which profits themselves act as determinants, not just outcomes.

Such a broader theory has advantages over both the causal-agnostic and the Sraffian accounts. It enables us to go beyond a simple, positive account of societies as they are, and develop a critical theory of societies as they might become. In this context, the analysis of structural limitations as a mode of determination becomes very important, for it is by grasping the limits of possibility within a given social structure that we can begin to understand scientifically the changes in those possibilities that will result from the transformation of the social structures themselves.

This assessment of the causal-agnostic and Sraffian models, it must be stressed, assumes the adequacy of the Marxist account itself. From the standpoint of the causal-agnostic theory advanced by Cutler *et al.*, both the Marxist and Sraffian accounts make totally arbitrary claims about the ordering of various causal processes. In particular, Cutler *et al.* argue that the Marxist claim about the centrality of surplus labour is a purely ideological claim. The category of surplus labour is introduced into the analysis because it is necessary in order

---

processes of policy outcomes within the state. But it is totally incapable of providing a theory of the limiting processes, of the determinations of the range of possible policies considered by legislative bodies or the range of possible candidates in elections. The Marxist theory of the class character of the state is precisely an account of such limiting processes. If all one wanted to do was to predict (calculate) which policy is actually passed in a legislature, the pluralist theory would be adequate to the task; but if one wants an explanation of the outcome, it is necessary to develop a theory of the limits, and this is what the Marxist theory of the state accomplishes.

to analyse capitalism as a system of exploitation. But there is no scientific basis, they insist, for arguing that exploitation or surplus labour have any particularly distinctive effects on *any* outcomes, including profits. And thus there is certainly no reason to elevate them to the status of 'fundamental' determinants.

Similarly, those who espouse the Sraffian framework would reject the claim of its incompleteness. Since an account of determination and calculation are seen as equivalent, and since the mathematical thought-experiment demonstrates that the calculation of profits can be entirely derived from the technical conditions of production and the real wage, surplus labour can play no role in a model of determination of profits. To be redundant in a calculation implies having no real effects in the world. 'Structural limits', therefore, are simply irrelevant and metaphysical.

If one accepts the methodological strictures of either the causal-agnostic or Sraffian stances, then the category surplus labour or surplus-value at most can be considered one of many causes (the first stance) or an irrelevant category (the second stance). But if we reject both of these methodological prescriptions and argue both that causes are structured in systematic ways and that certain causes establish limits within which other causes have their effects, then the possibility for surplus-value to play a pivotal role is reintroduced.

Rather than debate these methodological principles in the abstract, I would like to turn to the question of the empirical agendas which would flow from each of these models. In the end, the cogency of any defence of a particular methodological or epistemological stance within social science depends a great deal upon the richness of the research which it is capable of stimulating and the power of the explanations of social processes which emerge from that research.

3. Implication for Social Research

Theoretical frameworks impinge on empirical investigations in four basic ways.

1. *Questions.* Theory defines the range of possible questions that can be asked in an empirical investigation. As Althusser has stressed, this

implies both a positive and negative process: certain questions are 'unaskable' within a given theoretical framework. This is not to suggest that simply by knowing the broad theoretical framework we know precisely what questions will be asked. Theories impose limits on questioning, but there are many possible questions that can be posed within a given theory.

2. *Concepts.* Theories also provide the conceptual categories used to answer a given question. They define the range of admissible categories which could potentially enter into an explanation or be used to formulate specific hypotheses within a general explanation. Concepts are always produced within theories; they are never somehow given by a neutral cognitive process 'outside' of theory. Different theoretical frameworks, therefore, do not merely shape the questions we would ask of the world, but the categories we would use in framing an answer.

3. *Expectations.* Theories also contain specific types of expectations about the alternative possible answers to a given question. Obviously, if there was only one possible answer, there would be no need to conduct research at all. The importance of empirical investigation stems precisely from the fact that there are generally multiple possible answers to a particular question, given the conceptual tools available. But a theory generally does specify the relevant, interesting, alternative expectations; research then contributes to understanding the precise mechanisms or processes which lead to one alternative over another.

4. *Answers.* To the extent that a theoretical framework has been used to ask questions, with specific concepts exploring specific sets of expectations, then gradually the theory also develops a set of received answers, a set of substantive theses which have been examined through various investigations. These answers constitute the body of knowledge within the theory which is augmented through research. Such answers are always, of course, provisional and are subject to transformation in light of new research, new investigation. As is often remarked, there can be no final guarantee that an answer is 'true', but only a methodology for adjudicating the cogency of contending answers.

All of these elements are constantly in a process of transformation. New questions are posed in the light of unexpected answers (anomalies, to use Kuhn's expression); new concepts are produced to explore new questions; new expectations are formulated in the light of conceptual breakthroughs. The relationship between theory and research cannot be a static one, any more than can the relationship between theory and practice.

In the discussion which follows I shall focus on the first of these aspects, the ways in which a theoretical structure defines the relevant range of questions. In many ways this is the most decisive, for the specific concepts one adopts and the range of alternative expectations one might entertain are themselves shaped by the particular objects of investigation. In any event, the sharpest contrasts between the three perspectives we are examining centre on the kinds of questions they generate, so it is on this level that we will concentrate.

Causal-Agnostic Models

A causal-agnostic model of profit determination begins with the presumption that there are multiple, pertinent, necessary conditions for the existence and magnitude of profits. A theoretical argument would then be used to elaborate a list of such necessary conditions; an empirical investigation would be used to establish their relative importance in the actual determination of profits.

One of the critical general questions which a causal-agnostic might ask in this context would be: Under what conditions does factor A or B become relatively more important in the determination of profits? For example, it could be argued that the more agriculture is mechanized, the less do the profits generated within the agricultural sector vary with the weather. Both mechanization and meteorology are pertinent causes of profits, but the development of the former reduces the effectivity of the latter. Another example would centre on the relationship between scientific knowledge and profits. Cutler *et al.* argue, in passing, that as direct, living labour becomes a smaller portion of the total costs of production, scientific knowledge is likely to increase as a determinant of profits.[20]

[20] Cutler *et al.*, Marx's *'Capital' and Capitalism Today*, 1, pp. 43–4.

All such questions involve investigating the relative weight of different factors within a process of causation. Since there is no logical ordering of causes possible, the only task of research is to establish relative empirical importance, and the conditions under which that relative importance itself varies.

Such a research agenda is likely to produce a rather rich descriptive picture of the principal sources of variation in profits. As Cutler *et al.* suggest, one of the outcomes of the research could be a systematic account of the various forms of the production process as a whole (not just the labour process as one aspect of that production), and of the relationship of these different general processes to different levels of profit and forms of distribution.

What such research would not do, however, is provide an account of how these sources of variation produce their effects. A causal-agnostic stance is incapable of generating theories of the actual *mechanisms* through which profits are generated, since it rejects the possibility of a structural ordering of determinations. To say that the entire process is the 'mechanism' is to say no more than that profits are the outcome of everything which determines them; it is not to specify the internal logic which generates that outcome.

Both the Sraffian and Marxist models of profit determination organize their research agendas around such mechanisms.

The Sraffian Model

The heart of the Sraffian model is the claim that the socio-technical conditions of production and the real wage constitute the actual mechanisms which determine real profits. An empirical investigation of the determinants of these two processes, therefore, could be interpreted as an account of how the mechanisms which determine profits work in the real world, i.e., what role they play in translating the decisions of actors, the weather, or the political conditions of social conflict into a specific kind of outcome, profits.

The pivotal research question which this model generates is thus: What are the determinants of the real wage and of the technical conditions of production? This leads immediately to two general objects of empirical study: the determinants of the market power of wage labourers and capitalists, and technological change. The first of these concerns would involve investigations of such things as the impact of trade unionism on the collective bargaining power of workers; the effects of monopoly concentration on the relative power of capital; the role of the state, particularly the welfare state, in regulating the market conflict between labour and capital and in guaranteeing a certain real wage for workers; or the role of imperialism in making possible higher real wages for workers in the imperialist centres. All of these empirical questions would contribute to understanding the process through which the real wage was concretely determined.

The study of technological change would be equally important within the Sraffian model of profit determination. Such an investigation would include such things as the role of competition in technical change, the relationship of changing market conditions (including changes in the real wage) to technical innovation, and the role of social conflict within the labour process itself in technical change.

Taken together, all of these factors would define the broad social determinants of actual profits. The specific theory of profit determination within the Sraffian framework then provides an account of the structural mechanisms which link these determinants to the outcome.

The Marxist Model

All of the questions which are suggested by the Sraffian model of profit determination can be asked within a Marxist framework as well, since the Sraffian model is in a sense contained within the Marxist model. The difference between the two models centres on the ways in which class struggle intervenes in the process.

In the Sraffian model, as in the Marxist model, class struggle within the market plays a critical role in the determination of the real wage. The real wage is conceptualized as a zero-sum game between wage-earners and capitalists, in which every gain for workers is—at least in the short run—a loss for capital (a deduction from profits); thus the market conflict between labour and capital over the real wage is intrinsic to their very relationship.

But what about class struggle within production, within the labour process itself? In Sraffian theory, social conflict over the labour process is simply one of many influences on the technical conditions

The Value Controversy and Social Research 63

of production. Since the labour component of the technical conditions of production has no theoretically salient role in the socio-technical conditions of production, the social struggles within the labour process have no a priori importance. It may turn out, on examination, that such struggles are important, but there would be no particular reason for a Sraffian theorist to focus research on that aspect of the determination of the socio-technical conditions of production over any other aspect.

It is quite otherwise within Marxist theory. Because surplus-value is seen as defining the absolute limits on profits, the central research question immediately becomes: what are the social processes which influence the amount of surplus labour performed? On the one hand, as in Sraffian theory, this directs our attention to the process by which real wages are determined. But unlike Sraffian theory, the Marxist model also directs our research efforts toward those transformations of the socio-technical conditions of production that directly impinge on surplus labour. It is for this reason that the Marxist analysis of production revolves around the analysis of the *labour process* as such, and not simply the technical input-output matrices of production.

The distinctive questions that Marxists would ask in the investigation of the labour process all centre on the relationship between the labour process and the performance of surplus labour: In what ways does technical change impinge on the struggles over control of labour within the labour process?[21] What is the relationship between the changing structure of *skills* within production and the problem of extracting surplus labour from the working class?[22] Do the imperatives of social control within production mean that different categories of employees perform different amounts of surplus labour?[23]

[21] See especially David Noble, 'Social Choice in Machine Design', and Michael Burawoy, 'Towards a Marxist Theory of the Labor Process', both in *Politics & Society*, special issue on the labour process, vol. 8, nos. 3–4, 1978.
[22] See Harry Braverman, *Labor and Monopoly Capital*, New York 1974, for a discussion of the relationship of degradation of labour to exploitation.
[23] For discussion of income determination and the social relations of production, see Erik Olin Wright and Luca Perrone, 'Marxist Class Categories and Income Inequality', *American Sociological Review* (42:1), 1977; Erik Olin Wright, 'Race, Class and Income Inequality', *American Journal of Sociology*, May 1978, and *Class Structure and Income Determination*, New York 1979; and Christian Baudelot, Roger Establet,

At first glance it might seem that the differences between the Marxist and the Sraffian accounts are not so drastic. After all, it is in principle possible for these questions to be asked by a Sraffian, even if they would play a less central role in the theory. Ian Steedman certainly insists on this point when he argues that all of the basic Marxist questions about the labour process are compatible with the Sraffian account of the determination of profits.

On closer inspection, however, the centrality of surplus labour within the Marxist account produces certain fundamental differences from a Sraffian analysis. In particular, the concept of 'class' and 'class struggle' is different in the two frameworks. Within Sraffian theory, classes play a *systematic* role only in terms of the determination of the real wage, and the combatants in the class struggle are defined by their location within the market. All wage-earners, therefore, would be part of the working class, since the income of all wage-earners takes the form of a deduction from profits. The Sraffian account of the determination of profits is thus much more consistent with the Weberian definition of classes and class struggle than the Marxist conception.

In Marxist theory, the concept of class is closely linked to the question of surplus labour. Classes are defined by the social relations of production, not primarily by market relations. Within those social relations of production, the control over surplus labour is a particularly salient dimension. Not all wage-earners, in fact, fall into the working class, since not all wage-earners are excluded from control over surplus labour.[24] The class struggle within production, therefore, is structured by class relations, defined in terms of the social relations of domination within the labour process. While both Marxists and Sraffian theorists might look at the impact of class struggle on technical change, the content of the categories used in such an investigation would be different.

---

and Jacques Malemort, *La petite bourgeoisie en France*, Paris 1976. The work of Baudelot *et al.* in particular attempts to examine value relations in studying the income of various privileged categories of wage-earners.

[24] See Wright, *Class, Crisis and the State* (chapter 2) and 'Varieties of Conceptions of Class Structure', University of Wisconsin, for detailed discussions of the definition of the working class and of the problem of domination/subordination within production with respect to control over surplus labour.

There is, of course, one other alternative. A theorist could derive the categories of a class analysis from Marxist theory and the categories of the technical economic analysis from the Sraffian framework. This is very close to what Steedman, in fact, does. The advantage of such eclecticism is that it may enable a research project to draw on the theoretical strengths of different traditions; the limitation is that the categories drawn from the different traditions may cease to have any coherent theoretical relationship to each other. Given that surplus labour has no privileged status within Sraffian theory, it is hard to see why classes defined in terms of social relations of production should have any special role to play in the theory or its empirical applications.

The advantage of the developed Marxist model of determination in this respect is that it incorporates the predictive capacity of the Sraffian account while sustaining the theoretical centrality of surplus labour in the explanation of profits. Within this model, therefore, there is an internal basis for conceptualizing classes in terms of production relations and still empirically investigating the concrete determinants of profits in terms of the real wage and the technical conditions of production.

4. An Example: Value and the Labour Process

A great deal of solid empirical research has been done in recent years on the labour process, focusing both on the historical transformations of the labour process in the course of capitalist development and on the patterns of variations in the labour process in contemporary capitalism. While the labour theory of value has been implicit in most of this research, rarely is it explicitly incorporated into the conceptualization of the problem. What I would like to do here is show how the labour theory of value can directly inform the study of the labour process and its conflicts and transformations.

In order to link the labour theory of value to the study of the labour process, it will be helpful to systematically decompose the working day into a number of subcomponents. This is a familiar task in Marxist theory, since the fundamental division between 'necessary labour' (the labour needed to reproduce the direct producers) and

66

'surplus labour' is metaphorically conceived as a partition of the total number of hours worked within the working day. We can, however, make a number of additional distinctions within the working day which will facilitate our analysis of the labour process. These are schematically illustrated in figure 7.

Beginning at the bottom of the diagram, these components should be understood as follows.

1. *Physiological minimum necessary labour.* This is the amount of labour time it takes simply to reproduce the direct producers at a minimum subsistence level. With rare exceptions in advanced capitalist countries, the actual wage of workers is well above this level.

2. *Historical and moral component.* Above and beyond the physiological minimum labour, there is a component which Marx referred to as the 'historical and moral component' of the wage. It constitutes that part of the working day of an average worker (of average skills) devoted to producing the means of consumption of that worker beyond the physical minimum. Taken together, these first two components therefore constitute the social average value of labour power.

3. *Differential value of skilled labour-power.* Not all workers, however, have skills at the social average, and since skills themselves take labour time to produce and reproduce, an additional part of the working day must be devoted to covering the added value of skilled labour-power. The value of different types of labour-power, therefore, is the sum of the first three components of the working day. These constitute, together, what Marx referred to as 'necessary labour'.[25]

4. *Redistributed surplus-value.* Certain employees (some workers, but mainly people outside the working class who work for wages, such as managers) have incomes which are kept permanently above the value of their labour-power. That is, their wages do not reflect the costs of producing or reproducing their skills above and beyond

[25] Note that in many cases this third component will be insignificant or zero, and necessary labour becomes simply the first two components.

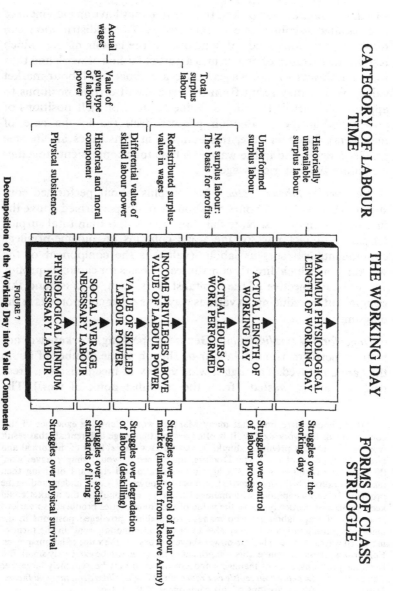

FIGURE 7
Decomposition of the Working Day into Value Components

socially average labour-power. In addition, they have an increment of redistributed surplus-value in their wage. This redistribution can result from various kinds of control over the labour market which restrict the entrance of people into a particular line of work and thus force employers to pay wages above a competitive labour-market value; or they may result from the capacity of certain positions to appropriate part of, the surplus-value because of their positions of power within the production process itself (as in the case of managers). In either case, this component constitutes an 'income privilege' embodied in the wage.[26] These four components together constitute the empirical wage.

5. *Net surplus labour (value).* Net surplus labour performed constitutes the number of hours of labour actually performed above the first four components. Note that this may be less than total surplus labour if in fact part of the wage contains an income-privilege component. Net surplus labour (value) is the component of the working day which directly constitutes the basis for capitalist profits. The critical objective of the capitalist class, then, is to expand this component by reducing, in various ways, the other components in the diagram.

6. *Unperformed surplus labour.* Generally speaking, workers will not actually perform as much labour on the job as the number of hours they are employed. Through a wide variety of mechanisms, a great deal of time is 'wasted' (from the capitalist point of view). The

[26] It is important to note that many Marxists would deny the existence of this component of the working day. It is often argued that wage differentials that result from special market privileges should be viewed as a special kind of 'historical and moral' component of the wage. Doctors, in this sense, would simply have 'won' through their forms of struggle a higher historical/moral standard of living than manual workers. This seems to me to be a much less powerful way of understanding the problem. Just as a capitalist who managed to gain a monopoly in the market could keep prices systematically above the value of the commodities produced, so various categories of wage-labourers who manage to establish privileged positions in the market or production are thereby able to obtain a 'monopoly rent' in the form of increased wages; a price of labour-power above and beyond the value of labour-power. For most workers, of course, this component of the wage will be extremely small. But for some positions, such as managers and executives, it may be extremely large. See Baudelot *et al.*, *La petite bourgeoisie en France*, and Wright, *Class Structure and Income Determination*, for discussions of this component of the wage.

difference between the length of the working day and the amount of labour actually performed can be referred to as unperformed potential surplus labour.

7. *Unavailable surplus labour.* The maximum possible amount of surplus labour technically possible, given a particular value of labour-power, is represented by the physiological maximum length of the working day. With extremely rare exceptions, the actual working day is much less than this. The difference between the two constitutes an historically unavailable quantity of surplus labour.

The diverse forms of economic class struggle can be interpreted as struggles which impinge differentially on each of these components of the working day. Although the research on these forms of struggle have not explicitly taken as their point of departure this entire schema, nevertheless the essential logic of this decomposition of the working day underlies many of the empirical studies of the labour process and class struggle.

Perhaps most obviously, class struggles over the length of the working day directly affect the amount of historically unavailable surplus labour. While such struggles were particularly salient in the nineteenth century, they continue today in the form of struggles over mandatory overtime and the thirty-hour week.

Struggles over the control of the labour process determine the amount of unperformed potential surplus labour. Much of the current research on the labour process has centred on this issue. Harry Braverman's discussion of the progressive separation of conception and execution is at root an argument about the loss of the capacity of workers to control the labour process, and conversely, the increasing capacity of capital to ensure that labour power is converted into labour within that process (i.e. that unperformed surplus labour is reduced).[27] Michael Burawoy's brilliant studies of the labour process within machine-tool production have also centred on this issue.[28] He argues that the pivotal problems facing capital within production are the 'securing' and 'obscuring' of the surplus.

[27] Harry Braverman, *Labor and Monopoly Capitalism.*
[28] Michael Burawoy, 'Towards a Marxist Theory of the Labor Process', *Politics & Society*, 8: 3–4, 1978; and *Manufacturing Consent*, Chicago 1979.

70

Securing surplus, in the present context, refers to minimizing
unperformed surplus labour. Burawoy argues that within the monopoly corporation which he studied there has been a basic change in
the form of control used to accomplish this securing of the surplus.
He has characterized this transformation as a change from the
despotic organization of consent on the shop floor to the hegemonic
organization of consent. In the former, the surplus is secured largely
through direct supervision and discipline; in the latter it is ensured
through a complex structure of 'games' which workers play within
the labour process, games which imply an accepted set of rules and
strategies which guarantee a relatively low level of unperformed
surplus labour.

Finally, Richard Edwards's research on forms of managerial
domination also revolves around the problem of this component of
the working day. His distinction between simple control, technical
control, and bureaucratic control is intended to identify the different
general mechanisms by which unperformed surplus labour is reduced
within the production process.[29]

The proportion of the working day represented by redistributed
surplus-value is in some ways the most complex element. Broadly
speaking, social struggles over the control of the labour market most
decisively impinge on this element. Where wage-earners are capable
of systematically restricting the supply of labour into a given
occupation so that a 'competitive equilibrium' price of labour-power
is prevented, then the actual wage will generally be above the value of
labour-power. Within monopoly capitalism, the development of
complex forms of internal labour markets—i.e. internal systems of
promotion and recruitment within the corporation such that certain
positions are insulated almost completely from the general labour
market (and thus from the reserve army of labour)—also directly
affects this component of the working day.[30]

In addition to dynamics embedded in restriction of the labour
market, there is an additional mechanism which generates re-

[29] Richard C. Edwards, *Contested Terrain*, New York 1979.
[30] For discussions of segmented labour markets and internal labour markets, see
Richard C. Edwards, Michael Reich, and David M. Gordon, *Labor Market
Segmentation*, Lexington 1975, and Peter Doeringer and Michael Piore, *Internal Labor
Markets and Manpower Analysis*, Lexington 1971.

distributed surplus-value in the wage, a mechanism which is particularly important in contemporary capitalism. Wages should not simply be seen as a reimbursement for costs of production (of labour-power) realized in an exchange relation; wages can also constitute an element in a strategy of social control within production. This is particularly important for those positions within the production process which I have characterized elsewhere as 'contradictory locations within class relations'.[31] Take the example of managers, the contradictory location between the working class and the capitalist class. Managers are defined as positions which while directly subordinated to capital also dominate workers. They thus have a certain amount of real power within the production process, delegated power to be sure, but power nonetheless. The delegation of power to managers poses certain problems to capital, in particular, the problem of ensuring that this power be used in responsible and creative ways. It is not enough to ensure conformity of managers to the bureaucratic rules of the corporation through the use of repressive controls; it is also important to stimulate responsible behaviour. Income, as a graded structure of bribes, is a crucial element in creating the motivational inducements for such behaviour. And this implies, in terms of the schema laid out in figure 7, that managers' incomes will contain an element above and beyond the costs of reproducing the value of their labour-power (i.e. reimbursing them for the costs of the production and reproduction of skills), an element which reflects their position as a contradictory location within class relations.

The work of Baudelot, Establet, and Malemort on the new petty-bourgeoisie in France has attempted to measure the amount of this component of the wage of various positions.[32] Their strategy was to take a skilled worker as the social standard and then attempt to monetize the costs of production/reproduction of the additional skills of various occupational positions by estimating training costs, retraining costs, even recreation costs needed to reproduce 'mental' energy. (In order to avoid any accusation of underestimating the value of labour-power of such privileged occupations, they also

---

[31] See *Class, Crisis and the State*, chapter 2.
[32] Baudelot *et al.*, *La petite bourgeoisie en France*.

72

included the costs of reproducing the next generation of incumbents in such positions.) Their estimates, therefore, represent a minimum estimate of the redistributed-surplus-value part of the wage among managers, professionals, and technicians. Their results indicate that among *cadres supérieurs* (top managers) some 55 per cent of the average wage is above and beyond the value of their labour-power; among *cadres moyens* the figure was 43 per cent, and among technicians 27 per cent.

My own research on class structure and income determination used a different strategy to assess the magnitude of this component among managers. By using statistical techniques of multiple regression analysis, it is possible to compare a worker and a manager (where a manager is defined as a wage-earner who has subordinates and who says that he/she has some say in the pay or promotions of the subordinates) who have approximately the same value of labour-power and see if their expected incomes would still differ.[33] Using this strategy, it was found that the expected income of male managers was some $3,200 higher than male workers with the same value of labour-power, which represents approximately 20 per cent of the manager income. What is more, this income differential can be shown to increase with the value of labour-power. To put it in more conventional Marxist terms, the rate of exploitation of managers compared to workers declines with the value of labour-power.

In all of these investigations of redistributed surplus-value, the ultimate issue is the extent to which a particular position is subject to pressures from the reserve army of labour. Either through restrictions on the movement of people into an occupation, or through restrictions on promotions and job ladders, or through contradictory locations within production relations, certain positions are systematically insulated from the full pressures of the reserve army of labour, and thus the tendential equalization of the price of labour-power and the value of labour-power is reduced. In some cases this may in fact generate a stable and more or less permanent divergence of the two.

[33] See Wright, *Class Structure and Income Determination*, and Wright and Perrone, 'Marxist Class Categories and Income Inequality', *American Journal of Sociology*, May 1978.

Struggles over the degradation of labour—the destruction of skills in various ways—directly affects the differential value of skilled labour-power. Economic struggles over redundancy (featherbedding) are the most common form of conflict over this component in contemporary capitalism.

Finally, struggles over the historical and moral component of the wage represent struggles over the basic, social, average standard of living of the working class. Increasingly in contemporary capitalism such struggles are waged through the state, in the form of demands for social welfare, social insurance, medical benefits, etc. It is also this component which is perhaps most bound up with the question of imperialism. The position within the world capitalist system of the imperialist centres has historically given their ruling classes considerable room to manoeuvre in conflicts over this component. Modest increases in the historical and moral component of the wage could be granted since they could be recuperated through the international transfers of surplus-value from Third World countries. The current squeeze on this component of the wage in the United States and Western Europe is in part at least a consequence of the disruption of imperialist domination due to class struggles in the Third World, coupled with the fiscal crisis of the state within the imperialist centres themselves.

5. Conclusion

Four basic conclusions can be drawn from the arguments of this essay.

First, a developed Marxist model of the profit determination process is formally compatible with much of the Sraffian and causal-agnostic accounts of profits. Most of the positive propositions within either perspective are consistent with a framework in which surplus labour (in the form of surplus-value) acts as a basic limiting determinant of profits within which technical conditions and the real wage have selection effects, as illustrated in figure 6.

Secondly, not only are all three models largely compatible, but we can also substantively incorporate the Sraffian and causal-agnostic models of profit determination within the Marxist model if they are viewed as representations of the process at lower levels of abstraction. Within the limiting process specified in the Marxist model, the Sraffian model defines the selection mechanisms for profits; and within the selection mechanisms specified in the Sraffian (and Marxist) accounts, the causal-agnostic model defines the range of concrete determinants of profits. What is incorrect about these models is not that they purport to represent real processes, but that they deny, in different ways, the more abstract levels at which these processes may be determined.

Third, the Marxist model provides us with a systematic way of introducing class struggle into the account of profit determination, at the level of both circulation and production. Furthermore, it does so in a way that sustains a definition of classes in terms of the social relations of production. While classes, understood in these terms, can be used in analysing the determinations in the Sraffian model as well, they play no organic role within that theory. In the absence of the Marxist model of determination, the classes within Sraffian theory could be no more than Weberian 'market classes'. If, on the other hand, we regard the Sraffian model as a specification of the Marxist model at a middle level of abstraction, then there is no difficulty in using Marxist class concepts in the empirical investigation of the elements in the model.

Finally, the Marxist model of determination of profits makes it possible to embed the specific analysis of profits within a broader social theory of structural limitations, selections, and transformations. On this basis, the theory moves beyond a positive account of the concrete determination of profits, and becomes part of a critique of the very structure of possibilities in the existing society.

Critique of Wright
1. Labour and Profits

Geoff Hodgson

The transfer of allegiance from paradigm to paradigm is a conversion experience that cannot be forced. Lifelong resistance, particularly from those whose productive careers have committed them to an older tradition of normal science, is not a violation of scientific standards but an index to the nature of scientific research itself. The source of resistance is the assurance that the older paradigm will ultimately solve all its problems, that nature can be shoved into the box the paradigm provides.

THOMAS KUHN
The Structure of Scientific Revolutions

Marxist theoreticians have been preoccupied with several key debates during the 1970s.* Perhaps the one that has drawn most attention is the controversy about value theory, in which one side has urged that drastic surgery is required on the body of theory laid down in *Capital*. Initially, the discussion was not primarily about acceptance or rejection of the labour theory of value, but it has since developed in that way. Opponents of the labour theory are perhaps more confident and intransigent. Its supporters are divided into groups ranging from repetitive fundamentalists to inventive and sophisticated defenders of its indispensability. Erik Olin Wright, in his contribution 'The Value Controversy and Social Research', comes close to the latter end of the spectrum. His graphic rigour, and his aversion to the fundamentalist habits of label-daubing the opposition or appealing to the hallowed

* In writing this paper I have been aided by discussions with Leo Panitch and by useful remarks by Ian Steedman on an earlier draft. Their help is acknowledged with gratitude. Responsibility for errors and omissions in the final version is, of course, entirely mine.

texts for support, make his article a refreshing change from other contributions on the subject. From the opposing side of the debate, however, there is a strong temptation to put a Kuhnian perspective on things, and to see Wright's article as a late but sophisticated attempt to shove the nature of capitalist reality into the old box of the labour theory of value.

Wright's Survey of Theories of Profit Determination

Wright discusses three accounts of how profits and prices are determined. For expository and other reasons he focuses on the central question of the level of profits. The first account of profit determination, which he calls 'causal agnostic', is that found in *Marx's 'Capital' and Capitalism Today*, by Anthony Cutler, Barry Hindess, Paul Hirst, and Athar Hussain. This he regards as an inferior account since it fails to identify any causes of the profit level as more important than others. No cause, or set of causes, has a privileged status in their analysis of profits, the state of the weather being just as significant, and useful, in informing us of the processes at work as the state of the class struggle. Wright's diagrammatic illustration of the 'causal-agnostic' account of profit determination is depicted in his figure 1 (p. 39).

His second step is to move on to an evaluation of the Sraffian contribution to the theory of profits, first presented in Piero Sraffa's *Production of Commodities by Means of Commodities*, and discussed and elaborated in Ian Steedman's *Marx After Sraffa*. In the Sraffian scheme it is accepted that there are many determinants of the real wage and the 'socio-technical' conditions of production, including, in the work of most of its exponents, the class struggle. But once these determinants have played their role, the socio-technical conditions and the real wage alone determine the rate of profit in the system. The latter are the proximate causes of profits. Class struggle, for example, can still play a pivotal role in the dynamics of profit determination. But such causes have their effect on profits by virtue of their effect on real wages and socio-technical conditions only. Wright illustrates this Sraffian account of the determination of profits in his figure 2 (p. 42).

Wright's preliminary critique of the Sraffian account includes some pertinent remarks on the difference between calculation and causality. If the socio-technical conditions of production and the real wage are sufficient to *calculate* the rate of profit in the system, they do not necessarily figure, Wright observes, as sufficient *causes* of the level of the rate of profit. This remark implies that there may be other causes of the profit level which, although redundant in the calculation of profits, play a full role as causes in the real world.

Third, Wright moves on to a discussion of previous Marxist accounts of the determination of profits: 'Traditional Marxist accounts share with Sraffian accounts a commitment to organizing the multiple determinants of profits into an ordered structure of determination. But they differ in assigning a privileged status to surplus labour (in the form of surplus-value) within the structural model of determination: in Marxist theory, real wages and technical conditions of production have their effects on profits by virtue of their effects on the creation of surplus-value. Other causes of variation in profits may be two steps removed from the final outcome. The weather, for example, may influence profits by virtue of its influence on socio-technical conditions and real wages; these, in turn, influence profits by virtue of their effects on surplus-value.' Wright's illustration of this basic model is shown in his figure 3 (p. 45).

Unlike many of the participants in the debate about value theory, Wright accepts that there is a fatal flaw in the traditional Marxist theory of profit determination. He agrees that it has been demonstrated, on the basis of Sraffian analysis, that it is possible to change the total magnitude of profits, or, presumably, the rate of profit, without any change in the amount of total surplus-value produced. This demonstration is based, partly, on a consideration of choice of production technique and has been discussed by Morishima and others.[1] Surplus-value, therefore, cannot be regarded as the proximate cause of profits. The traditional account of profit determination in Marxist theory must be either recast or abandoned.

Wright's Account of Profit Determination

Wright chooses to recast the traditional Marxist theory of value rather than abandon it. His crucial innovation is to introduce a more

[1] Michio Morishima, *Marx's Economics*, London 1973.

complex and diversified notion of causation, one in which there are different kinds of causal relations between elements in a theory. For his immediate purposes, in order to set up a first approximation to his recast version of Marxist value theory, Wright defines two different kinds of causation, or 'modes of determination': '1. *Structural limitation*, in which one structure or element systematically sets limits of possible variation on another structure or element. Within these limits, there is a variety of possible outcomes, but the limits themselves are determinate.

'2. *Selection* of specific outcomes from a range of structurally limited possibilities. In a sense, this is a mode of determination which establishes limits within limits. Depending upon the specific process being investigated, there could be several nested layers of such selection processes.'

The 'recasting' process then takes place in the light of these differentiated modes of determination. Real wages and socio-technical conditions 'select' the profit level. But surplus-value places a 'structural limitation' on it. In turn, surplus-value is 'selected' by the real wage and 'limited' by socio-technical conditions. Wright's diagram of this simplified Marxist account is illustrated in his figure 4 (reproduced as figure 1, p. 79).

Wright thus develops a model that involves a 'mutual interdependence' of surplus-value, real wages, technical conditions, and profits: 'surplus-value establishes the fundamental limits on the range of possible profits. With a given quantity of surplus-value, there is an absolute ceiling on the possible quantity of profits. When surplus-value is zero, no profits at all are possible; as surplus-value increases, the possible maximum profit also increases monotonically. Within these limits, however, both the socio-technical conditions of production and the real wage have a selection effect on profits.' (In making this assertion, Wright makes indirect and allusive reference to Morishima's 'fundamental Marxian theorem': that the profit rate is positive if and only if surplus labour, as defined by Morishima, is positive.[2] Wright thus recognizes the problem of ambiguity in the

[2] See M. Morishima, 'Marx in the Light of Modern Economic Theory', *Econometrica*, vol. 42, 1974, pp. 611–32, and M. Morishima and G. Catephores, *Value, Exploitation and Growth*, London 1978.

general definitions of embodied labour and surplus labour, and rests his account on the Morishima definitions, which cannot give negative values even in cases of joint production.)

According to Wright, therefore, for any given amount of surplus labour there is an upper and lower bound on the amount of profits produced: 'The amount of surplus-value, then, constitutes the explanation of those levels of profits that are impossible; the socio-technical conditions of production and the real wage explain—"predict"—which of the many possible levels of profits actually occurs.'

Several pages later Wright moves on to integrate his simplified Marxist model into a more sophisticated account of profit determination. To do this he introduces two additional modes of determination, and he grafts on the various causes that, in different ways, have an effect on socio-technical conditions and the real wage; he also indicates the effect of profits on other elements within the system. His diagram of this 'complex approximation' is depicted in his figure 6 (p. 54).

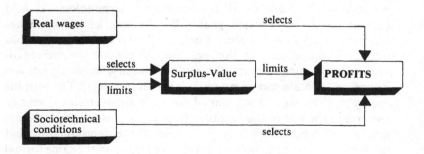

FIGURE 1

As can be seen in the various figures, the simplified 'first approximation' in figure 4 is contained within the 'complex approximation' in figure 6. The two do not contradict each other. In contrast, the traditional Marxist account in figure 3 is inconsistent with both figure 4 and figure 6.

It is both necessary and convenient to concentrate our critique of Wright's paper on the simplified model in figure 4 (reproduced above), for if flaws are found in it, they will also exist in figure 6. In doing this we recognize the value and importance of Wright's analysis of class structure and class struggle, which is elaborated in detail in his *Class, Crisis and the State*.[3] Figure 4 is the core of Wright's attempt to recast Marxist value theory, and to its critique we now turn.

The Arbitrariness of Embodied Labour

Wright anticipates our first line of critical attack. But he does not give a true measure of its strength, nor provide an adequate defence against it. This first line of attack is based on a simple formal observation. In Wright's model, surplus labour is identified as the limiting factor on profits. But, as he himself is aware, if any 'factor of production' (or basic input, to use Sraffian terminology) is held constant, then it too will limit profits. For example, let us assume that energy is an input of the system. Energy will enter into the production of most commodities and also, perhaps, the production and reproduction of labour-power itself. Every commodity, including labour-power, will contain some amount of 'embodied energy'. The 'surplus energy' will be the net amount of energy coming from the energy sector into the rest of the economy (just as surplus labour is the net amount of labour-time transmitted after the reproduction and performance of labour-power). Profits are limited in the same formal manner by 'surplus energy' as they are by 'surplus-value'. We can therefore construct an 'energy theory of value' with the diagram in figure 4'. I do not mean to suggest seriously that such a theory of value would have the same meaning or explanatory power as the

[3] Erik Olin Wright, *Class, Crisis and the State*, London, NLB, 1978.

labour theory, or that labour-power does not have special characteristics that are worthy of identification and must be understood if the inner workings of the capitalist system are to be explained. Labour-power is important, central, and unique. But we have to demonstrate this uniqueness and centrality, not assume it at the outset. At this stage the important point is to note that there can be no formal objection if we proceed from any other basic input of the system and view it as placing limits on profits. Wright's elaborate and elegant account does begin to look blinkered by the preconceptions of its author.

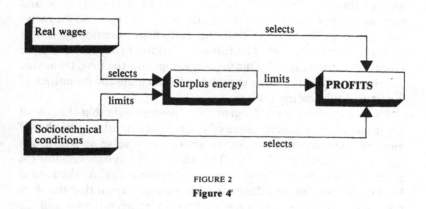

FIGURE 2

Figure 4'

The main argument in the previous paragraph can be restated in a more rigorous fashion. For a complete mathematical proof the reader is advised to consult a work by Bródy.[4] The proof is discussed further in a subsequent book by Vegara.[5] The essentials of the Bródy proof are as follows. The material inputs of a capitalist economy are

[4] A. Bródy, *Proportions, Prices and Planning*, Amsterdam 1970.

[5] Josep M. Vegara, *Economía Política y Modelos Multisectoriales*, Biblioteca Tecnos de Ciencias Económicas, Madrid 1979.

presented in the usual matrix form. One column (or row) is added to the nth position to represent the labour inputs in each industry, and one row (or column) is added in the nth position to represent the real wage, in other words, the 'inputs' in the domestic sphere of the economy. A zero occupies the diagonal at the nth position. This augmented matrix is sufficient (along with data for the outputs in the economy in the case of joint production) to determine prices and the rate of profit.

If we wish to calculate the amounts of labour embodied in each commodity we detach the nth column and the nth row, leaving the original material inputs. The embodied-labour values are calculated with a well-known expression that includes the truncated matrix and the vector representing the labour inputs. The point, however, is that we can formally carry out the same operation for any row and corresponding column. Detach, say, the forty-fifth row and the forty-fifth column. We assume that the forty-fifth commodity is, for example, lubricating oil. The forty-fifth column (or row) gives the inputs of lubricating oil. This vector, along with the new, truncated matrix, is used in the same expression to calculate the quantities of 'embodied lubricating oil'.

The point of this formal algebra is to demonstrate that the role of labour as a source and measure of value is indiscernible from that of any other commodity. Any other 'source' may serve as well in the formal determination of prices. The relative price system remains the same whether we start from labour or anything else. At the formal level there is simply no difference. (But we must repeat that this does not mean that there are no real differences between labour and the other inputs in the system.)

Wright's Defence and the Collapse into Circularity

In defence against the argument that any input could be chosen to supply the 'structural limitation' on profits, Wright adduces special reasons for selecting labour and surplus labour:

'The focus on surplus labour as the underlying process which establishes limits on profits . . . is itself derived from the class analysis of exploitation in general and of the specific forms of such exploitation in capitalism. There is, therefore, an element of truth in the charge that the choice of surplus-value as a limiting condition is "arbitrary". It is arbitrary with respect to the specific problem of *calculating* profits, and if this was the only reason for a theory of profit determination then indeed there would be no grounds for choosing surplus-value over any other factor as a limiting condition. . . . But the choice is far from arbitrary with respect to a broader theoretical project—understanding classes and class struggle in terms of social relations of production, and linking such class struggles to the specific analysis of capitalist mechanisms of appropriating surplus labour through surplus-value and profits. It is because we are interested in understanding class relations and class struggle that we seek a model of determination of profits that allows us to link classes to profits, not because we have an autonomous interest in profits as such, independently of their social determinants and consequences. In these terms, the specific way in which one formalizes the model for the calculation of profits is conceptually subordinated to the qualitative theory of social relations within which profits acquire their social content.'

The same point is repeated, in slightly different terms, in a footnote: 'Because Marxists are subjectively committed to a certain set of values and thus have an interest in studying exploitation, an ideal-type model revolving around surplus labour is appropriate. In fact, the argument does not rest simply on the value preferences of the theorist, but on the realist claim that classes and class struggle, defined in terms of production relations, are the decisive social forces which shape social change. Classes are real, not simply analytical conventions. Surplus labour also establishes real limits on possible profits, not simply analytical limits.'

In short, then, we must focus on labour and surplus labour because it leads us to an examination of classes, class struggle, and exploitation. Classes are real, and they are the key elements in social change.

This leads us to the obvious question: how are classes defined? Wright attempts a definition: 'For our present purposes, the key point is that classes are defined above all by positions within production relations, not by their positions within market relations or other aspects of social relations. The decisive aspect of those production relations centres on the ability of one class to force another class—the direct producers—to perform labour beyond what is needed for the reproduction of the direct producers themselves, and to appropriate the products of that "surplus labour". *In all class modes of production, the dominant class is defined by those positions which appropriate surplus labour; the subordinate class by those positions which have their surplus labour appropriated.*' (Emphasis added.)

The argument has now turned full circle. According to Wright, behind the need to focus on surplus labour is the need to examine classes; behind the examination of classes lie relations of production; and, fundamentally, these relations are about which class performs and which appropriates surplus labour. We can put the relevant question to Wright again: Why is surplus labour, and not surplus-anything-else selected out as the structural limitation on profits? Wright's answer, it seems, is as follows. We focus on surplus labour because it helps us understand classes and class struggle in terms of relations of production. Classes, however, are understood in terms of their relation to the extraction of surplus labour. In Wright's answer, 'surplus labour' and 'classes' are like two words in a badly designed dictionary. We look up one word and we find it defined in terms of the other, and when we look up the other word we are referred back to the first. Wright's defence against the charge that the selection of surplus labour is arbitrary is thus nothing but a circular argument, in which the terms 'classes' and 'surplus labour' play leap-frog with each other through the crucial passages of his paper.

We can also note that Wright has similarly failed to give substantive support to his assertion that classes are 'real'. In his terms, they are real only because they relate to the extraction of surplus labour. In the selection of surplus labour as the key category Wright thus falls into the Weberian mire that he himself detects along the route of his argument: 'This . . . comes perilously close to a Weberian methodological stance on theory construction, namely that the categories we choose are strictly subordinated to the subjective preference of the analyst.'

Wright, however, is not aware that he has actually slid into the mire. The solid ground on which he believes to stand is nothing but a self-sustaining invention of his own mind, and not a support in the real world. The result is methodological chaos. We can simply adapt

Wright's theoretical apparatus to fit in with our own preconceptions. Imagine the reaction of a modern ecologist to Wright's essay. This person believes that the fundamental force in the world is the flow and transformation of energy and therefore understands the world in these terms. Wright's apparatus can be accepted eagerly by the ecologist: 'This shows that Sraffa is wrong!' he cries. 'There is a place for another cause. Surplus energy is the limit on profits. I believe this because it fits in with a true picture of the world as I understand it.' We shall not pursue this line of argument further, by examining, for example, the reaction of a Christian evangelist to Wright's scheme (the evangelist believing that profit is the result of and reward for pain).

Calculation and Causality

Wright's first main assault on the Sraffian account of profit determination, as we have seen, is to point out that to assemble a set of factors necessary and sufficient to *calculate* profits is not the same as to assemble a set of *causes* of the profit level. At first sight this seems plausible, but on closer examination it is as empty as his justification for the selection of surplus labour.

In reply to Wright it must first be pointed out that he has not demonstrated causality in his own model. His attempt to distinguish three or four different types of causes, or 'modes of determination', is impressive, but does not help. In his scheme he asserts that surplus labour *limits* profits, and the nature of these limits are mathematical maxima and minima. So the allegation against Sraffa can be turned against Wright: to point out a factor, or set of factors, that *limit* profits is not the same as to point out a *cause*, of any type, of the profit level or of a range of possible profit levels. There is no difference here. Sraffa identifies a set of factors that are sufficient to calculate the precise level of profits; Wright identifies a factor (surplus labour) that is sufficient to *calculate* limits on profits. Both are calculations and not, at this stage, demonstrations of cause and effect. The only difference worth noting is that Wright's calculation is a weaker and less precise version of the one provided by Sraffa; Sraffa's is sufficient to provide an exact answer, whereas Wright's is not.

To reinforce the point let us consider Wright's diagram that is alleged to show a relationship between surplus labour and profits, the former setting limits on the latter. This diagram is represented in his figure 5 (p. 48). According to Wright, surplus labour is the independent variable and profits are the dependent variable— dependent, that is, in the sense of being 'structurally limited' by surplus-value. But why is one a cause of the other? We are offered no reason. There is no argument in Wright's paper to prevent us making profits the independent variable and surplus labour the dependent variable. In other words, surplus labour will be structurally limited by profits, and profits will be the proximate cause of surplus labour and surplus-value. Wright's 'first approximation' can be changed, reversing the position of profits and surplus labour. This is done in figure 3 below.

Again, let me make my argument clear: I do not suggest that profits do, in fact, limit surplus labour, just as I do not seriously suggest an 'energy theory of value', nor propose that labour-power can be treated in the same way as any other commodity. The counter-examples, absurd as they may seem, are designed simply to demonstrate that Wright is assuming what he has to prove. He *assumes*

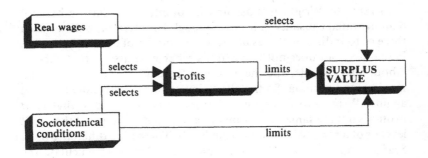

FIGURE 3

Figure 4″

that surplus labour is *the* cause limiting profits, and he *assumes* that there is a uni-directional, causal link between the two. He *proves* none of this. My point is to show that other analysts, using Wright's methodology, may well assume other plausible connections. The only problem with them is that they do not square with the Marxist preconceptions that are the very objects of dispute in the post-Sraffa debate. Wright's article may have been welcomed by those Marxists who were seriously worried by the impact of the Sraffa system on traditional Marxist theory. With its relative rigour and apparent elegance, it would appear to rescue the labour theory of value. But on closer inspection, Wright proves 'nothing. Despite claims to the contrary, he does not lay bare real processes in the real world: real chains of cause and effect. His work is nothing but a scholastic attempt to fit new theories into old boxes. But, as we shall argue, they simply do not fit.

Nested Modes of Determination

The next line of criticism, like the previous one, requires that we tackle Wright's methodology on its own terms. According to Wright, socio-technical conditions of production plus the real wage *select* the profit level; that is, no other factors are required to determine the level of profits. But also, according to Wright, surplus labour *limits* profits. This raises an obvious question: if selection is sufficient to determine the result, what then is the status of structural limitation? The level of profits selected will always be within the limits provided by surplus labour, because *by definition* the limits contain all the feasible profit rates for a given amount of surplus-value. So surplus labour is a 'cause' that plays no role, because the other causes act to determine the outcome. Surplus labour will never actually bring itself to bear upon the result. Wright has *defined* these limits in such a way that they are *redundant*.

In general, it is difficult to envisage a causal role for *structural* limits if other factors, through the process of *selection*, are entirely sufficient to determine the outcome. It is like saying that the height of *Homo sapiens* is caused, through 'structural limitation', by the thickness of the atmosphere. Certainly, humanoids could not survive on Earth if they were ten miles high! The invention of structural limits is arbitrary for any real phenomenon, and it is completely erroneous simply to assume, as Wright does, that they play a causal role.

Wright's error is compounded, in this case, by the fact that the structural limits he has chosen—those laid down by given amounts of surplus labour—must lie outside any reasonable selected level of profits. This is because the limits are *defined* to include all possible rates of profit, as stated above. We have argued that a structural limit can be a cause only if it actually bears upon the outcome. In the case of surplus labour, however, this structural limit can *never* be a cause, because it *never* bears upon the result. It never does this because it never affects socio-technical conditions or the real wage. We are thus led to conclude that surplus labour does not affect profits either.

Causality in the Sraffa System

Let us examine the notion of causality implicit in the Sraffa system. At one level the Sraffa model is merely a mental construction, a 'thought experiment'. Read in this way it is certainly not devoid of meaning. For example, the prices that are derived in the system are the prices that are *logically* necessary to ensure an equalized profit rate. Prices and profits depend, logically, on socio-technical conditions and the real wage, and factors that influence them, *and nothing else*. These formal results enable us to order and arrange data about the real world, and they help us to skirt the trap of logical inconsistency when analysing problems of value and distribution. It is at this formal level that logical problems have been identified, by means of the Sraffa system, in the neo-classical theory of distribution and the neo-classical aggregate production function.

In logic, however, there are no causes or effects, merely assumptions and conclusions. To successfully criticize such a formal system only two courses of action are possible: to challenge the initial assumptions or to find a fault in the logic of the argument. A great deal of the misunderstanding about the Sraffa system lies in a failure to appreciate that the model is being used, most of the time, as a purely formal construction.

It is possible, however, to interpret the Sraffa system in various ways, and to posit statements about the real world. It must be made clear—and this is another frequent source of misunderstanding—that many such interpretations are possible, even if only one of them is valid. The formal Sraffa system does not lead us automatically to any particular view of the production process, or, for example, to see the sphere of exchange as primary and that of production as secondary. All these things can be, legitimately or illegitimately, *read into* the formal construction, but they are not there at the outset.

I wish now to put forward a certain partial interpretation of the Sraffa system that will have something to say about cause and effect. It will be clear from the remarks above that there is no reason for all adherents of Sraffa automatically to accept what I say. They may wish to put forward a modified, or even a distinct, interpretation.

It is not for the sake of convenience or uniformity that Sraffa, like many other value theorists (including Marx), assumes an equalized rate of profit. An equalized, or general, rate of profit is assumed because there are real forces in a capitalist economy that tend to bring the rates of profit in different industries into line. These forces are the forces of competition. Marx himself makes this clear in several passages of his writings. For example: 'What competition between the different spheres of production brings about is the creation of the same general rate of profit in the different spheres.'[6] This competition flows from the nature of capitalism itself, and prevails within that system: 'There is no doubt . . . that aside from unessential, incidental and mutually compensating distinctions, differences in the average rate of profit in the various branches of industry do not exist in reality, and could not exist without abolishing the entire system of capitalist production.'[7] For Marx, then, the equalization of the rate of profit, the formation of a general rate of profit, is an 'actual process' corresponding to 'real phenomena'[8] in the capitalist world. It is not simply a mental equalization, but one that corresponds to real processes outside the minds of economists. At the same time, Marx recognized that there may be barriers or limitations to the full equalization of the rate of profit, but he regards these as 'incidental'.

[6] K. Marx, *Theories of Surplus-Value*, Part 2, London 1969, p. 208, emphasis removed.
[7] K. Marx, *Capital* Volume 3, London 1962, p. 151.
[8] Ibid.

Marx may have underestimated the barriers to a full equalization. This may be due to the fact that he did not perceive the results of monopolization under capitalism, and he wrote at a time when capital was fragmented into many small competitive units. Even if this is so, his account of profit-rate equalization is still relevant. The essence of capitalism is competition, and insofar as capitalism is competitive there will be forces tending to bring different rates of profit into line, even if an equal and general rate of profit is not formed. Insofar as there are barriers to this equalization, there is a modification or distortion of capitalism's fundamental character—it is capitalism near the brink of a transformation into an entirely different mode of production: 'The centralization of the means of production and the socialization of labour reach a point at which they become incompatible with their capitalist integument.'[9]

If capital is competitive and mobile, then it will flow to the industries and firms with higher rates of profit. This will cause an excess supply of certain goods, their price will be forced down, and the rate of profit in the formerly attractive industries and firms will be brought down. A general equilibrium will arise when rates of profit are more or less equal, and a general rate of profit is formed in the system. That is the *real* process, in my view, behind the *assumption* of an equalized rate of profit in the Sraffa system. Sraffa, therefore, is discussing a certain type of equilibrium state. However, the dynamics of the process are not discussed in Sraffa as they are in Marx. Causality in Sraffa has to be discussed in terms of comparative statics. This, of course, gives the exercise a limited scope, but it is not without value. A full dynamic analysis will expose other causal factors, but, to repeat our earlier warning, such factors have to be *detected*, and not simply imputed into the model.

Let us assume that in a certain capitalist economy, at a certain time, the forces of competition have succeeded in bringing about an equalization of the rate of profit. Things change, but ten years later the forces of competition triumph once more and a general rate of profit is formed again. However, it is quantitatively different from the rate of profit ten years before. What factors have *caused* such a

[9] K. Marx, *Capital*, Volume 1, Penguin Books in association with New Left Review, Harmondsworth 1976, p. 929.

change in the rate of profit? Sraffian analysis shows us that the proximate causes are the socio-technical conditions and the real wage. There is no other proximate cause. It is not simply a question of calculation. These factors are *causes*, in the sense that we have described. They operate in the real world.

Marx, of course, held that embodied labour played a central role in the transformation of values into prices and the formation of a general rate of profit. The causal role of labour and surplus labour, however, is asserted rather than proved. Furthermore, for the reasons that are outlined in Steedman's book, labour and surplus labour cannot be regarded as causal factors in the same way and sense as the socio-technical conditions and the real wage. Embodied labour values are not sufficient, for example, to determine prices or the general rate of profit: the technical structure of production will also play a role. Steedman shows that in some circumstances the attempt to calculate the rate of profit from embodied labour values will give an incorrect answer, even if we add the necessary extra information. These arguments are clearly laid out in Steedman's book, and there is no need to repeat them here. What has to be added is an explanation of their significance in the light of Wright's remarks on causation. At the abstract level of analysis of Sraffa's *Production of Commodities by Means of Commodities* or Marx's chapter in *Capital* on the formation of a general rate of profit (volume 3, chapter 9), the Sraffian critique of the labour theory of value demonstrates that embodied labour values are redundant not only in the *calculation* of profits but also in their *causal determination*.

(It may be suggested, in response, that there is a role for embodied labour and surplus labour outside the level of abstraction discussed above. I am aware of no rigorous theory of the capitalist system that includes such a role. The reader may recall Anwar Shaikh's 'vindication' of Marx's solution to the problem of transforming values into prices.[10] Shaikh shows that embodied labour values can be used as a first approximation to prices, under certain conditions, and after successive adjustments in the light of differences in the

[10] Anwar Shaikh, 'Marx's Theory of Value and the "Transformation Problem"', in Jesse Schwartz (ed.), *The Subtle Anatomy of Capitalism*, Santa Monica 1977, pp. 106–139.

calculated rates of profit, these values can be gradually 'transformed', in an iterative manner, into prices. However, Shaikh does not succeed in showing that such a process occurs in the real world. Furthermore, there are an *infinite number* of 'first approximations' that can be used, in the same iterative process, to derive the same results. Conceivably, we could start with our old friend 'embodied energy' or even the number of letters in the name of the commodity when translated into Serbo-Croatian. Subject to certain conditions, all these 'first approximations' will lead us to the same end point. What matters in the iterative process is not the starting point but the process itself, and embodied labour plays no part in Shaikh's *process*. There is no evidence to show that this is anything more than a *calculation*; embodied labour values play no apparent role in the real dynamic of the capitalist world.[11])

Embodied Labour and Production

As if to reinforce his earlier assertion that surplus labour is important because it leads us to understand the role of classes, an argument that assumes what it had to prove, Wright makes the following point about the application of his recast version of Marxian value theory:

'Because surplus-value is seen as defining the absolute limits on profits, the central research question immediately becomes: what are the social processes which influence the amount of surplus labour performed? . . . the Marxist model also directs our research efforts towards those transformations of the socio-technical conditions of production that directly impinge on surplus labour. It is for this reason that the Marxist analysis of production revolves around the *labour process* as such, and not simply the technical input-output matrices of production.'

If casual reading of this passage gives a favourable impression at first glance, much will be due to the careful phraseology. Good Marxist words like 'social' and 'labour process' are contrasted with the formidable 'technical input-output matrices of production'.

---

[11] For a further criticism of Shaikh, see Heinz D. Kurz, 'Sraffa After Marx', *Australian Economic Papers*, June 1979, p. 55n.

Much of this is mere artistry. Surplus labour as such does not necessarily have any immediate associations, in the mind of the run-of-the-mill theorist, with a social process. A Marxist of technological-determinist hue would immediately focus on the technological determinants of surplus labour, not the social processes of production. There is nothing attached to the concept of surplus labour that leads us to the analytical haven of the labour process.

After all, we can calculate surplus labour only by reference to the economy as a whole. Surplus labour is not to be detected, whether directly or indirectly, as a phenomenal substance within the firm. The association of terms like 'surplus labour' and 'value' with 'production' and 'labour process' is little more than prejudice. Whilst our choice of categories does indeed influence our area and mode of theoretical investigation, it simply has not been demonstrated that terms like these necessarily lead to the area of study that Wright, myself, and others would agree is central: the sphere of production.

A study of the history of Marxist economic analysis will support these remarks. Since the publication of the first volume of *Capital* in 1867 there has been much discussion of embodied labour values. But although large sections of Volume 1 are devoted to the labour process, there has been little discussion of it in the literature. In his 1904 reply to Böhm-Bawerk's criticisms of Marx,[12] the highly regarded Marxist Rudolf Hilferding asserted the importance of the labour theory of value because it involves a 'social' rather than 'subjective' category. There is no substantial discussion of the labour process, and he does not assert that Marxian value theory leads us to regard this as central in the process of capitalist production. In the two unrivalled classics of Marxist economic theory to appear outside Germany or the Soviet Union since the death of Marx, Paul Sweezy's *Theory of Capitalist Development* and Ernest Mandel's *Marxist Economic Theory*, we find nothing more than scanty discussion of the labour process, despite these authors' adherence to the labour theory of value. In fact, most of the important literature on the labour process, such as Braverman's *Labour and Monopoly Capital*, has appeared only since 1970. It may be necessary to recast

[12] Reproduced in P. Sweezy (ed.), *Karl Marx and the Close of His System*, London 1975.

Marxian value theory, but it would be an indignity to rewrite the history of Marxian economic thought as well.

It is the view of this author, which may be noted in passing, that it is not the categories of embodied labour and surplus labour that are crucial in leading us to an understanding of the central role of the labour process, and of the unique features of labour itself. The crucial element in the Marxist theory of capitalist production is Marx's distinction between labour and labour-power. It is labour-power, the capacity to work, that is bought and sold on the market; but it is labour, the activity of work itself, that must be extracted for production to take place. The distinction between labour and labour-power draws us towards an examination of the processes of coercion and management that are utilized to extract this labour from labour-power. I have discussed the significance of this elsewhere, [13] and it has been noted in an important article by Bob Rowthorn. [14]

Prejudices Against Sraffa

Wright assumes, wrongly, that categories like embodied labour and surplus labour automatically direct us towards a study of the labour process. He is also mistaken in asserting that the Sraffian categories deter us from such study and lead instead to concentration on market relations. According to Wright, the pivotal research question the Sraffa model generates is this:

'What are the determinants of the real wage and of the technical conditions of production? This leads immediately to two general objects of empirical study: the determinants of the market power of wage labourers and capitalists, and technological change. The first of these concerns would involve investigations of such things as . . . trade unionism . . . monopoly concentration . . . the role of the state . . . in regulating the market conflict between labour and capital . . . or the role of imperialism.' No other factors have been excluded from the last sentence. Two things are to be noted in this

[13] G. Hodgson, 'Exploitation and Embodied Labour Time', *Bulletin of the Conference of Socialist Economists*, June 1976.

[14] Bob Rowthorn, 'Neo-Classicism, Neo-Ricardianism and Marxism', *New Left Review*, No. 86, July–August 1974.

quotation. First, Wright carefully inserts the word 'market' in two critical places where it does not follow from the course of the argument. The passage would be no less valid if the word 'market' was deleted. We could even replace 'market', a derogatory term for some Marxists, by terms with the Marxist stamp of approval, and the argument would lose no validity. Replace 'market power of wage labourers and capitalists' by 'class power of wage labourers and capitalists at the point of production', and replace 'market conflict between labour and capital' by 'class conflict between labour and capital over the length of the working day and coercion of labour by capital to extract an ever higher output' and loud applause can be heard in the gallery. These things can be read into Sraffa, as easily as a predilection for the market can be read in to tarnish the Sraffa system by association. But the accredited Marxist interpretation of Sraffa is just as valid, for the length of the working day and the level of output do appear prominently amongst the coefficients of the Sraffa system. Wright's association of Sraffa with a concentration on the market is mere prejudice, nothing more.

This prejudice is manifest on more than one occasion. Such misinterpretations of Sraffa are so widespread that it is worth discussing them in more detail. In Wright we find passages like this: 'Within Sraffian theory, classes play a *systematic* role only in terms of the determination of the real wage, and the combatants in the class struggle are defined by their location within the market. All wage-earners, therefore, would be part of the working class, since the income of all wage-earners takes the form of a deduction from profits. . . . In Marxist theory, the concept of class is closely linked to the question of surplus labour. Classes are defined by the social relations of production, not primarily by market relations.' This is wrong, through and through. If Wright read Sraffa more attentively he would find that classes are not defined, and the results of market forces are taken as given. There is no explicit or implicit definition of class in terms of the market, production, property, or anything else. It is just as valid to say that in Sraffa profits are a deduction from wages as it is to say that wages are a deduction from profits. Both are false propositions, and neither is to be found in Sraffa. It does not follow from Sraffa, therefore, that all wage-earners are part of the working class. Wright can interpret the Sraffa system in one of several ways.

But he should not impute an obviously false interpretation in order to knock down the formal propositions of the system.

We have noted that Sraffa presents no definition of class. That is an important omission, and in my view class is indeed an essential socio-economic category. But it must also be noted that there is no clear and explicit definition of class in *Capital*. Marx moves towards such a definition at the very end of the unfinished notes for Volume 3. Of course, a focus on production and the labour process is clear in Marx, but Wright has not shown that this focus is inconsistent with Sraffa. The drift of his paper, that the recast Marxist theory of value leads to an appropriate investigation, or 'social research', into the labour process, whereas Sraffian theory does not, is supported by no serious or rigorous theoretical argument.

Summary and Concluding Remarks

Unlike some critics, Wright does not reject Sraffa, but instead tries to subsume his work into a modified Marxist model. This is done by asserting that there are elements of causality in the Marxist theory that can be integrated with the Sraffa approach and retain their bearing on the real world. We have argued that the elements of causality Wright wishes to retain are not causes in the real sense at all. Furthermore, his choice of 'causes' is somewhat arbitrary, and others could follow his example and invent a multitude of different causes of the same type. His attempt to justify the category of surplus labour as a proximate cause is based on a circular argument about classes that assumes what he has to prove. And finally, his suggestion that the Marxist categories alone add something because they direct us towards the important area of the sphere of production and the labour process is simply unfounded.

Wright's article, impressive as it appears at first sight, includes a dubious phraseology and a measure of unfounded fundamentalist prejudice. For example, consider the passage, quoted above, in which Wright asserts that 'surplus-value establishes the fundamental limits on the range of possible profits'. Such key passages are riddled with ambiguity. What does 'establishes' mean? Does it mean establish in thought, or establish in the real world? The latter interpretation is not demonstrated, but it is implied by such a word, with its associations with real-world things like institutions and buildings. What does 'fundamental limits' mean? Limits that are narrower than other limits? If that is the assertion, then it is not demonstrated. What else could it mean? A solid sounding sentence, highly ranked for quotation and approval, is rife with ambiguity and bereft of rigorous demonstration. Stripped of these linguistic supports, his argument collapses.

On other occasions Wright constructs statements that are formally correct but suggest something erroneous. Consider the following: 'to the extent that the organic compositions of capital in highly integrated economies tend to be relatively homogeneous across sectors and the rate of accumulation tends to be close to the maximum, the limits on possible profits will be fairly narrow.' Formally, the passage is correct. But the words 'in highly integrated economies' are redundant. The statement would be true for *any* capitalist economy, highly integrated or not. Why is the phrase inserted? It is hard to avoid the supposition that it is put there to evoke this sort of response from the reader: (1) modern economies are highly integrated; therefore, (2) organic compositions of capital will tend to be relatively homogeneous across sectors, and if (3) the rate of accumulation tends to be close to the maximum, then (4) the limits on possible profits will be fairly narrow. Such a response, however, would be incorrect. Proposition (2) does not follow from (1). If we have a highly integrated economy, there is simply no reason to assume that organic compositions of capital are fairly uniform—the opposite could well be the case.

It is to be noted that our critique of Wright's argument has not involved a discussion of joint production, problems with negative surplus labour, and so on. In rather cavalier fashion, Wright dismisses these problems in a footnote. For our purposes, however, this does not matter, for our critique of Wright is not based on any assumption of joint production. The reader can assume the most 'well behaved' capitalist economy in the world; Wright's model still has its glaring faults and fails to apply. We have attacked it in its firmest citadel: the well-behaved, single product capitalist economy. If the model is measured against the more realistic world of fixed capital and joint production, it must face other problems as well, but we have no need to elaborate on them here.

It is sufficient to note that Wright's assumption that the real world

98

is well behaved and will conform to his single-product (and relatively uniform organic composition of capital?) model is reminiscent of the neo-classicist faith in the well-behaved aggregate-production function, despite the fact that the Sraffian critique of neo-classical distribution theory has shown that there are no reasons for assuming such special, 'well-behaved' cases. In response, many neo-classical economists hold to their aggregate-production function merely as an article of faith. It would be dangerous to retain 'structural limitation', and such a well-behaved causal relation between surplus labour and profits, for the same reason.

The faithful might find some solace in Wright's essay. It postpones the demise of the old paradigm when it is the new one that should be adopted and enriched with fresh scientific insight. To me, the state of value theory in the classical-Marxist/Sraffian tradition can be compared to the state of astronomy after Copernicus. The analogy should not be pushed too far: Sraffa is not Copernicus and neither Marx nor Adam Smith were Ptolemy. Common features, however, can be found. The Ptolemaic model was an elaborate construction designed to demonstrate the geocentricity of the universe. It involved a complex system of thirty-nine 'wheels' to 'carry' sun, moon, planets, and stars in their heavenly motion. The problem with the Ptolemaic universe, and similar labours of his Alexandrian colleagues, was not that of failure to make correct predictions, nor of failure to be of practical use: 'Hipparchus's Catalogue of the fixed stars, and Ptolemy's Tables for calculating planetary motions, were so reliable and precise that they served, with some insignificant corrections, as navigational guides to Columbus and Vasco da Gama.'[15] The Ptolemaic theory was not refuted by evidence, nor made redundant through any failure to construct a practical view of the world. It was eventually displaced, after more than a millennium and a half had passed, by a different view, in which the earth moved around the sun and the stars were not requested to describe circles for the benefit of a static Earth.

What were the reasons for its displacement? The Ptolemaic system could claim to explain the universe in terms of elaborate sky geometry, of cycles and epicycles, centrics and eccentrics. It served

[15] Arthur Koestler, *The Sleepwalkers*, London 1968, p. 70.

the purpose of elevating the Earth, and thereby its dominant species, humans, to the status of supreme being within the world of the Creator. It was resilient and impressive. But it was displaced because it failed to construct an adequate explanation of cause and effect. It was not the hint of a heliocentric universe in Copernicus, nor the telescope of Galileo, nor the ellipses of Kepler, that led to the abandonment of the Ptolemaic system. It was Newton's mechanics, in which motion through space is explained by three laws of motion, that crushed the Ptolemaic system. Nevertheless, if we wish, we can go on believing in Ptolemy even to this day, because there is no final proof of the validity of the Newtonian system.

An analogy is suggested with Sraffa and traditional Marxian value theory. The defect of the latter is not that it fails to make predictions, nor that it fails to be of practical use. As Ptolemy's Tables guided Columbus to a New World across the ocean, so Marx's labour theory of value led him to the labour process and to begin to examine the process of exploitation under capitalism. But that does not mean that Ptolemy's or Marx's theories are valid.[16] Yet Wright and others continue to uphold the latter's labour theory of value. In an effort to reconcile it with new insights and arguments, he constructs an elaborate typology of 'modes of determination', analogous to the wheels of the Ptolemaic system. The result, however, is not science. In the words of Milton in *Paradise Lost*, it is an elaborate effort 'to save appearances':

> 'Hereafter, when they come to model Heaven
> And calculate the stars, how they will wield
> The mighty frame, how build, unbuild, contrive
> To save appearances, how gird the sphere
> With centric and eccentric scribbled o'er,
> Cycle and epicycle, orb in orb.'

---

[16] For an analysis of the labour process and exploitation without the labour theory of value, see my *Capitalism, Value and Exploitation*, Oxford 1981.

Critique of Wright
2. In Defence of
a Post-Sraffian Approach

Pradeep Bandyopadhyay

In his article 'The Value Controversy and Social Research' Erik Olin Wright has attempted to confront two of the past decade's most serious attempts to reassess Marx's legacy and scientific impact: the sustained post-Althusserian work of Cutler, Hindess, Hirst, and Hussain,[1] concerned chiefly to develop a *methodological-epistemological* critique of Marx's claims; and that of Ian Steedman (whose work can be considered in conjunction with a broader set of findings sometimes labelled neo-Ricardian by critics), concerned more directly with Marx's *economic* claims, and in particular with the labour theory of value and its associated concepts—surplus-value, value rate of exploitation, the structure of capital in value concepts like constant and variable capital, the value-related law of the tendency of the rate of profit to fall, etc. It is Wright's aim to explore the relation of these two challenges to what he terms a 'reconstructed version of the traditional Marxist account based on the labour theory of value'. In conducting his comparison and assessment, Wright chooses to view them all from the 'vantage point of the Marxist labour theory of value itself'. I assume that this means in terms of how well each of the approaches can deal with the concerns, questions, and problems that the labour theory of value presumably handles successfully, or at least puts on the research agenda in a resolvable manner. To focus the analysis and restrict its length he chooses the examination of profits as the basis of comparison. By his own

---

[1] Anthony Cutler, Barry Hindess, Paul Hirst, and Athar Hussain, *Marx's Capital and Capitalism Today*, 2 vols., London 1977, 1978.

admission, Wright seems unsure of the results of his work, for he cautiously declares that his essay should be 'seen more as attempting to redefine in certain critical ways the terms of the debate rather than definitively resolving all of the points in dispute.'

When concluding, however, he claims to have established four results about the three approaches to the analysis of profits. My contribution, concerned mainly with Wright's characterization of what he calls the 'Sraffian account', will argue that each of his four conclusions regarding the 'Marx-after-Sraffa' position is either unwarranted wholly or in part, misleading, or simply false. These four conclusions may be summarized as follows.

1. A developed Marxist model of the process of profit determination is 'formally compatible' with much of the Sraffian account of profits; indeed, most of the 'positive propositions' in a Sraffian account are consistent with 'a framework in which surplus labour in the form of surplus-value' acts as 'a basic limiting determinant of profits'. This may be termed the *general compatibility* thesis.

2. The reconstructed Marxian account can incorporate the Sraffian account as a representation of the process of profit determination at a lower level of abstraction: 'Within the limiting process specified in the Marxist model, the Sraffian model defines the selection mechanisms for profits.' This claim that the Marxian model possesses greater generality may be termed the *incorporation thesis*.

3. The Marxist model is sociologically more relevant and powerful than the Sraffian. This contention comprises two parts. First, the Marxist model can introduce class struggle systematically, whereas classes (as Marxists define them) play no 'organic role' in the Sraffian model; second, the Marxian model is required if both circulation and production relations are to be incorporated in the concept of class, whereas in a Sraffian model 'classes' can be no more than Weberian 'market classes'. This may be called the *absence-of-production-relations thesis*, or the *Sraffian-as-Weberian* thesis.

4. Finally, the Marxian model makes it possible to embed a theory of

the determination of capitalist profits within a broader 'theory of structural limitations, selections, and transformations'. The implicit suggestion is that the Sraffian model is intrinsically unable to accommodate such integration. Moreover, through its critiques the Marxist model can reveal the 'possibilities' in existing society, while the Sraffian model is strictly positive and thus cannot reveal 'possibilities'. Two additional claims form part of the ultimate conclusion. First, as a research programme the reconstructed Marxist position is richer, especially as regards the labour process, than the research programme associated with the Sraffian position. Second, Steedman and others like him have been concerned only to *calculate* the rate of profit, and success in calculation alone is not to be confused with a genuine *causal* determination of the real process.[2]

Wright's statement of Steedman's position is admirably concise and largely correct. In two important respects, however, it needs amplification. To start with, the problem of fixed capital and joint production *cannot* be ignored in an argument that claims to establish the greater generality of a reconstructed Marxian approach and seeks to incorporate the Sraffian approach into it. For, as will be evident to every reader, greater generality will be an attribute of the theory/model that can accommodate more states of affairs and greater complexity than a model that is consistent or workable only under simple or restrictive assumptions. The existence in any real capitalist economy of fixed capital and joint production (either in the 'pure' case or as a characterization of the existence of fixed capital) is both evident and pervasive. If the labour theory of value (in Marx's formulation) cannot be successfully applied in a capitalist economy with fixed capital and joint production, and if the Sraffian model can be so applied, then it is the latter that must be ascribed greater

[2] The charge that mere calculation of profit rates avoids a causal account of the profit-determining process was raised earlier by Anwar Shaikh: 'Marx's Theory of Value and the "Transformation Problem"', in Jesse Schwartz (ed.), *The Subtle Anatomy of Capitalism*, Santa Monica 1977, pp. 106–139. Shaikh also argued that the 'transformation' was from a direct expression of values to a more complex, modified expression of values, in other words, that 'prices of production' were modified values and had nothing to do with the prices of orthodox economics.

generality. Moreover, were that the case, then in so far as an empirical research programme was at all feasible, the Sraffian model would provide more adequate support for it, just because of the pervasive role of fixed capital and joint production in real capitalist economies. Then, if the Marxian model was consistent and relevant in the simpler and more restrictive situations, it would be incorporated into the more general Sraffian model, as relating to a subset of special cases— if indeed any incorporation was to be done.

Second, Wright's assertion that Steedman considers the determination of value categories redundant, and therefore an unnecessary detour, is not quite correct. It is true that Steedman shows that values are wholly determined when the socio-technical conditions of production (STCP) and the real wage are known, and that in this respect they are determined by the same factors as are prices of production and the rate of profit. But value categories are not merely redundant: if conceived in the manner of Marx they can be found, in well-defined contexts, to be *negative* and as such puzzling. Moreover, they are obstacles to and misleading about the analysis of such central issues as the capitalists' decisions about choice of technique, the rate of profit, changes in the quantity and distribution of surplus labour, etc. This is partly because values cannot be known without specifying the technical conditions of production, which are themselves variable and affected by decisions taken by capitalists and other agents in a capitalist economy. But it is also because of the limitations of value categories that arise from the fact that, as Marx realized, if values *are* to be the basis of analysis, then a transformation of values into prices of production and of surplus-value into profits, interest, and so on, is requisite. In other words, if value categories are taken as the basic concepts, then the transformation problem is a relevant question and its accompanying difficulties become significant scientific problems. But, as Steedman has argued,[3] the transformation problem is a trivial non-issue if the conditions that generate it are unnecessary for a coherent analysis of profits, exploitation, etc.

The same point can be put more sharply: if Marxian values can (at least in the simple cases) be coherently calculated from the STCP and

---

[3] Ian Steedman, 'The Transformation Problem Again', in *Bulletin of the Conference of Socialist Economists*, autumn 1973, pp. 37–42.

real wages, and if prices and profits can be calculated from the same data, then no transformation whatever is required for a scientific theory of capitalist profits and dynamics. Not that the transformation of values into prices of production cannot be achieved in well-defined situations, for this has been precisely and carefully demonstrated by several analysts since Dmitriev.[4] Rather, no theoretical gain is achieved by attempting to follow this route. In any case, in its most general formulation, no transformation can be achieved without returning to the STCP and the real wage.[5]

It is true that in footnote 9 Wright recognizes that Steedman maintains that *puzzles* result from the use of value categories, but he dismisses the grounds for this claim by noting that if Morishima's redefinition of surplus labour and values is accepted, then the mistakes to which Steedman has called attention can be rectified. But readers are given no indication of what Morishima proposes or why, nor of the wider implications of the conceptual shifts involved. It is not merely that values cease to be *additive* (additive values generate the difficulties discovered by Steedman); moreover, they can no longer be considered as embodying or incorporating identifiable quantities of 'socially necessary labour time'—at least not in Marx's sense of depending on the *average* conditions of production in a particular branch of industry in which several actual processes of production (techniques) are in use. On the contrary, Morishima's definition of 'surplus labour' requires that we discover, by linear programming methods, for instance, the *minimum* amount of labour time needed to produce the consumption basket for workers if this consumption is set at subsistence.[6] This *notional* minimum quantity of labour-time is

[4] Some relevant works are: V.K. Dmitriev, *Economic Essays on Value, Competition and Utility*, London 1974; L. von Bortkiewicz, 'Value and Price in the Marxian System', in *International Economic Papers*, 1952; Francis Seton, 'The Transformation Problem', in *Review of Economic Studies*, vol. 24, 1957, reproduced in M.C. Howard and J.E. King (eds.), *The Economics of Marx*, Harmondsworth 1976; M. Morishima, *Marx's Economics: A Dual Theory of Value and Growth*, London 1973, Part III; Luigi Pasinetti, *Lectures on the Theory of Production*, New York 1977, appendix to chapter V, pp. 122–150. The list is ordered in terms of mathematical difficulty from the least to the most demanding.

[5] Arguments and demonstrations to this effect are to be found in Morishima, and Steedman, *Marx After Sraffa*, London, NLB, 1977, chapters 2, 3, and 4.

[6] M. Morishima, 'Marx in the Light of Modern Economic Theory', in *Econometrica*, vol. 42, 1974, pp. 611–632. This is Morishima's inaugural lecture on his appointment to the Chair of Mathematical Economics at the London School of Economics.

then taken as 'necessary labour', and the difference between it and the labour-time *actually consumed* is 'surplus labour'.

Here 'necessary labour' is strictly the minimum labour-time needed to produce workers' subsistence consumption, given *all available techniques of production*, and not simply those actually in use. Since capitalists select their production techniques from the available set according to the highest profit rate yielded and not in an effort to minimize the employment of labour-time, considerable differences may arise between the technology (and hence the physical coefficients of production) actually in use and those that would minimize the labour-time strictly required to reproduce the workers at subsistence level. The actual employment of labour-time in the economy will also be higher than this notional minimum, because positive amounts of labour are employed in the production of luxuries (all consumption goods other than those composing subsistence consumption of workers) and investment goods. Finally, the actual labour-time employed may also differ from the notional minimum defining 'necessary labour' owing to non-equilibrium conditions and sub-optimal operation in the real economy.

It will be noted that the Morishima method leads to an *abstract* conception of 'necessary labour'—not the *actual* labour-time spent in producing wage-goods. Moreover, it is arrived at by taking all available techniques of production into account and solving a minimization problem for the *whole economy*, treating all processes for producing all commodities. It cannot be calculated for particular factories or firms. The rate of exploitation is established for the economy as a whole, and this cannot be assumed to characterize conditions in each production process.

Given the linear-programming problem that yielded the minimum labour-time required to produce the subsistence consumption of workers, it is possible to solve a 'dual' linear-programming problem to obtain 'shadow prices' of the output of subsistence-consumption goods for workers. These 'shadow prices' can be treated as 'optimum values'. As Morishima himself puts it, 'there is an alternative way to formulate the labour theory of value, *not* as the theory of "actual values" calculating the embodied labour contents of commodities on the basis of the *prevailing production coefficients* as Marx did, but as the theory of "optimum values" considering values as shadow prices determined by a linear-programming problem that is dual to another linear-programming problem for the efficient utilization of labour' (emphasis added).[7]

This is indeed a theoretical advance important to research programmes. But as Steedman has pointed out,[8] the advance goes *beyond* Marx's use of value categories. His value categories referred to production methods actually used; they were additive, whether for a single commodity, a particular process of production, a sector of the economy, or the whole economy, since values were determined as the sum of the values of all the means of production expended plus the living labour (as abstract labour) performed, and they were *always positive*. Since the exploration of labour-value analysis with fixed capital and joint production has revealed the possibility of negative additive values for some commodities and negative surplus-value, it is clear that all three features of Marx's use of values cannot obtain simultaneously.

It is at this juncture that Morishima takes us further, by showing us that the puzzle of negative values can be eliminated if we re-conceptualize values so as to attain greater generality, in terms of the 'optimum values' mentioned above. But whilst value categories are now positive again, they are neither actual nor additive. The difference of opinion between Morishima and Steedman relates only to whether Morishima's proposals can continue to be regarded as basically a version of Marx's labour theory of value. Steedman thinks not. But as regards the central issue in the assessment of the Sraffian model, which is Wright's main concern, Morishima does not help the 'reconstructed Marxian model' at all. He himself emphasizes the objectivity of the calculation of the rate of exploitation under his approach. This rate is now obtained either as the ratio of 'surplus labour' to 'necessary labour' as reconceptualized, or as the ratio of paid to unpaid labour when paid labour is taken to be the subsistence consumption of workers evaluated at the 'optimum values' instead of the actual embodied-labour values. In both cases the rate of exploitation and the corresponding 'optimum value' of workers' subsistence consumption, or the 'necessary labour' in the economy,

[7] Ibid., pp. 615–616.
[8] Ian Steedman, 'Positive Profits with Negative Surplus-Value: A Reply', in *The Economic Journal*, vol. 86, 1976.

are uniquely determined by these factors: the output coefficient matrix, the physical-input coefficient matrix, the labour-input coefficient row vector, the number of workers actually employed, and the subsistence consumption of workers in physical units.[9] This is just what the Sraffian model as developed by Steedman terms the socio-technical conditions of production and a *given* subsistence real wage, namely the minimum possible wage.

It must also be remembered that since we have notional 'necessary labour' and 'optimum values' and are admitting joint production, the STCP here include all feasible technologies known to the capitalists. While Marx's labour values cannot be known until and *unless the problem of choice of techniques is resolved by the relevant agents*,[10] Morishima's notional values and related apparatus can be determined independently of the *actual* choice of techniques. The actual techniques chosen are determined by a number of factors, including the process of class struggle. The point is that nothing in the Morishima proposals contradicts the generality and conceptual precision of the Marx-after-Sraffa approach of Steedman, as will be evident to anyone who has actually worked through Steedman's book, especially chapter 13, where the Morishima proposals are explicitly discussed.

Later in his paper, Wright notes that Steedman and Morishima agree that 'the profit rate and growth rate are positive if and only if surplus labour, as newly defined by Morishima, is positive'. Morishima has called this the Generalized Fundamental Marxian Theorem, which holds for capitalist economies with very few restrictive assumptions. Morishima thinks that the only important restriction (besides the usual qualification that the theory applies only to reproducible commodities) is the absence of *heterogeneous labour*, i.e. the assumption that all labour inputs can be treated as reducible to a common scale, an assumption widely applied in all economic analysis. But Wright allows his readers to be misled into thinking that this vindicates what he has termed the reconstructed Marxian model—without a hint that the 'surplus labour' at issue here is a very

[9] Morishima, 'Marx in the Light of Modern Economic Theory', p. 618.

[10] Ian Steedman, *Marx After Sraffa*, particularly chapter 4, 'Value, Price and Profit Further Considered'.

different concept from that arrived at on the basis of Marx's labour theory of value. Indeed, it is for this reason that Steedman consistently refers to 'surplus labour' and not 'surplus-value'.

This brings us to a second serious weakness in Wright's article: his casual identification of 'surplus labour' and 'surplus-value'. In footnote 10 he writes: 'For convenience in this discussion I will not constantly refer to "surplus labour in the form of surplus-value", but simply to "surplus-value". Surplus labour is appropriated by dominant classes in all societies but it only takes the form of surplus-value in capitalist ones. . . . It is only that surplus labour which is performed in productive sectors of the economy and thus embodied in commodities as surplus-value that constitutes the basis of profits within Marxist theory. For simplicity, therefore, I will generally refer directly to surplus-value in this exposition.'

Thereafter he consistently *assumes* that whenever 'surplus labour' as a concept is warranted, it is also appropriate to speak of surplus-value in the traditional Marxist sense. This is a *petitio principii*, since among the points of contention between the Sraffian and re-constructed Marxian models is first and foremost precisely whether the labour theory of value and the Marxist conception of 'surplus-value' are apposite for the analysis of surplus labour and its quantitative assessment. Neither party in this debate disputes the existence of 'surplus labour' in some appropriate sense as a fundamental characteristic of capitalist economies; nor is there any dispute about the *existence* of identifiable relationships between this 'surplus labour', properly understood, and the level and rate of profits. As any reader of his fundamental work knows, it was Sraffa who rigorously demonstrated the existence of a maximum rate of profit given a set of physical production data.[11] He himself attributed the idea to Marx, who spoke of a limit to the rate of profit even if the workers could live on air.[12] Marx in turn seems to have taken the idea from the physiocrats, especially Quesnay, whose notion of a net product in a circular conception of the production system contains the idea that

[11] Piero Sraffa, *Production of Commodities by Means of Commodities*, London 1960, pp. 12–18.
[12] Ibid., p. 94.

the physical input and output proportions set a limit on the potential rate of profit under given production conditions. What is at issue, however, is whether the STCP and the real wage (treated as a variable) determine the rate of profit or whether some additional determinants *not indicated by or related to the* STCP *and the real wage* are required; and whether the traditional 'labour-embodied' conception of values is appropriate for an understanding of 'surplus labour' and its measurement—in other words, whether 'surplus-value' can be taken as an adequate representation of 'surplus labour' for all capitalist economies (even under the least restrictive assumptions). Wright simply assumes and asserts this, thus either failing to understand what the argument is about or misleading his readers into thinking that if 'surplus labour' exists in any sense whatever, then the labour-value concept of 'surplus-value' is legitimated.

This point is crucial to the rest of Wright's argument. His diagrammatic representation of the *reconstructed* Marxian model (his figure 4) differs from the equally schematic representation of the Sraffian model (his figure 2) in just this respect: the 'surplus labour' of his figure 2 is *not connected* to profits, whereas in his figure 4 there is no reference to 'surplus labour' but only to 'surplus-value', which is given some prominence and *connected* by a line, marked 'limits', to profits. These diagrams are based on a distinction between several modes of determination that Wright elaborated in his book *Class, Crisis and the State.*[13] There, developing an Althusser-influenced, structuralist-Marxist position, Wright listed limitation, selection mediation, transformation, and reproduction/non-reproduction as the basic modes of causal determination. Models, as distinct from modes of determination, were represented diagrammatically in the manner of systems-theorists, with boxed-in variables and/or structures mutually related by lines representing one or several of the modes of determination. This is the procedure Wright now uses to characterize the differences between the Marxian and Sraffian models. In the 'first approximation' given in his figure 4 only two modes of determination are presented: *selection* and *limitation*.

He argues that the STCP establish a limit on the maximum amount of surplus-value given by a real wage of zero. The actual level of real

[13] Erik Olin Wright, *Class, Crisis and the State*, London, NLB, 1978.

wages then acts as a 'selection determinant' of the actual level of surplus-value, within the upper limit set by the socio-technical conditions of production. Wright uses 'limits' in the plural, thus suggesting that there is a lower limit to surplus-value. Presumably this is zero, and obtains when the full value created by labour-power is received by the workers as real wages. Profits in this case are also zero, and there is no exploitation. So far the analysis parallels the Sraffian approach, the only difference being that the latter would speak of 'surplus labour' instead of values, for the proper conceptualization and role of the value categories is at issue. The treatment of the real wage as variable and distinct from the STCP is a major feature of Sraffa's models in *Production of Commodities by Means of Commodities*. It is in this manner that he establishes that the rate of profit and real wages are *inversely related*, given the STCP and, therefore, the 'net product' including wages.

At this point, it will be evident that in two important respects Wright differs from some others who have attempted criticisms of the Sraffa and so-called neo-Ricardian analysis.[14] First, Wright acknowledges that the STCP *determine values*, since they determine the upper limit of surplus-value. This admission—that the physical input-output data (socially determined in various ways) is sufficient to calculate values—is often disputed,[15] although no better way of arriving at values in order to compare them quantitatively has been proposed. Second, Wright admits the *variability of the real wage*, a position not always granted by those who insist that the equilibrium wage is the 'value of labour-power', presumably determined, like other values, by the STCP at any *given time*, and therefore given once the STCP are given. The problem is the theory of wages in a Marxian analysis. Marx's writings appear to evince two theories of wages. In *Capital* Volume 1 wages are said to fluctuate around the value of labour-power, determined, like other values, by the labour-time required to reproduce it (but incorporating in the reproduction process a 'cultural' component, which over short periods is a given of the society or civilization under consideration). In *Value, Price and*

[14] He differs, for example, from Ira Gerstein, 'Production, Circulation and Value', in *Economy and Society*, 1976.

[15] In addition to Gerstein, see also S. Himmelweit and S. Mohun, 'The Anomalies of Capital', in *Capital and Class*, 1978.

Profit Marx expounds a somewhat different, clearly class-struggle theory of wages, according to which wages are inversely related to profits and are indeterminate if only the STCP are given.[16] Wright agrees with Sraffa, Steedman, etc. in treating wages in conformity with Marx's second position rather than in terms of a labour-embodied 'value of labour-power'.

In his recently published lectures Pasinetti[17] suggests that we might think of the wage rate as consisting of two parts: one bare subsistence and determined biologically (this varying according to geographical and ecological conditions), the other a 'surplus' over and above subsistence requirements. The subsistence component can then be written into the technical coefficients of the physical data as itself a technical datum, and the 'surplus' part of the wage would vary as a result of class struggles and 'civilization'. In these matrices the maximum 'surplus-value' in Wright's sense would not require wages to be zero, but the minimum subsistence level. Morishima's 'surplus labour' and 'optimal values', however, require us to go one step further: not only do we put workers' consumption at the subsistence level, but we compute the surplus in terms of the *minimum labour input* requirements *possible* for the economy, given all the available techniques of production. This reduces 'necessary labour' not only to an actual biological minimum, but also to a conceptually meaningful *possible* minimum.

Apart from these two similarities between Wright and Steedman, Wright also judges, at least initially, that there is nothing fundamentally wrong with Steedman's approach, which is merely too limited. It is only on this basis that the incorporation thesis can be convincingly affirmed.

An idea of the source of Wright's confusion may be gleaned from careful examination of his diagrams. In figure 2, representing the Sraffian model, nothing is said of the modes of determination, limitation and selection. But they are relevant to an understanding of the Sraffian model. The STCP establish the *limits* on the level of profit, and the real wage, determined 'exogenously' by the conjunction of various forces (including class struggles, population growth, state

[16] For a discussion of this matter, see M.C. Howard and J.E. King, *The Political Economy of Marx*, London 1976.
[17] Pasinetti, *Lectures on the Theory of Production*.

intervention, limited-access training facilities, demand for labour on the part of capitalists, etc.), *selects* the prevailing rate of profit. The amount of 'surplus labour', of course, can be calculated by subtracting the aggregate real-wage bundle from the 'net product'; alternatively, the Morishima redefinition of 'surplus labour' can be accepted. In general, however, in neither method will 'surplus labour' equal what Marx would call 'surplus-value'. (There are, of course, simple situations, subject to many *restrictions*, in which Sraffian 'surplus labour' would indeed equal Marx's 'surplus-value'. It is Sraffa's formulation that has the greater generality and that reveals the limitations of Marx's formulation of the labour theory of value). In figure 4, representing the reconstructed Marxian position, the modes of determination are written in, but with several puzzles. Why should the connection between the STCP and profits be one of *selection*, when in the Sraffian model and by Wright's own words it is one of *limitation*? It is *in fact* one of limitation, since by themselves the STCP establish only the maximum rate of profit, while the real wage must be known to *select* the actual rate of profit. In other words, the very same relations that Wright claims exist between the STCP, real wages, and surplus-value exist between the STCP, real wages, and profits. Indeed, it would be odd if both real wages and the STCP exercised a selecting determination on profits without one exercising subordinate selection within the limits established by the other.

Another puzzle is the *limiting* determination exercised by surplus-value. At first, this could seem to make sense if the role of both the STCP and the real wage were that of selection. But that is itself dubious, or at any rate calls for a hierarchical listing of the roles of the STCP, surplus-value, and real wages. By Wright's own account, the STCP exercise a limiting determination on surplus-value, and it is thus an enigma in what sense it *selects* profits. After all, the surplus-value that is limited by the STCP itself establishes only *limits* for profits. For figure 4 to be a serious model alternative to the Sraffian, and for surplus-value to exercise some *limiting* determination on profits not already exercised directly by the STCP, there must be some determinant of surplus-value independent of the STCP and real wages. The model requires at least one missing 'structure', to be placed, say, between real wages and the STCP and establishing limits on surplus-value, these limits either being nested within the limits established by the STCP or exercising an independent determination that must be somehow 'combined' or 'articulated' with the limits determined by the STCP, as in my figure 1 below.

Without the 'missing structure' to exercise an *independent* limiting determination on surplus-value, the *limits* on possible profits exercised by surplus-value are reducible to those exercised by the STCP, in which case Wright's figure 4 reduces to a correctly identified figure 2, with 'surplus-value' reverting to 'surplus labour' in the general case and becoming 'surplus-value' only in well-defined special cases. The impression that figure 4 represents an informative model different from the Sraffian rests entirely on the unargued decision to describe the effect of the STCP on profits as one of *selection*, for this apparently leaves a niche for surplus-value to establish *limits*! A comparison of my figure 1 and Wright's figure 4 (reproduced below) will show that Wright's representation of a reconstructed first-approximation Marxian model is either confused or quite incomplete. Actually, there is evidence that Wright *is* confused. On pp. 45–6 he writes that the 'socio-technical conditions of production establish the basic limits on the creation of surplus-value'; but on page 47, after producing a diagram

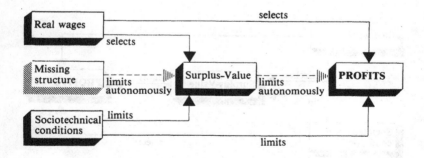

FIGURE 1

114

that, we are warned, should not be taken to show what it seems to show, he writes: 'The amount of surplus-value, then, constitutes the explanation of those levels of profits that are impossible; the socio-technical conditions of production and the real wage explain—"predict"—which of the many possible levels of profits actually occurs.' These two claims are contradictory, for according to the second, the STCP are nested within the limits of surplus-value, whereas according to the first the STCP establish those limits.

Wright anticipates some aspects of the above argument. He notes that one possible objection to the model depicted in his figure 4 is that 'since surplus-value is itself determined by the socio-technical conditions and the real wage, it plays no autonomous role in the process and is thus still "redundant"'. His answer, however, is unsatisfactory, for it begs the question. He asserts that 'it is precisely because surplus-value is an endogenous factor within that process that it can be viewed as a privileged determinant.' He then shifts attention from the model in his figure 4 to that in his figure 3 (the *unreconstructed* Marxian model) and argues that the figure 3 model would be quite adequate in a world of equal organic compositions of

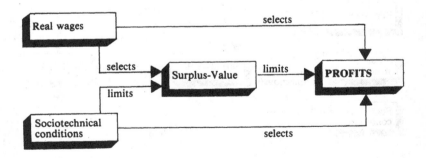

FIGURE 2

Wright's Figure 4

capital, that in such a case 'surplus-value' would be *endogenous* since entirely determined by the STCP and real wages, and that 'these two factors have their effects on profits only by virtue of their effects on surplus-value'. Finally, he affirms that even when the organic compositions of capital are not equal, the basic relationship between surplus-values and profits remains the same. Except that now, in the more realistic case, changes in surplus-value are not the necessary and sufficient condition for changes in profits; instead, 'they remain necessary and sufficient conditions for changes in the *limits* on possible profits'. But these assertions are by no means self-evident, and once we leave the world of equal organic compositions of capital, we face, if we persist in using Marxian labour-values, the transformation problem. The long history of discussion of this problem has shown that the transformation can be achieved (at least in the absence of fixed capital and joint production), given a normalization condition.[18] But whatever proposed solution is adopted, one or both of two equalities upheld by Marx—the equality of total values and total prices of production and of total surplus-value and total profits—must be lost.

The whole debate about the re-examination of Marx and the reconstruction of a materialist (Marx-inspired but not necessarily Marx-repeating) analysis of capitalist economies with a central focus on the exploitation process arises because of the implications of the discussion about the transformation of values into prices of production. Some have worried about an invariant measure of value and found that socially necessary labour-time, in the most general case, will not do the job.[19] Others have worried about the relation between values and surplus-values on the one hand and prices and profits on the other and found that under *some* conditions the value system is a 'double' of the price system, but that in more general models (admitting fixed capital and joint production) values are not strictly determinate and could be negative, or require drastic redefinition.[20]

[18] See the references in note 4.

[19] For example Sraffa, who devised the 'standard commodity' as a way of solving the problem of an invariant measure of value.

[20] For example, Morishima in his book on Marx's economics, and Andras Bródy in his *Prices, Proportions and Planning. A Mathematical Restatement of the Labour Theory of Value*, Amsterdam 1970. Ian Steedman showed by illustrative hypothetical cases how values could be negative, see *Marx After Sraffa*, pp. 150–162.

One result of these studies has been to view Marx's values and prices, in so far as they are related at all, as twins arising from the physical data once the real wage is given and incorporated into the relevant matrices or equations. Both change with alterations in the physical production data, but neither directly determines the other. They are related as two tines of a fork stemming from the STCP and real wages. But even whilst admitting this duality, some would argue that the price and profit analysis (on the basis of the STCP and the real wage) is more basic, since questions about choice of technique when various techniques are available can be answered in terms of that analysis, whereas the value analysis, by its nature, can be completed only *after* the choice of techniques has been made; alone, it cannot illuminate how the choice will be made. Wright's casual dismissal of one objection that he does anticipate therefore amounts merely to a profession of faith in a dogma; he neither confronts nor refutes the argument. Besides, what is to be made of the notion of a *privileged* endogenous determinant? Why ascribe privileged status to surplus-value except as the re-affirmation of dogma?

Wright uses the problem of natural-resource scarcities largely as a pretext to adumbrate some aspects of the classical Marxian theory of classes and social relations of production. But in the process he appears to concede too much to 'factor-scarcity' approaches to profits and prices, since he writes that the choice of a theory of labour-values with surplus-value as the limiting condition is arbitrary in *calculating* profits and that the reasons for focusing on surplus-value have to do with understanding classes and class struggles and linking them to the specifically capitalist mechanisms by which surplus labour is appropriated. This may strike some readers as a startling admission, coming as it does after so many belaboured points about the importance of surplus-value during the discussion of the Sraffian model. It certainly will not be seen as a strong argument by anyone not already convinced that the Marxist concepts of classes and the details of class struggle provide the correct approach to the study of human history and politics in capitalist societies. It comes perilously close to the popular adage that for those who believe in god no reasons are necessary and for those who do not no reasons can be given.

The issues raised in a comparison of the Sraffian theoretical approach with mainstream neo-classical factor-scarcity analysis of prices and profits cannot be enumerated here. A few brief indications may be offered, however. First, there are some important differences between 'production-reproduction' approaches descending from the work of Quesnay, Ricardo, and Marx and the 'factors of production combined to satisfy consumer demand' approaches enshrined in orthodox textbooks. These have to do with the explanation of profits, the theory of distribution, recognition or not of the class monopoly over the means of production, and conflicting theories of growth and fluctuations in capitalist economies.[21] Second, the labour theory of value, as treated by both Ricardo and Marx, was explicitly intended to apply to freely reproducible commodities (those not subject to a natural-resource or other input limitation). The theory will therefore not directly 'cover' all real-world situations in which various 'constraints' on natural resources, land, and locations might arise (at least for definite time periods). To determine what difference this makes to an *empirical* analysis of profits in a given economy requires both a theoretical method of incorporating such situations into the general model and the particular data for the given case (including, of course, such other 'excluded' phenomena as monopolies, oligopolies, state taxes and subsidies, and so on).

The theoretical method of incorporating all scarcities arising from non-reproducible inputs is dealt with in Sraffa's treatment of rents, since lands of varying fertility, for example, can be considered a particular case of non-reproducible inputs subject to scarcity and exhaustion. In other words, there is a way to incorporate these into the matrices that describe the STCP, although the details cannot be

---

[21] Luigi Pasinetti, chapter 1, 'A Brief Historical Excursus'. Also see the excellent paper by Mario Nuti, 'The Transformation of Labour Values into Production Prices and the Marxian Theory of Exploitation', originally published in the Polish journal *Ekonomista*, 1974, and reproduced in Jesse Schwartz (ed.), *The Subtle Anatomy of Capitalism*. Nuti writes: 'The *evaluation* of the surplus product at prices (in terms of labour embodied) equal to values and at transformed prices is not necessarily the same, except for a few special cases; the transformation process affects the evaluation of the surplus product, and not merely its distribution among capitalists. This, however, does not alter the findings of Marx's analysis on the origin of profit, his view of profits as exploitation, and his measurement of the degree of exploitation.' This statement, on the whole, would be accepted by those adhering to a Sraffian approach.

discussed here. (Some indications of the relevant sorts of work is provided below.[22]) The point of interest here is that in principle the Sraffa analysis *has* a means of incorporating non-reproducible factor-scarcities while still preserving its structure as a circular production model that maintains the demonstration that profits and wages are inversely related and shows that real wages exogenously determined (i.e. determined by causes not strictly technical-economic) will then determine what surplus product is available to capitalists. This remains more than simply the capitalists' consumption, since it includes investment in means of production and the material basis for the reproduction of capitalists as capitalists and workers as workers.[23]

The Sraffian will concede relatively little to the problem of factor scarcities. The models will be rendered more complex, but not fundamentally different or untenable. To observe this is to identify another point of superiority of the Sraffian over the traditional Marxist approach, with or without Wright's reconstruction. This is *not* to say that there are no difficulties with the Sraffian analysis, especially as regards the introduction of monopolies, changing demand conditions, exhaustible resources, the incorporation of services and public goods, etc. These problems *do* constitute the research frontiers for theoretical work and elaboration for those interested in developing Marx-after-Sraffa. These are the problems that require critical attention. The issues Wright considers still unresolved and excludes from consideration in his paper—fixed capital, varying time-structures of capital, and joint production—are in fact quite well clarified in the work of Sraffa, Von Neumann, Morishima, Steedman, and others.[24]

For Wright, however, the whole issue of input scarcities and their role in the determination of profits was merely a pretext to introduce a complicated systems-theoretic schema representing the Complex Approximation (as opposed to the earlier First Approximation)

[22] Piero Sraffa, *Production of Commodities by Means of Commodities*, pp. 74–91, and Gilbert Abraham-Frois and Edmond Berrebi, *Théorie de la Valeur, des Prix et de l'Accumulation*, Paris 1976, chapter III, pp. 90–165.

[23] Mario Nuti, pp. 101–103.

[24] Sraffa, chapters VII–X, pp. 43–62; Morishima, *Marx's Economics*, chapters 13 and 14, pp. 164–196; Steedman, *Marx After Sraffa*, chapter 12, pp. 163–183.

version of the reconstructed Marxist model: his figure 6. Class struggle and class structure are now introduced as boxed-in structures/variables along with the previous real wages, STCP, profits, and surplus-value. Wright states, correctly, that under capitalism 'precisely because the performance of surplus labour is disguised through the exchange process and the organization of production as a capitalist labour process, class struggles are never over surplus labour as such.' Class struggles transform the STCP and real wages, as well as the class structure itself. Two modes of determination absent from the first approximation now make their appearance: transformation and reproduction. The STCP are seen as exercising a reproductive determination on the class structure. The box with surplus-value now stands on the far right side, and profits are placed left of surplus-value so as to be connected by a selection-determination arrow to class struggles.

Two points must be made immediately. First, this diagram in itself is a *programmatic* statement of connections more than a well-developed model, or even a model with some well-specified relationships. In the absence of greater detail or more precise specification of the nature of the 'limits', 'transformations', and 'selections' suggested, it is a statement of broad orientation more than a model. It represents, however, the normal claims that most Marxists generally consider warranted.[25] Second, if and in so far as it may be elaborated so as truly to 'model' the structures and processes represented, there is little in it that would not be acceptable, *without any inconsistency*, to any Sraffian model analyst who was also a Marxist in matters of sociological and political analysis. The only Sraffians who might not be willing to assent to the broad connections are those who are strictly neo-Ricardian and agnostic or unconvinced about the role and relative importance of class struggles and the inter-dependence of class structure and the STCP. All the Sraffians would do would be to jettison the right-hand box—'surplus-value', and the three arrows associated with it—as *unnecessary*. More strictly, they would simply remove the arrow labelled *limits* arising from 'surplus-value' with its

[25] Steedman probably would include much or all of this in what he takes 'as read' in order to focus with precision on a set of very well defined issues. See *Marx After Sraffa*, pp. 15–16.

head pointed at 'profits', on the grounds that this is unwarranted and, without an appropriate re-definition of 'surplus-value', erroneous.

The statement that 'class struggles do not directly affect surplus-value and exploitation' because they operate through effects on the STCP and the real wage would not be acceptable to Sraffians as regards exploitation. For in a Sraffian analysis, the rate of exploitation depends on the proportion of the net product that goes to workers as real wages. Class struggles over the real wage will therefore directly affect the rate of exploitation and indirectly influence the proportion of 'surplus labour' (in the Morishima definition) that goes to the capitalists.

With regard to his figure 6, Wright re-affirms the dogma noted earlier, without any further argument, namely that 'it is still the case that class struggles have their most decisive impact on profits *by virtue of their effects on surplus-value*' (Wright's emphasis). Perhaps unconvinced of the dogma himself, he adds in a teleological vein that this has 'very important implications' for the empirical research agendas that will emerge, as though these outcomes constitute the best support for the dogma (that Marxian surplus-value is unambiguously identifiable and sets the limits on the possible rates of profit).

Finally, in drawing together his assessment of the Sraffian model, Wright advances a number of claims, some simply stated, one developed at length through a review of some recent studies of the labour process in capitalist industry. He repeats the allegation that the Sraffian analysis is concerned solely with calculation of profits and cannot account for the social possibility of profits. This is quite false. True, Sraffa's own work *is* monastically austere, devoid of any social comment. But it can be used, when combined with socio-historical data, to demonstrate that profits are appropriated by those who own and control the means of production, that their level is the outcome of social processes that determine how much of the net product must be paid out as real wages, and that if real wages rise under given STCP, then profit receivers will garner less profits and will thus attempt to reduce real wages or alter the STCP so as either to bring about a result equivalent to a fall in real wages or to raise the maximum possible level of profits, i.e. raise the net product. All these results arise from Sraffa-type analyses and show that they *do* raise problems of social process and can provide answers, or a locus for answers, in objective and, in principle, measurable ways. It is false that the concept of 'surplus labour' plays no role in the Sraffian analysis. On the contrary, a precise theoretical sense is ascribed 'surplus labour', and in principle it, too, becomes calculable, at least over the economy as a whole. It is the concept of surplus-value that Steedman urges us to drop, not the concept of surplus labour. The latter is more basic and generic, and is required both for Marxist investigation of modes of production and for the formulation of a theory of social classes and their relations. Surplus-value, on the other hand, is a specific concept proposed by Marx for the analysis of the *specific* features of a capitalist economy, and is found, when used systematically, to be inadequate to its purpose. It is therefore being replaced by new concepts and theoretical proposals, from Morishima and Steedman, among others.

As to the claim that the Marxist account 'embeds its analysis of the determination of profits in a larger theory of social relations and determinations, a theory in which profits themselves act as determinants, not just outcomes', one may easily agree that this is correct, but deny the implied suggestion that such bedding rights are not available to Sraffians. Sraffian models are eminently of the 'circular production' type, so that profits as outcomes do have determinate effects on the STCP, on real wages, and, as Steedman forcefully demonstrates, on the choice of technique and decisions affecting the labour process.[26] It is surprising that one who has actually read *Marx After Sraffa* could make the claim Wright does, for one of its central ideas is that capitalists *take their decisions with reference to prices and profits* and not values and surplus-values, so that profits do indeed become determinants of the structure and dynamic path of capitalist economies. In so far as well specified and determinate theoretical models of the larger theory of social relations are available, they may be accepted by Sraffians (those who see themselves as extending and not merely refuting Marx's work)[27] provided their formulation does not require Marx's theory of surplus-value and his value concepts.

[26] Ian Steedman, *Marx After Sraffa*, pp. 64–65.

[27] Not all those who agree with the importance of Sraffa for economic analysis and take his work as a point of departure would accept Marxist claims regarding historical processes, the theory of modes of production, etc. They would therefore *not* be interested in the construction of *Marxist* theory after Sraffa.

Some, including many proponents of Sraffian theory, may hold that this broader sociology-cum-theory-of-history, insightful and fecund though it is as a framework of analysis, has not yet received a rigorous theoretical expression that would allow the sort of penetrating debate that characterizes assessment of Marx's theoretical work in *Capital*. In the context of very precise analytical issues in the study of production and distribution systems, these wider theories and arguments would therefore be needlessly distracting. Acceptance or rejection of the wider social theory in Marx has little to do with the precise conceptual issues raised in the shadow of Sraffa, by Steedman. Marx's theory of modes of production and the conditions for their reproduction or collapse, or the social and political correlates of his theory of capitalist crises, could, when given a particularly clear exposition, incorporate the Sraffian analysis of commodity-producing economies and be the stronger for it. It is hard to imagine that such an elaboration of the broader aspects of Marx's *scientific* work would be unable to survive dispensing with his formulation of labour-values and surplus-value. What Marxist analysis has to say about human potentialities and feasible futures growing out of present conditions would also be available to Sraffians, if found satisfactory in terms of the knowledge and chain of reasoning advanced. The Sraffians' silence on these matters no more disqualifies them from accepting warranted and rigorously articulated theory about these issues than their silence regarding brain functions excludes them from accepting warranted neurological theory. The apparent silence probably has to do with the difficulty of developing rigorous and (in principle) quantifiable theory on these matters rather than with any principled rejection of the possibility of scientific work in these areas. In fact, it can be argued that the Sraffian theory actually grants greater precision and detail to the investigation of alternative courses of action and the problems of the socialist re-organization of the economy, since in terms of both generality and measurable objectivity, the Sraffa-type models accommodate more situations than do the classical Marxian models.[28] That argument, however, would go beyond the purpose of this article.

[28] For an interesting discussion of how the 'unified' theory of production emerging from the work of Marx, Von Neumann, and Sraffa relates to economic problems of socialist economies, see A. Bródy.

Finally, Wright's *pièce de resistance*, the core of his disquiet with the Sraffian approach, is the question of how the various theories treat the analysis of the labour process and the formulation of a theory of classes and class-based conflicts. Here he impugns the Sraffian approach on two serious counts, and thus finds the reconstructed Marxian approach doubly superior. First, he argues, the Sraffians have a 'market-determined' notion of class, more akin to Max Weber's theory of social stratification than to a Marxist conception. The Marxist theory of class is stated in terms of the social relations of production and is therefore production-oriented and not merely market-oriented. Second, since surplus labour (which Wright takes as equivalent to surplus-value in capitalist economies) is a central concern of Marxists but not of Sraffians, the former can place on their research agenda penetrating questions about the labour process that cannot be seriously and centrally raised in the latter framework. Many interesting empirical questions about monopolies, state intervention, the impact of trade-unionism, game-theoretic studies of collective bargaining and the wage-struggle, imperialism, and real wages, technological change, innovation, and the impact of labour-process conflicts on technical change are allowed the Sraffian approach. These questions are seen to relate to the determination of real wages and the STCP and so are part of the research agenda of Sraffian theory. The alleged superiority of the Marxist theory is that not only can all these be raised as part of its research agenda, but in addition something more can be and is being researched: the changes in surplus labour, the means of controlling workers, and the social relations of domination in the labour process.

I believe that both these claims are mistaken. The reasons for the mistake lie in what we have discussed previously: the confusion of surplus labour with surplus-value, and the failure to understand the 'production-model' aspects of the Sraffian theory. Before examining Wright's claims, it is well to state an important respect in which he, most Marxists, and, I believe, Sraffians would agree. It is that the basic concepts of class theory must be established *independently* of a theory of value, relative prices, and profits in a capitalist economy— so that the theory of classes can be deployed more generally than simply with reference to capitalist societies; and that the theory should contain, as a sub-region, a specific theory of the identification and relations of classes in a capitalist society—and this with reference to profits and wages, amongst other things.

It is this requirement that gives surplus labour and its specific identity in different modes of production *primacy* over surplus-value, which is a concept in a specific theory designed to account for the basic properties of a capitalist economy. If one assumes, as Wright does, that surplus labour *is* surplus-value (in Marx's understanding of the concept) and that together they stand or fall as relevant scientific concepts (with regard to capitalist economies), then one is likely to consider that all Sraffians have lost a central locus for the exploration of the various ways in which the magnitude of surplus labour can be altered in a capitalist economy. The recommendation that no more time be wasted on surplus-value is interpreted as implying that the analysis of surplus labour and its variation is of no importance. But as I have suggested, this assumption of Wright's is an error, and even a cursory reading of *Marx After Sraffa* will reveal a sustained interest in the formation, magnitude, and variation of surplus labour. The concept itself is understood in some respects differently than in, say, *Capital* Volume 1, although the concern with the length of the working day, the relation of paid to unpaid labour, the intensity of the work process, etc. is preserved. This should suffice to show that there is no reason to assume a priori that Sraffians who also accept a Marxian theory of classes are uninterested in the labour process.

The charge that Sraffians are inclined by their theory to a Weberian market-oriented theory of class is the sociological version of the frequently levelled charge that Sraffa-type analysis is concerned with the 'sphere of circulation'—the mechanisms of distribution (for example, the share of output making up real wages)—and not the 'sphere of production', with the production of surplus-value and the structuring of the labour process. It is puzzling why this misconception is so persistent. First, the division of the net product explored in Sraffa-type production models is examined specifically to clarify what happens to profits and relative prices *if and when* the real-wage rate is altered. Such exercises do *not* imply that the net product actually is or can be so casually divided up. Whether or not the real wage *can* rise depends on the exogenous (i.e. exogenous to relative pricing) determinants: class power, alternatives to wage labour, competitive conditions, etc. Second, the division of the net product is not the same as the sharing out of consumer goods and personal services; it is the distribution of investible resources and funds as well as of what is generally understood as income distribution. Thus, in a highly abstract manner, it includes company expansion funds, transactions in financial asset markets, and capital transactions generally. In this sense, 'primitive accumulation' and the Ricardian-Marxian inquiry into the production and distribution of profits, rents, and wages is also a 'distributive' investigation: the distribution that engenders and reproduces the class monopolies over land and means of production. The distribution and repeated reproduction of a given pattern of distribution of the means of production and financial assets should not be viewed as identical to the distribution of consumption between capitalists and workers. Third, the charge of market orientation appears also to rest on a confusion, on a failure to distinguish between the 'market' for production inputs and the 'market' for final consumer goods. Both exist *simultaneously* in capitalist economies, and so production activities cannot get started without transactions—conducted by agents very differently related to the means of production and selling very different commodities, from labour-power to company shares—in the market for production inputs. In this sense, even the Marx of *Capital* Volume 1 is market-oriented: labour markets and the level of employment are major concerns. In a later volume of *Capital*, Marx is again market-oriented: the transactions between capitalists of Departments I and II are the focus of interest; and so one could go on. In a capitalist economy one *has* to be market-oriented. The difference is between those who see the whole economy as a *coherent reproducible structure* in which the outputs of some production processes, after passing through markets, become inputs to other production processes, and those who see the economy as an exchange counter in which various individuals with different 'assets' enjoy mutual benefits through exchanges that increase their level of satisfaction. The latter tend to treat primarily the consumer-goods market (the purchase of fish or bread in the standard textbook examples), taking the initial distribution of productive assets and occupations as a given, as a microcosm of the basic features of the whole economy. This is clearly not the method of Marx, but nor was it of Ricardo or Quesnay. And it is likewise not true of the work of Sraffa or Pasinetti, and in this respect the Sraffa-type analysis is directly concerned with the material basis for social classes and how it is reproduced by and finds expression in the organization of production.

This is not to say that the implications of the Sraffian analysis for a theory of social class are crystal clear. There are still too many unresolved issues in the conceptualization of social classes, let alone empirical measurements, for anyone to be certain of whether the Sraffian work is capable of supporting other than an income-strata notion of social class, or whether it must treat all wage-earners as necessarily belonging to a single class. It may'turn out that social class is a highly abstract concept with several subsets of characteristics that may not be well-ordered; conversely it may be so strictly a matter of the modalities of the extraction and distribution of surplus labour as to leave indeterminate its effects on relations in other social spaces. This is an area of analysis that has benefited from Wright's previous work, but which still remains, in important respects, theoretically open.

Finally, there is the important and related (to the theory of class) question of whether the Sraffian analysis inhibits rigorous study of the labour process and how the magnitude of surplus labour available to capital can be varied within it, along with the associated long-term strategies of the organization of work, jobs, and careers. Again, a detailed re-examination of the studies Wright cites in his support, though quite relevant, will not be attempted here. Only three counter claims will be made, which the reader may evaluate in the light of both the studies cited by Wright and the work of Steedman.

First, the studies cited are of very uneven merit, at least in terms of the clarity and precision with which their theoretical claims are developed. They raise several problems for *exploration*, but none presents a theory of the labour process comparable in conceptual rigour and deductive fecundity to, say, Steedman's theoretical discussion of the labour process and the problem of hetrogeneous labour in Sraffa-type models. I say this not because I believe that mathematically expressed pure theory is indispensable to scientific work, but because in the absence of such clarity one *can* reasonably remain unconvinced and discover unresolved ambiguities. The debate is then difficult to conduct with the sharpness that has characterized the debates arising from Sraffa's work.

Second, apart from the work by Baudelot and Establet,[29] none of the studies *necessarily requires* the labour theory of value and surplus-value to state its arguments and findings, which are sociological and have to do with relations of domination, decision-making powers, strategic options regarding long-term growth or profitability, etc. That is, if these studies were judged to be sound conceptually and empirically, one could agree with their claims whilst holding to a Sraffa-type analysis of exploitation, the importance of struggles over real wages, and the profit-oriented decisions regarding choice of technique, if certain organizational forms, including wage differentiation etc. are treated as constituting alternative techniques of production or processes.

Third, the Sraffian analysis provides a method of clearly analysing the outcomes of various changes in the labour process and thus provides a basis for assessing alternative strategies for workers (or capitalists) and for de-mystifying the real implications of certain changes. Steedman's book includes a chapter entitled 'Within the Labour Process'; it is concerned to unfreeze the assumption that there is a fixed relation between the real wage paid to the workers and the amount of work they actually perform: 'the given real wage will be taken to be the wage paid, by the capitalist, for the use of the worker's capacity to work; but while that wage will be held constant, the work actually performed will be assumed to be variable: it will be seen how the rate of profit depends on the amount and the intensity of work which the capitalist is able to obtain from the worker. While the analysis presented will certainly not *determine* the "balance of forces" in the workplace, and thus the outcome of coercion and resistance in the labour process, it will show the importance of that balance for the determination of the rate of profit.'[30]

He goes on to list various contradictory objectives capitalists and workers will pursue as regards the organization and functioning of the labour process. Whilst the list is not exhaustive, and in particular does not include strategic objectives such as division of the workers, promotion of a pro-capitalist ideology (e.g. social partnership of capitalists and workers) etc., it does include a great many issues

[29] Christian Baudelot, Roger Establet, Jacques Malemort, *La petite bourgeoisie en France*, Paris 1974.
[30] Ian Steedman, *Marx After Sraffa*, pp. 77–87.

connected with the labour process. In a considerably more complex analysis all these aspects could be studied in a Sraffian model. With simple illustrations, however, Steedman shows how some of the standard issues in shop-floor struggles are related to the rate of profit, and how many courses of action available to capitalists will have the effects of a wage-cut, although the experience of the workers will be different according to whether there is an actual cut in real wages or, say, an intensification of the work-process that has effects similar to a wage cut. In principle, virtually all Marx's concerns in *Capital* Volume 1 regarding the labour process could be analysed in an appropriately complex Sraffian model (which will, of course, continue to be successful in determining prices, profits, and rents in the general case).

It would seem that *as long as changes in labour-process social relations have effects on and can be indicated or measured by changes in the* STCP *data and/or real wages*, they can be analysed precisely within Sraffian models. There may, of course, be aspects of the labour process that have no concomitant indicators or measures in terms of the STCP or real-wage data: such as, say, purely ideological effects. These will have to be analysed with the help of appropriate sociological/socio-psychological theories, and such analyses will in no sense be *incompatible* with a Sraffian analysis of those problems with which it is best equipped to deal. The choice between a post-Sraffa Marxian analysis and a traditional, labour-theory-of-value Marxist analysis will not be decided by these *sociological* analyses of the political and ideological processes accompanying the exploitation of labour in the production and consumption of commodities in capitalist economies, because such analyses would be compatible with either type of model.

To conclude, it may be noted that this discussion has attempted to show that Wright's conclusions 1, 2, and 4 are unwarranted; indeed, 1 is false and 2 ought to be *inverted*: it is the Sraffian model that incorporates the traditional Marxist model as a limited, special case. As regards 4, neither model has an intrinsic advantage over the other: the strict-Sraffian is silent on these matters, but a Marxist Sraffian accepts the warrant of Marxist sociological and philosophical claims. The Sraffians may be able to analyse some problems of socialist economies more clearly than traditional Marxists, whose labour theory of value is a cumbersome and unhelpful tool for the study of socialist economies. Finally, as regards Wright's third claim, it is partly based on a misunderstanding of the 'production relations' aspects of the Sraffian approach, but in an important sense the question of an appropriately specified *theory* of social classes and their relations and effects, as distinct from a typology or classification scheme for empirically identified social classes, remains an open one.

There are, therefore, no research-agenda advantages that can be claimed by reconstructed traditional Marxist models over reformulated post-Sraffa Marxian models. There are, in fact, a few needless handicaps and obstacles in continuing to use the former.[31]

---

[31] This article, following Wright's contribution, does not use any mathematical demonstrations, although many of the claims advanced rest on mathematical formulations, especially the treatment of joint production and the Morishima redefinition of surplus labour. The rigorous demonstrations will be found in the works cited in the relevant footnotes.

Reconsiderations

Erik Olin Wright

Like most Marxists, I have considered the labour theory of value (LTV) to be one of the essential elements in the conceptual framework of Marxist theory.* It provides an elegant and intuitively gripping way of talking about exploitation in capitalist society, and on the basis of this account of exploitation provides a way of linking such diverse concepts as class, class struggle, accumulation, crisis and so on into an overall theory of capitalist development. While it is true that my empirical research has never been directly based on the categories of the labour theory of value, nevertheless it always seemed that value concepts provided a very general point of departure and inspiration for the questions and direction of that research.

It was in this context that I wrote 'The Value Controversy and Social Research'. That paper was primarily an attempt to come to terms with the Sraffian critique of the labour theory of value as formulated in the work of Ian Steedman. I attempted to establish two principal theses: 1. That if the Marxist account of the relationship between surplus-value and profits is properly reconstructed, then it is possible to demonstrate the formal compatibility of the labour theory of value and the Sraffian account of the determination of profits. This compatibility rested on the argument that the Marxist account specifies a process of structural limitation on profits whereas the Sraffian account specifies a process of concrete selection of profits within those limits. (This distinction will be explained below.) 2. That the labour theory of value generated a different research agenda and provided the basis for a different theory of class relations than did the

* I would like to thank Michael Burawoy and Herb Gintis for their helpful comments on an earlier draft of this paper.

Sraffian alternative. In particular I argued that the LTV supported a conceptualization of classes in terms of exploitation based in the relations of production, whereas Sraffian theory more naturally supported a market-based (Weberian) notion of class, and that as a result the LTV more systematically directed research towards questions of the labour process and its relationship to classes.

In the two years since I wrote that paper I have had many occasions to reflect on its core arguments. It now seems to me that some of those arguments were incorrectly formulated and the conclusions overstated. I therefore welcome the opportunity provided by P. Bandyopadhyay's critique of my paper, 'In Defence of a Post-Sraffian Approach', and Geoff Hodgson's critique, 'Labour and Profits' to rethink and elaborate some of the positions I defended in the initial paper.

After briefly summarizing my original argument, this essay will be organized around three clusters of issues raised by Bandyopadhyay and Hodgson: 1. The concept of structural limitation and its role in a theory of profit determination; 2. The problem of the distinction between formal and real determination; 3. The relationship between the labour theory of value, the Sraffian approach to profits and prices, and class analysis. In each section I will address criticisms raised by Bandyopadhyay and Hodgson, but the objective will not be to provide a point-by-point defence of my earlier positions. Rather, I will try to use these criticisms as a point of departure for a clarification and reconsideration of my initial arguments and conclusions.

Before proceeding, one general disclaimer needs to be made. As in the original essay, this paper will not deal with any of the technical issues surrounding the problem of joint production and fixed capital. Bandyopadhyay argues that this issue cannot be 'abstracted from' since it is at the heart of the general debate and bears directly on all other issues. If, after further theoretical work, debate, and clarification it turns out that Marxists do not produce a fully satisfactory reply to the criticisms associated with the joint production problem, then indeed this will have serious implications for the validity of the labour theory of value. I cannot provide such a reply, and if a reader feels that this silence preempts the usefulness of the discussion of any other issues associated with the debate on the LTV, then there is little reason for reading further in this essay.[1]

Summary of Original Argument

The heart of the original argument I advanced revolved around what I termed a 'model of determination' of profits. This model contained four principal elements: profits, surplus-value, the real wage and the socio-technical conditions of production (STCP). I argued that these elements were connected in the manner depicted in my figure 4 (p. 46). This model should be read in the following way: With a given quantity of surplus-value generated in an economy, there is an upper and lower boundary to the quantity of profits possible in that economy. As long as that quantity of surplus-value remains unchanged, then profits cannot exceed that maximum regardless of how one might change the STCP or the real wage. Changes in the STCP and real wage, however, can affect the level of profits within those limits, and thus a selection determination links these two variables directly to profits.[2] Surplus-value is itself structurally determined by the STCP and the real wage: the STCP determine the range of possible levels of surplus-value within which limits the real wage has a selection effect.

This model implies that the STCP and the real wage can influence profits through two routes, one direct and one indirect. Indirectly,

---

[1] Since I will not treat any of the issues associated with joint production in this essay, I will not discuss many of the criticisms raised by Bandyopadhyay. Much of his essay directly or indirectly springs from this issue since he emphasizes the 'puzzles' of negative surplus-value, negative prices, etc. His long discussion of the ways in which I confuse or conflate surplus labour with surplus-value also is really based on the problems associated with joint production, since in the absence of joint production surplus labour can be interpreted as the actual difference between total labour performed and necessary labour in a straightforward way. I do not mean to dismiss these criticisms out of hand, and eventually a Marxist economist needs to produce a rigorous solution to joint production within a value framework (or, at a minimum, a rigorous critique of the Sraffian solution), but these concerns are outside of the domain of this paper.

[2] Although in the model these two selection-determinations are not themselves hierarchically ordered, there is nothing in the concept of selection which precludes such ordering. Thus, as Bandyopadhyay argues, the selection-determination from the real wage should be seen as operating within limits established by the selection-determination from the STCP.

they influence profits through their impact on the level of surplus-value produced in the economy, and thus on the limits to profits; directly they select the level of profits within those limits.

Within this model of determination, the Sraffian account of profits describes the selection-determinations of profits, while the Marxist account describes the limitation-determinations. As Sraffa has demonstrated, profits are positively determined (selected) by the STCP and the real wage. With these variables known, it is possible to specify the actual level of profits (and prices) without needing any other information. The Marxist account, on the other hand, defines the range of possible profits. Under certain conditions—when the organic composition of capital is the same in all sectors of the economy—these limits collapse and the quantity of surplus-value determines a unique level of profits.[3]

Let us now examine the criticisms of this model.

Structural Limitation

Two quite different objections were raised against the argument about limits, one by Bandyopadhyay and one by Hodgson: 1. If surplus-value is itself determined by the STCP and the real wage, then there is no meaning to the claim that it in turn imposes limits on profits. To count as a cause of profits, surplus-value must have 'autonomous effects', that is, effects which are not themselves 'reducible' to the STCP and the real wage. 2. If an outcome—in this case profits—is completely determined positively by various selection determinations, then it is meaningless to talk about structural limitation being a 'real' causal process. Real causes must always have a direct impact on the outcome. I will discuss each of these issues in turn.

1. The Problem of Autonomous Effects

Bandyopadhyay argues that in order for surplus-value to act as a limiting determinant of profits there must be a 'determinant of surplus-value independent of the STCP and real wages. The model

---

[3] This is, of course, the condition assumed in *Capital* Volume 1.

requires at least one missing "structure" to be placed, say, between real wages and the STCP and establishing limits to surplus-value . . . Without the "missing structure" exercising *independent* limiting determination on surplus-value, the limits on possible profits exercised by surplus-value are reducible to those exercised by the STCP.' He goes on to say that it is flatly contradictory to simultaneously claim that the STCP impose limits on the amount of surplus-value and that the amount of surplus-value imposes limits on profits within which the STCP have a selection effect.

The issue here is whether it is meaningful to attribute causal efficacy to elements in a system of determination which are themselves endogenously determined, by other elements in the system. Bandyopadhyay insists on a strictly transitive notion of causation: If X causes Y and Y causes Z, then X causes Z and any discussion of Y is strictly 'redundant' or irrelevant. There are two reasons why such a reductionist approach to causation is inadequate. First, even if Y is completely determined by X, it may be the case that once it is produced it has effects which are no longer reducible to X. Y can, in a sense, be 'institutionalized' and cease to respond to subsequent changes in X. This issue is particularly important in problems of state theory, where it may well be the case that even though the structures of the state are determined by class struggle, once those structures are created and institutionalized they produce effects which persist even if the conditions of class struggle change. In the present case—the analysis of profit determination—the argument of institutionalization is less relevant than a second reason for rejecting reductionist approaches to causation: X may vary in many different ways and have many different effects in the world, but only some of these forms of variations and effects influence Y. In such a situation even if Y is completely determined by X, variation in Y is still an essential part of the explanation for variation in Z. Not all variations in X will have effects on Z; only those variations which operate through their effects on Y will effect Z. Thus, unless there is a simple, one-to-one, isomorphic relationship between X and Y, it is not redundant to argue that Y has effects on Z even if it is in turn completely caused by X.

This second situation is precisely the situation that pertains in the relationship between the STCP, the real wage, surplus-value, and profits. As I argued in the original paper, this logic of interdependence is more obvious in the simplified case in which the organic compositions of capital are equal in all sectors and thus surplus-value determines a unique level of profits (i.e. the limits collapse). In such a situation there are many changes in the real wage or the STCP which have no effects on the level of surplus-value. The vector of commodities in the wage basket could change in certain ways—some commodities replacing others—without the amount of surplus-value changing; or the choice of technologies could change without the productivity of labour changing, and thus surplus-value would remain constant. In such instances, no change in the level of profits would occur. In the simple case, then, profits change only by virtue of the ways in which changes in the STCP and the real wage affect the level of surplus-value. The fact that surplus-value is totally determined by the socio-technical conditions of production and the real wage in no way implies that it is irrelevant or redundant in a causal explanation.

The story becomes a bit more complex when we move to a situation with heterogeneous organic compositions of capital. Under such circumstances it is no longer the case that profits change only when surplus-value changes: it is possible to have a change in the level of profits without there being any change whatsoever in the level of surplus-value. However, the degree of possible variation in profits is still constrained by the level of surplus-value, and it is in this sense that I argued surplus-value imposes limits on profits.[4] If one is willing to accept that 'structural limitation' is a legitimate form of determination, then there is no contradiction at all in saying that the STCP impose limits on surplus-value and surplus-value imposes limits on profits, any more than in the simpler case it is contradictory to say that the STCP and real wage directly determine surplus-value, which determines a unique level of profits.[5]

---

[4] When the organic composition of capital is homogeneous across sectors, then changes in surplus-value become the necessary and sufficient condition for changes in profits; when the organic compositions are not homogeneous, then changes in surplus-value become necessary and sufficient conditions for changes in the limits on profits, but not the specific level of profits. It should be noted that in the equal organic composition of capital case, changes in the STCP and real wage are still necessary conditions for changes in profits, but they are not sufficient conditions: it is entirely possible to have changes in these two variables which have no effects whatsoever on profit levels (namely, changes which leave the total surplus-value constant).

[5] Hodgson also seems to fall into the same error as Bandyopadhyay when he argues that surplus labour cannot constitute the basis for real limits on profits since it does not affect the real wage and the STCP:

2. *Structural Limitation as a Mode of Determination*

The above argument presupposes that 'structural limitation' is a form of real determination. This claim is challenged by Hodgson. In order for something to count as a cause, he argues, it must have a positive impact on the outcome in question: 'In general, it is difficult to envisage a causal role for structural limits if other factors, via the process of selection, are entirely sufficient to determine the outcome.' Since the concept of limits plays such an important role in the strategy I adopted for linking the Marxist labour theory of value to the Sraffian analysis of profits, it is important to explain the sense in which a cause can be real and yet not determine a specific outcome.

The concept of limits may be somewhat clearer if, for the moment, we shift our attention from the problem of the determination of profits to the theory of the state. (This example was used in footnote 19 in the original paper.) If we want to explain fully the policies of a given state, we are faced with two complementary explanatory tasks. First, we need to explain the determinants of the range of possible policies open to the state, the determinants of alternatives within the agenda of state policies. Second, we need to explain the determination of the specific policy option within that range which is actually selected by the state, which concretely becomes state policy. These are quite distinct tasks, and they may involve quite different explanatory principles. Thus, pluralist interest-group theory, with its emphasis on active bargaining/negotiations between organized interest groups in the process of decision-making, may provide a reasonably accurate account of the selection-determination of specific state policies within the range of alternatives, and yet be totally unable to understand

---

'In the case of surplus labour, this structural limit can never be a cause because it never . . . affects socio-technical conditions or the real wage. We are led to conclude that surplus labour does not affect profits either.' This formulation by Hodgson would apply equally well to the situation in which all organic compositions of capital were equal and thus the level of surplus-value directly defined a unique level of profits, since it would still be the case that surplus-value would not affect the STCP or the real wage. Thus, even though in the simple case, variation in surplus-value is a necessary *and* sufficient condition for changes in the level of profits, while changes in the STCP and the real wage are not sufficient conditions (since they may vary in ways which do not affect surplus-value), Hodgson would reject a treatment of surplus-value as causally effective on profits.

anything about the process through which the alternatives are themselves determined. The Marxist theory of the state is, in large part, precisely a theory of such structural limits on the state, of the determinants of what the state cannot do rather than simply what it does do. The central thesis of the Marxist theory of the state in these terms is that such limits are inscribed with a class content.

The important point in the present context is that a full-fledged 'explanation' of the state policy in question must involve *both* an account of the concrete selection-determinations and the structural limitation-determinations. But note: it is possible that a theory of the selection determinations could effectively *predict* the outcome in all empirical situations. A refined pluralist theory of interest-group coalition-formation could conceivably predict the passage or failure of legislation in parliament with perfect accuracy, and indeed explain causally why one piece or another was successful. What such a theory would be unable to explain was why the choices were the way they were. For that, a theory of limits is needed.

Analyses of limits of these sorts are an essential aspect of a Marxist methodology. Indeed, it could be argued that the investigation of structural limits constitutes one of the decisive differences between Marxist social science and most mainstream work. Marxism is not just a theory of the existing society as it is; it is also a theory of historical alternatives to capitalism. The analysis of socialism in large part revolves around decoding the limits of structural possibility in capitalism and the contradictions generated *within* those limits which pose the potential of a rupture *of* the limits themselves.

It is not enough, of course, to argue that limits on state policy (or any other outcome of interest) exist. The important theoretical problem is to specify the form and content of those limits. And this is where the difficulties begin. If limits are to form the basis of an explanation for possibilities which cannot occur (under given structural conditions) rather than simply an empirical inventory of alternatives which do not occur, then a fully developed argument about limits must specify the causal mechanisms which impose the exclusions, which substantively demarcate the boundaries.[6]

[6] For a penetrating discussion of the problems of studying systematic 'non-events' in the theory of the state, see Claus Offe, 'The Structural Problem of the State', in von Beyme (ed.), *German Political Studies*, vol. I, Beverly Hills 1974.

In the analysis of profits, as in the analysis of any other social process, it is thus legitimate to construct arguments about the structural limitations at work in the process. The fact that a concrete level of profits is uniquely selected (determined) by the STCP and the real wage does not imply that such determinations do not themselves take place within limits, in this case limits imposed by the level of surplus-value. As long as the account of such limits includes an analysis of the actual mechanisms through which the limits are imposed, then limits can designate real causal processes.

Hodgson is thus wrong in rejecting structural limitation as a mode of determination simply because it does not positively bear on concrete outcomes. But he is correct in pointing out that the analysis of limits which I propose remains largely formal in character and that I have not presented any arguments whatsoever concerning the causal mechanisms operative in the relationship between surplus-value and profits. This is a serious weakness in my analysis and undermines the force of my critique of the Sraffian perspective as well. Let us examine this problem in more detail.

Formal vs. Real Determinations

In my critique of the Sraffian account of profits I argued that Steedman and others had collapsed the distinction between formal calculation and explanation. While they had established that surplus-value was a redundant concept in the calculation of profits, they had not at all established that it was redundant in the causal process through which profits were actually determined. Using the example of explaining vs. predicting state policies cited above, I argued that it was entirely possible to be redundant or irrelevant in a formal mathematical process of calculation and yet play a pivotal role in a real process of causation.

Hodgson correctly points out that I have failed in my own analysis to provide any account of causation: 'In reply to Wright it must first be pointed out that he has not demonstrated causality in his own model. His attempt to distinguish three or four different types of causes, or "modes of determination", is impressive, but does not help. In his scheme he asserts that surplus labour *limits* profits, and the nature of these limits are mathematical maxima and minima. So the allegation against Sraffa can be turned against Wright: to point out a factor, or set of factors, that *limit* profits is not the same as to point out a *cause*, of any type, of the profit level or of a range of possible profit levels. There is no difference here. Sraffa identifies a set of factors that are sufficient to calculate the precise level of profits; Wright identifies a factor (surplus labour) that is sufficient to *calculate* limits on profits. Both are calculations and not, at this stage, demonstrations of cause and effect.'

What makes matters more serious is that in general Marxist defences of the labour theory of value have not very effectively built causal arguments for the relationship of embodied-labour times (values) to prices of production, prices, profits, and other variables in the system. The causal relationship is often proclaimed, but the arguments in support of such claims generally turn out to be rather unconvincing.

Four sorts of arguments have traditionally been advanced by Marxists to support a causal basis for the labour theory of value. 1. An account which argues that the only logically possible solution to the 'riddle of profits' is the labour theory of value. 2. An account based on behavioural assumptions of individual rationality. 3. An account based on the necessary conditions for exchange to take place at all. 4. An account based on the functional requirements for general social reproduction. Let us briefly look at each of these in turn and assess their adequacy.[7]

1. *The* LTV *as the logically necessary solution to the riddle of profits.*
Perhaps the most common causal defence of the labour theory of value is that it is the only logically coherent way of explaining how at the end of a production cycle in which all commodities exchange at their values it is possible to end up with a profit. Martin Nicolaus poses the problem in this way: 'Marx brings up the central problem of the theory of capitalism and proceeds to solve it. How is it, he asks, that at the end of the production process the capitalist has a commodity which is worth more than the elements that went into it?

[7] For a contrasting set of criticisms to these same causal arguments, see A. Cutler, B. Hindess, P. Hirst, and A. Hussain, *Marx's 'Capital' and Capitalism Today*, vol. 1, London 1977.

140

He pays the price of machinery, raw materials and the price of labour, yet the product is worth more than all three together. What, in other words, is the source of surplus-value which the capitalist appropriates?'[8]

The solution to this riddle, Nicolaus argues, following Marx, lies in the capacity of labour-power 'to produce more value than is necessary to reproduce it'. Thus capitalists end up with a profit because they are able to force workers to work more hours than is embodied in the commodities which they purchase with their wages.

The labour theory of value certainly does provide an elegant solution to this problem, but if the Sraffa vs. Marx debate has demonstrated anything, it has shown that the LTV does not provide the only logically possible solution. An account of exchange-value based on the STCP and the real wage can also formally solve the riddle. This of course does not imply anything about which solution is correct, but simply that the argument for the logical necessity of the LTV to account for profits is inadequate.

2. *Behavioural account of value.* The behavioural argument for the labour theory of value usually makes some reference to Adam Smith's famous parable of beaver- and deer-hunters.[9] In this story it is demonstrated that beaver and deer will exchange proportionately to the amount of time it takes their respective hunters to catch them, since it would be irrational for the hunters to exchange their prey in any other ratio (as long as it was possible for hunters to switch back and forth between beaver- and deer-hunting). If it is assumed that the actors in the system can choose what they will produce and that they have knowledge of the time it takes to produce the commodities in question, then such minimal behavioural assumptions of time-efficiency rationality make this account plausible.

The problem with this causal defence of the labour theory of value, as has often been noted, is that the behavioural mechanisms break down as soon as we leave the simple world of directly exchanged (or

[8] Martin Nicolaus, 'Proletariat and Middle Class in Marx', *Studies on the Left*, No. 7, 1967, pp. 266–267. For a more extended commentary on this argument, see my *Class, Crisis and the State*, London, NLB, 1978, pp. 117–118.

[9] For example, Paul Sweezy in *The Theory of Capitalist Development* uses the beaver- and deer-hunter story as a vehicle for defending the plausibility of labour-time calculations of exchange-values.

bartered) commodities produced only by direct labour (i.e. the labour embodied in the means of production is negligible). Once commodities are produced for an impersonal market and once the costs of production are not simply directly experienced labour times, but include the costs of machines, raw materials, buildings, etc., as well, then the producers themselves no longer operate with a subjective calculation of labour times. Instead, their subjective orientation is directly geared towards market prices. To be sure, the behaviour of the actors may still be regulated by labour times in the way postulated by the LTV, but the mechanism can no longer be directly ascribed to the conscious calculation of labour times. Thus, the rational-behavioural causal explanation is no longer adequate.

3. *Labour-values as the logically necessary condition for exchange.* Marx uses this kind of causal argument for labour time as the substance of value. In order for commodities to exchange, Marx argues, they must share a common substance. In terms of their use, commodities are radically heterogeneous. There is no basis in their use-characteristics for one apple to be the equivalent of x safety pins. The commensurability of commodities thus must lie in their sharing a common quantitative characteristic. The only plausible such common substance, Marx and others have argued, is the labour time embodied in their production (or, more rigorously: the socially necessary labour time used in their production). This argument works backwards from the empirical fact of quantitative exchange between heterogeneous commodities and argues that the only possible basis for such exchange is labour time.

This argument has been criticized in various ways. First of all, it is simply not correct that the only possible common substance of commodities-in-exchange is labour time. All commodities also embody calories of energy, human and mechanical. And all commodities embody 'machine time' as well, in which human beings would constitute simply one type of machine. Even if having a common substance was a necessary condition for exchange, it is not logically required that labour be that common substance.

Second, as Marx himself stressed, the actual concrete labour that is expended in production is not homogeneous, but rather is qualitatively distinguished by its skills, specializations, etc. The homogenization of such concrete labour—its transformation into 'abstract labour'—is thus itself a social process that occurs by virtue of the exchange process itself and its generalization throughout the society. But if concrete labour is transformed into abstract labour through such a social process—the particular process of the interconnection of production and exchange in capitalism—then it could equally well be the case that a concrete vector of inputs could be seen as transformed into an 'abstract' metric through this same process. This would be the kind of story the Sraffians would tell: the transformation of the concrete physical inputs in the production of a commodity into a homogeneous metric which makes it quantitatively exchangeable (units of the standard commodity) is a process that takes place through the social process of commodity exchange.

Third, it is not obvious that exchange does presuppose a common substance embodied in the production of commodities (or even imputed to the commodity through the exchange process). Imagine a fanciful society in which all commodities grew on trees which required no labour inputs at all. And imagine that each tree was the private property of a different person and that a state apparatus existed to enforce property rights to trees. In such a society tree-produced commodities would have regular exchange ratios based on such things as relative scarcities and demands, even though they had no costs of production. This is not to suggest that in an economy where there are costs of production of whatever sort such a model of exchange-ratio determination would be adequate, but merely to point out that a common 'substance' based in the production of commodities is not a logical precondition for exchangeability as such.

4. *Functional requirements for social reproduction.* A fourth causal argument sometimes used to support the labour theory of value revolves around an account of the functional requirements for the reproduction of society. All societies, it is argued, require a certain distribution of social labour into different tasks in order to continue to exist. A certain quantity of labour is needed in agriculture, in transportation, in the manufacture of different industrial products, and so on. Every society, therefore, must develop some sort of mechanism for adequately distributing labour to these tasks. The capitalist economy poses this problem in a peculiar way, since the

production of use-values in such an economy is organized anarchically (i.e. each unit of production makes its own decisions about what and how much to produce). What mechanism guarantees the functional requirement that labour be distributed in the socially necessary quantities? The answer that is offered is that the exchange of the products of labour (commodities) in ratios proportional to the labour-time socially necessary for their production provides such a mechanism. The labour theory of value, therefore, is seen as identifying the necessary causal process which must exist if society itself is to continue to exist under conditions of capitalist production.[10]

This kind of functional argument seems to me to be legitimate in principle. That is, if one indeed does identify a functional requirement (i.e. a necessary condition for reproduction) of a society and establishes that a particular structure or mechanism provides a solution to that functional imperative (and no other structure or mechanism provides such a solution), then one has gone at least part of the way in 'explaining' that structure and decoding its effects. I say 'at least part of the way' since a full functional explanation also requires an account of the chain of causes and effects that regulate the functional relations. But functional explanations are not in principle illegitimate aspects of causal/historical explanations.[11]

In this particular case, however, the functional explanation as a causal defence of the labour theory of value is quite shaky. Several objections can be raised against it. First of all, it is clearly not the case that there exists 'a necessary distribution of social labour' for social reproduction. Rather, there exist a multitude of socially possible distributions all of which are compatible with social reproduction. To be sure, there are some distributions of social labour which would make social reproduction impossible—if all labour produced toothbrushes the population would starve. But the fact that radically catastrophic distributions exist does not imply at all that a unique functional distribution is needed.

[10] One of the most extended defences of the LTV in terms of the functional imperatives for the distribution of social labour can be found in I.I. Rubin, *Essays in Marx's Theory of Value*, Detroit 1972.

[11] For a defence of the use of functional arguments in Marxist theory, see G.A. Cohen, *Karl Marx's Theory of History: A Defence*, Oxford 1979.

Now, it is still true that a society must somehow or other prevent catastrophic allocations of labour if the society is to continue to exist. But this is a much weaker requirement than producing a specific functional distribution. All that is needed, in fact, is a mechanism which reallocates social labour when relatively dysfunctional distributions of social labour occur. All that is needed for such a mechanism to work is that there exist a non-random (systematic) relationship between the prices of commodities and the social labour needed for their production, not that social labour actually regulates those prices. Again, this does not demonstrate that social labour times do not so regulate prices, but simply that such regulation is not functionally required for the reproduction of society as such under capitalist conditions of production.

A second objection to the functional defence of the LTV as a causal theory is that the distribution of social labour to the various branches of production is not the only distributive-functional requirement for social reproduction. One could just as well argue that it is crucial to avoid catastrophic distributions of energy or land. Indeed, in certain historical situations it can be argued that the dysfunctional distribution of resources other than labour posed the central problems of social reproduction. The shift of land from food production to wool production in England during the transition to capitalism could be considered such an example, and possibly the dysfunctional use of energy resources for private transportation in the United States today is another. Of course, in each of these cases there is a collateral issue of the distribution of social labour to various tasks, but the functional/dysfunctional dilemmas centre less on the labour distributions as such than on the associated physical resource distributions. This is not to argue that the distribution of social labour to various branches of production is not an issue in capitalist economies, but simply that it is not the only resource distributional issue, and thus it cannot provide a firm defence of the LTV as such.[12]

---

[12] Indeed, in these terms, the functional requirements argument lends greater support to the Sraffian account, since the Sraffian metric of exchange can be viewed as a way of talking about effects of a weighted average of all social resources (inputs into production) on prices. The formal structure of the Sraffian approach thus links the functional requirements of a vector of resources and their social allocation to the market structure of price determination.

Thus, the causal defence of the labour theory of value has not been adequately established through any of the conventional Marxist arguments. 1. The LTV is not the only logically possible causal basis for the existence of profits. 2. The behavioural causal arguments are inadequate whenever producers do not directly calculate the value of their commodities in labour times. 3. Labour time as the substance of value is not a logical necessity for the very possibility of the exchange of qualitatively heterogeneous use-values. 4. The functional requirements of social reproduction do not necessitate that the exchange of commodities be regulated by embodied labour times. Hodgson is thus quite correct in criticizing my arguments as being just as formal as the Sraffian account.

It should be noted in this context that the Sraffians, including the Marxist-Sraffians, have also not established a systematic causal argument about the relationship between physical inputs, the real wage, and prices/profits. What they have accomplished, in a way quite parallel to the traditional Marxist analysis, is to provide a causal argument for the social process which pushes prices back towards values when market-based deviations occur (i.e. through the movement of capital into sectors in which prices are above values). [13] This is the causal story that Hodgson tells in his essay. But they have not as far as I'm aware provided a causal account of the mechanisms that translate the STCP into real determinants of prices and profits. In terms of the debate over the labour theory of value, then, there is little basis for a choice between positions on this particular problem, important though it may be.

To restate the issue: while it is possible to argue formally that surplus labour/value imposes limits on the range of possible profits, no satisfactory causal argument in support of this formal limit has been offered. This is an important weakness, since from a strictly formal point of view a wide range of other limits could equally well be posed. As I pointed out in the original essay—and Hodgson also

[13] This is the heart of the 'law of value': that capital will move to sectors of production in which prices deviate above values (and thus in which the rate of profit is above the average). The law of value, however, does not require the full edifice of the labour theory of value. It merely needs a theory of equilibrium prices and the average rate of profit, and of the response of capitalists to situations in which prices are above such equilibria. Both the LTV and the Sraffian approach to prices and profits provide such a framework.

stresses—if any input to production is held constant, it will formally impose maxima and minima on the level of profits. From a formal-mathematical point of view, all of these limits have the same status, and there would be no reason for selecting out surplus labour as the 'fundamental' limiting relationship.

My way out of this problem in the initial paper was to argue that unlike other possible limits, surplus labour enabled us to link the theory of profits to the general theory of class. Let us now turn to this claim.

The Labour Theory of Value and Class Theory

What I have (I hope) established thus far is the following: 1. An argument based on structural limitations in a process of determination is legitimate, even if those limits are themselves completely determined by other elements in the system. 2. Formally, surplus-value can be viewed as imposing limits on the range of profits within which the STCP and the real wage constitute selection-determinants of profits. 3. But no coherent causal account of the mechanisms which impose those limits has yet been developed, and thus they remain a purely formal construction.

Is there any other basis upon which one might adjudicate the debate between the defenders and critics of the LTV? In my essay I argued that the LTV had the great merit over the available alternatives of providing a basis for systematically linking the Marxist theory of class to the theory of accumulation. Such a linkage, I insisted, did not naturally flow from the structure of the Sraffian account, whereas it did from the Marxian account.

This argument met with two basic criticisms in the essays by Hodgson and Bandyopadhyay: first, that the defence of the LTV on the basis of a concept of class rooted in the appropriation of surplus labour was circular, since it had to presuppose what it intended to establish; second, the Sraffian account of profits is just as compatible with the Marxian notion of class as it is with any other class concept. In what follows I will attempt to show that the first criticism is incorrect, while the second is largely accurate and requires a modification of my initial position.

1. Class and Surplus Labour

Hodgson levels the charge of circularity in the following terms. 'The argument has now turned full circle. According to Wright, behind the need to focus on surplus labour is the need to examine classes; behind the examination of classes lie relations of production; and, fundamentally, these relations are about which class performs and which appropriates surplus labour. We can put the relevant question to Wright again: Why is surplus labour and not surplus-anything-else selected out as the structural limitation on profits? Wright's answer, it seems, is as follows. We focus on surplus labour because it helps us understand classes and class struggle in terms of relations of production. Classes, however, are understood in terms of their relation to the extraction of surplus labour. In Wright's answer, "surplus labour" and "classes" are like two words in a badly designed dictionary.'

In order to respond to this charge it is necessary to provide an argument for defining classes in terms of the relations of appropriation of surplus labour which does not itself depend upon the labour theory of value. If there is an independent basis for such a definition, then the argument that the LTV provides a vehicle for linking this concept of class to questions of accumulation, profit determination, etc., is not circular. Hodgson is correct that I did not explicitly provide such an independent argument in the original paper, but it is not difficult to fill this gap here.

It would take me far too long to provide a comprehensive defence and exposition of the theoretical basis for defining classes on the basis of the relations of exploitation (appropriation of surplus labour). What I will do instead is briefly sketch out the central steps in the argument so as to establish the plausibility of the claim.

The Marxist definition of classes is based on a number of more basic concepts. Five of these are particularly important in the present context: labour, necessary and surplus labour, alienation, necessary and surplus products, and exploitation.

Labour. Labour is the activity of consciously transforming nature in order to produce useful things which satisfy human needs.[14] While

---

[14] The importance of stressing that the concept of labour implies the conscious transformation of nature is defended in G.A. Cohen's book.

148

not all human activity is 'labour' in this sense, labour is un-questionably one of the most fundamental aspects of human activity.[15] Furthermore, Marxists have usually argued that labouring activity is one of the fundamental ways—if not the most fundamental way—by which human beings create and transform themselves as conscious, social beings. Certainly throughout most of human history this activity has been the central preoccupation of the vast majority of people most of the time. If labour is such a basic dimension of human, social activity, then the social relations within which this activity takes place can plausibly be considered a critical aspect of the social structure of any society. This is one central reason why Marxists emphasize to such an extent the social relations of production.

Necessary and surplus labour. The activity of producing useful things can be divided into two segments: a duration within which the useful things needed for the reproduction of the people performing the activity occurs, and a duration within which other things (a surplus) are produced. The latter is particularly important, for it represents human time which is available for social development, for expanding the material basis of subsequent production. Surplus labour is thus time available for social tasks beyond the simple reproduction of the society as it is. How that time is organized, dominated, controlled, is thus of great importance for the character of social reproduction and social change.

Alienation. When the social relations within which labour is performed are organized in such a manner that the people who perform the activity of labour lose control over some or all aspects of that activity, we say that their labour is 'alienated'. Alienation, in this sense, is a social relation which is variable in form and degree, ranging from the alienation of a small part of labouring activity in the case of tribute-paying organic peasant communities to the pervasive alienation of capitalist industrial production. In the latter case the worker not only loses control over surplus labour, but over the entire labour process.

---

[15] There is no necessity to assume that labour is *the* most fundamental aspect of human practice in order to legitimately root the concept of class in the social relations within which labour is performed.

Necessary and surplus products. Why should anyone ever want to control the labour of someone else? What prevents those who are so controlled from simply reasserting their self-control, individually or collectively, of their labour? What keeps them from simply refusing to perform surplus labour for someone else? To answer these questions we must shift the discussion from labour to the products of labour, and in particular to the concept of surplus product.

Corresponding to the distinction between necessary and surplus labour is the distinction between necessary and surplus products: the products used to reproduce the producers and the surplus to be used for other purposes. Dominant classes do not simply control surplus labour; they appropriate surplus products. This appropriation provides the material explanation for both the subjective motivation for controlling the labour of others and the objective foundation for the reproduction of that control. In terms of subjective motivation, the appropriation of surplus products enables the appropriator to live without toil, and potentially to live extravagantly without toil. Throughout most of human history the *only* way to escape a life of toil was to become an appropriator of surplus products through one means or another.

In terms of the material basis for the reproduction of control, appropriation of surplus products gives the appropriator the ability to organize various specialized apparatuses specifically designed to ensure that control (i.e. the state and other apparatuses of domination). The surplus product thus provides material resources needed for the protection of that domination. It is almost impossible to imagine a dominant class which controlled the labour of a subordinate class without appropriating the surplus product. Such a ruling class would have a very weak subjective basis for the continuation of its rule and it certainly would have an extremely precarious material basis for reproducing the security of its rule.

Exploitation. The Marxist concept of exploitation is designed precisely to link these various aspects of social relations, i.e. to link the reality of labour as one of the fundamental dimensions of human social activity, the social relations of domination over labour (alienation) and the material basis for the reproduction of that domination (appropriation of surplus products). When the appropriation of surplus products does not involve the alienation of labour, then exploitation has not occurred. This would be the case, for example, when a group of people raid or poach the produce of forests they did not own without appropriating the labour of any producers in the forest. Similarly, the domination of labour which does not involve the appropriation of products is not exploitation. For example, in a prison where inmates are forced to prepare their own food under the domination of guards, but in which the guards do not appropriate the food (or any other products of prisoners), no exploitation has occurred. Domination without appropriation and appropriation without domination are not exploitation. *Exploitation can thus be defined as a social relationship within which surplus labour is appropriated through the domination of labour and the appropriation of surplus products.* Since labour once performed is materially embodied in the products of labour, we can speak in shorthand of exploitation as the process of the appropriation of surplus labour.

We can now provide a structural definition of classes: class may be structurally defined as the social positions within the social relations of exploitation.[16] Classes are thus always defined relationally, those relations are situated within the process of production, and the pivot of those production relations are the relations of exploitation. It will be seen that nowhere in this definition of class has the labour theory of value itself been presupposed. All of the essential concepts— necessary and surplus labour, necessary and surplus products, exploitation—can be defined independently of the thesis that commodities in capitalist societies exchange in ratios regulated by embodied labour times. The concept of class is based on the general concept of surplus labour and the relations of its domination/appropriation, but it does not posit a priori any specific relationship to the LTV as such. This conceptualization of class may have a number of serious limitations, but it is not circular.

---

[16] Note that this is strictly a *structural* definition of class. The concept of class, however, is not purely a structural concept. The global concept of class also encompasses the concept of class formation (the creation of social relations within classes and class consciousness) and class struggle. For an elaboration of this point see *Class, Crisis and the State*, pp. 97–108. For a more extended discussion of this definition and its difference from various alternative definitions of class, see my *Class Structure and Income Determination*, New York 1979, chapter 1, 'What Is Class?'

2. Class and the Sraffian Approach to Profits

While the conceptualization of class outlined above does not presuppose the labour theory of value, the two sets of concepts clearly have a systematic affinity to each other. Traditionally, the LTV has provided the answer to a specific problem of class analysis, namely: how does it happen that surplus labour is appropriated in a capitalist society in which, it appears, workers are paid the full value of their labour power when they work for capitalists. At first glance capitalism seems precisely to be an example of a social system within which the capitalist class appropriates a surplus product without actually appropriating any surplus labour, since all labour-power is paid its full equivalent in products (via the wage). In such a view, exploitation is absent from capitalism. The labour theory of value is, in these terms, an account of the mechanism by which surplus labour is 'pumped out' of workers, namely through forcing workers to perform more labour than is embodied in the commodities which they consume. On the assumption that the value of commodities is regulated by embodied labour times, this mechanism provides the basis for exploitation in capitalism. In this way the LTV links the theory of class to the theory of capital accumulation, profits, etc.

In my original article I argued that the Sraffian account of profits did not spontaneously lend itself to a concept of class rooted in production relations.[17] While the formal structure of Sraffa's argument was not actually incompatible with a production-based

[17] It is important to stress that Sraffa and most theorists working in his tradition never explicitly define classes or reflect on the broader problems of class analysis. Whenever I speak of a definition of class 'based on' or 'derived from' the Sraffian approach I do not mean to suggest that such a definition has been actively adopted by any particular theorist in the Sraffian tradition. A notable exception to this silence on questions of the concept of class within work that is heavily informed by the Sraffian tradition is the very important recent work by John Roemer. Perhaps more than any other theorist, Roemer's work can be characterized as an attempted synthesis of the theoretical thrust of Marxist social-historical theory and the technical economic strategies in the Sraffian tradition. The result is a reconstruction of the analytical foundations of Marxian economic theory which in principle does not sacrifice its sociological, historical, and political logic. See in particular his *Analytical Foundations of Marxian Economic Theory*, Cambridge 1981; *A General Theory of Exploitation and Class*, Harvard University Press (forthcoming 1982), and 'New Directions in the Marxian Theory of Exploitation and Class', Working Paper Series No. 161, Department of Economics, University of California-Davis, November 1980.

concept of class, it much more naturally suggested a Weberian notion of classes as positions within market relations.

It now seems to me that this initial conclusion was considerably overstated. My argument was based on the observation that the basic actors posed within the Sraffian account were the receivers and givers of the real wage. The real wage is one of the two elements in the determination of profits in the Sraffian system, and it suggests a class structure rooted in the social categories bound up with the social relations of the wage: those who purchase labour-power; those who sell labour-power; and perhaps those who sell skills. Such a schema is precisely what Weber proposed in the analysis of market classes.

My critique was incorrect. The Sraffian scheme does not simply suggest market actors, but production-level actors as well. The socio-technical conditions of production implicitly pose a structure of social relations within production itself, and a corresponding set of social positions which could form the basis of a class analysis. The physical coefficients of the STCP are actual expenditures of various inputs into production: hours of labour, tons of steel, kilowatts of electricity, etc. These do not necessarily correspond to the quantities of those inputs purchased by the owners of the means of production. Owners thus are faced with a problem: how to guarantee that when they purchase eight hours of labour-time they get eight hours of work performed. That problem—the translation of labour-power into labour—is precisely the problem which is at the heart of the Marxist analysis of the labour process, and as in the Marxist analysis it would draw the social analysis within the Sraffian perspective into an examination of classes rooted in production. The forms of conflict within production, the elaboration of managerial control hierarchies, the degradation of labour, etc. are all part of the implied sociological agenda of a Sraffian theory.

While a production-level concept of class is implicit in the Sraffian framework, there remain two differences with the Marxian frame-work that may have significant consequences. First, it is impossible to use the labour theory of value without adopting at least a primitive production-based concept of class, whereas the Sraffian system can be employed without ever mentioning class understood in this way. In the Sraffian framework there is no formal difference whatsoever between the problem of transforming labour-power into labour and the problem of transforming the quantity of steel purchased into the steel actually used or electricity purchased into electricity actually used. With respect to every purchased input of production there is a problem of potential waste, of a difference between the potential input represented in the market transaction and the real input represented in the production process. The structure of concepts in the Sraffian framework thus does not distinguish between the engineering problem of physical waste (including the engineering aspects of the problem of waste of labour time) and the social problem of labour control. Unless one brought to the Sraffian framework a theoretical commitment to the special importance of labour as such, there would be little impulse to draw out the implications of the Sraffian concepts for a class analysis. In the case of the labour theory of value, on the other hand, class relations are inscribed in the core concepts themselves, and thus one is insistently pushed towards a class analysis.

Second, if one does decide to draw out the implications of the Sraffian framework for a production-relations class analysis one would be led more naturally towards a theory of *domination* in production rather than *exploitation*.[18] While the Sraffian framework does suggest a relational, production-level concept of class, it would not suggest building that concept around the problem of the appropriation of surplus labour as such. While labour and its relation to labour-power do have a status in Sraffian theory, the concept of surplus labour has, at most, a marginal status. (And as Bandyopadhyay pointed out in his analysis, when it is discussed it has little to do with the actual division between necessary and surplus labour performed by producers, but rather is a purely technical parameter derived from the technically minimum amount of labour needed to produce various commodities.) The Sraffian analysis of prices and profits and other economic issues could proceed perfectly well without ever mentioning surplus labour. The Sraffian approach to production, therefore, suggests a concept of class structure based on

[18] Note that this is still a concept of domination *in production*, and not simply domination in society. The implied concept of class in the Sraffian framework is thus not subject to the criticisms sometimes levelled against the concept of class used by Ralf Dahrendorf, Gerhard Lenski, and others based on a generalized concept of authority unhinged from the process of production.

154

the ownership/non-ownership of the means of production (the aspect related to the real wage) and the control/non-control over the performance of labour (the aspect related to STCP), but not formalized around the problem of the appropriation of surplus labour as such. Thus, while the labour theory of value implies a concept of class that links exploitation and domination, the Sraffian framework implies a concept of class more strictly based on domination of labour alone.

The question then becomes how much of a real difference this makes for a class analysis. While the emphasis on exploitation rather than just domination certainly has significant polemical implications, it is far less clear that it has much substantive effect on the theoretical elaborations and uses of the concept of class (e.g., the theory of the state, class formation, class consciousness, etc.) or on concrete programmes of research. When Marxists begin to systematically decode the social relations of production, the concern with the appropriation of surplus labour generally plays the role of serving to justify the concern with the labour process and the relations of domination/control within it. Certainly in my own work this is the case.[19] While I do discuss the problem of the mechanisms through which surplus labour is appropriated, the concrete strategy I advocate for defining the structure of class relations revolves much more on the social relations of domination/subordination within production. With some variations, the same could be said of the class analysis of Poulantzas, Therborn, Carchedi, and others. In practical terms, then, many Marxist treatments of class shift their focus from surplus labour as such to the relations of control over the performance of labour.

Indeed, we can make an even stronger statement: in those cases where Marxist treatments of class do attempt to directly derive classes from the categories of the labour theory of value (rather than using the LTV as a point of departure for designating the relevant dimensions of social relations), they tend to fall into serious errors. This is most clearly the case in the preoccupation with the productive/unproductive labour distinction in some treatments of

[19] See especially, *Class, Crisis and the State*, chapter 2; *Class Structure and Income Determination*, and 'Varieties of Marxist Conceptions of Class', *Politics & Society*, 9:3, 1980.

class. Poulantzas, for example, argued that unproductive labourers cannot be in the working class, since they are not directly exploited in the distinctively capitalist way, i.e. surplus labour is not appropriated in the form of surplus-value. Such locations Poulantzas placed in the 'new petty bourgeoisie'. The result, as has often been pointed out, is that a janitor in a bank is in a different class from a janitor in a factory, even though they may have identical conditions of work. The attempt to derive directly the criteria for classes in real capitalist societies from the categories of the labour theory of value thus tends to fracture the relationship between class structure and class interests, and this in turn undermines any analysis of the link between class structure and problems such class formation, class consciousness, class struggles.[20]

The one area of research and theory where one might expect the Marxist emphasis on exploitation to generate significant differences from a concept of class based solely on the relations of domination in production would be the problem of income determination. A Marxist account might attempt to measure the differential rates of exploitation of different categories of labour-power, and such an attempt would presuppose the concepts of class based on surplus labour. This is precisely what Baudelot, Establet, and Malemort attempted to do in *Les petites bourgeoisies en France* (Paris 1974) and, somewhat less directly, I attempted to do in *Class Structure and Income Determination*. The theory of income inequality among wage-earners would thus revolve around the account of the determinants of the different rates of exploitation of different class locations and different strata within the working class. Such a project necessarily involves, directly or indirectly, assessing the amount of surplus labour performed by different categories of labour (i.e. the amount of labour they perform above and beyond the imputed labour-time equivalents of their wage). This kind of effort would not be made by a Sraffian.

It is less clear that the Marxist and Sraffian accounts would necessarily differ in their structural explanations of the results so obtained. They could both, at least in principle, explore such things as

[20] For a more extended critique of the productive/unproductive labour distinction in the conceptualization of class relations, see *Class, Crisis and the State* and Carchedi, *On the Economic Identification of Social Classes*, London 1977.

156

problems of social control within production, market barriers which protect the wages of certain strata of workers, forms of shop-floor struggles, etc. In the end, therefore, the emphasis on surplus labour might not make as much difference even in the study of income inequality as it might first seem. While the idiom of the discussions would differ, the substantive causal explanations might in fact be rather similar.

It appears, then, that the substantive distance between a Marxist concept of class explicitly based on exploitation and a Sraffian-derived concept of class based on domination-in-production is not as great as I originally argued. Indeed, some theorists would argue that for all practical purposes the Sraffian-derived concept of class is equivalent to exploitation. This would seem to be the upshot of G. A. Cohen's argument in 'The Labour Theory of Value and the Concept of Exploitation'. Cohen argues that the concept of exploitation is meaningful whenever one class appropriates the surplus *products of labour* of another class. In capitalism workers produce all commodities. It is their labour and not the labour of capitalists which actually transforms nature and produces use-values. That labour is exploited simply by virtue of capitalists appropriating the products of that labour, irrespective of any relationship between a notion of 'embodied labour times' and prices. The magnitude of that exploitation would be defined (presumably) by how much less labour they would have to perform to produce their same standard of living without producing anything for the capitalist's own consumption and capital accumulation. This concept of exploitation requires only two elements: a) that capitalists own the means of production (and thus have property rights in the commodities produced), and b) that capitalists can force workers to work long and hard enough to produce more than their own subsistence (i.e. that capitalists have at least some control over the labour process).[21] Both of these elements

21 This second condition is not explicitly included in Cohen's argument, but it does seem to me to be necessary. The capitalist ownership of the means of production (and the corresponding dispossession of the means of production from the working class) gives the capitalist class the right to appropriate the surplus product *if a surplus product is produced*. But, by itself, it does not guarantee that there will be a surplus product. For an actual surplus product to be produced the second condition must also exist, namely that capitalists must have enough control over the labour process to get their workers

would be satisfied by a Sraffian-derived production-relations concept of class. The Sraffian concept would be built around the property relations which give capitalists the capacity to appropriate the surplus product and the relations of domination within production that give capitalists the capacity to achieve at least the minimum necessary control of the labour process. If one accepts Cohen's arguments about the requirements for a coherent concept of exploitation, then indeed this is an exploitation-based concept.

It might appear from all these arguments that there are really no significant implications of the distinction between the two concepts of class we have been discussing—a concept based on the appropriation of surplus labour and a concept based on the appropriation of surplus products. In one important context, however, it does seem to me that a difference remains, namely in the way each concept implicitly poses the problem of socialism.

When class domination is understood as the appropriation of surplus labour, then the destruction and transcendence of capitalism is seen as opening up the possibility of the collective, democratic control not only of resources and production, but of the general use of social time. Surplus labour is a quantity of time, of human labouring activity with a duration. In capitalism, social time is monopolized by the imperatives of accumulation. Instead of being available for the collective direction of social life, labouring time beyond what is needed for social reproduction is directed towards ever-expanding production. This is one of the senses in which capitalist relations impose real, material limits on forms of social practice: those practices which require a radically different allocation of social time are precluded by the dominance of capitalist relations. This is crucial because for socialism to be a viable social order it is necessary for people to spend considerable time engaged in collective social-political activity. While it is always problematic to make pronouncements on the institutional forms socialism in advanced industrial societies might take, one thing is certain: the average person will have to spend a much greater proportion of the week

---

to produce more than their own subsistence. Some notion of domination over labouring activity is needed for exploitation to exist even if appropriation is understood solely in terms of the appropriation of the surplus product.

engaged in political activity (broadly understood) than in capitalist society.

This conception of socialism is clearly linked to the traditional Marxist distinction between necessary and surplus labour: necessary labour is that amount of labour-time that must be spent in the production of use-values needed for the reproduction of the producers; surplus labour is labouring time beyond that quantity. The surplus labour performed in capitalism is thus a rough index of the time available for alternative purposes in a socialist transition, especially for the political tasks of collective control of social life and development.[22] The usual Marxist claim that socialism becomes increasingly possible as capitalism develops is in large part a thesis about the decreasing amount of necessary labour time resulting from the development of the forces of production, and thus the increasing time potentially available for the social and political tasks of socialism.

The grounding of the concept of class in the appropriation of surplus labour thus serves to link together a number of critical concepts: class domination, the development of the forces of production, and the emergence and development of historical alternatives to a given set of class relations. The power of the Marxist concept of class lies precisely in the ways these different concepts are tied together within a single conceptual field. The definition of class relations in terms of the appropriation of surplus products does not preclude the analysis of the social use and control of time, but the concept itself does not underwrite the centrality of this issue.

The net effect of these various arguments is that I must significantly modify my original conclusion about the implications of the Sraffian approach to profits for a class analysis. While it may still be the case that Sraffians in practice are less likely to talk about class and that those who do may tend to adopt uncritically a quasi-Weberian notion of market classes, this is not logically entailed by the categories within

---

[22] The amount of surplus labour (surplus-value + unproductively performed surplus labour) in capitalism is an indicator of the minimum amount of time available for collective, social tasks in a socialist society. A certain amount of necessary labour under capitalism would probably be easily eliminated in a socialist society, since capitalism itself generates certain costs of reproduction which might be absent or reduced in socialism.

the formal edifice of the Sraffian schema. Those categories can equally well point towards a production-level, relational concept of class. The one remaining difference of potential importance is that a Sraffian-derived concept of class would not naturally be built around the concept of surplus labour and its appropriation. This, as I have argued, may have some implications for the critical use of the concept of class in the understanding of socialism as the historical transcendence of capitalism. It probably does not, however, have pervasive consequences for the use of the concept of class for various research agendas focused on the analysis of problems within capitalist societies. Most of the research programme which I suggested flowed more naturally from the labour theory of value than from the Sraffian account of profits could thus probably be pursued with equal facility within a Sraffian framework.[23]

Conclusion

The analysis of this paper can be summarized in several general conclusions.

1. It is methodologically legitimate to argue that surplus-value imposes limits on profits within which the STCP and the real wage have selection effects. Thus, while there is not a simple, monotonic relationship between surplus-value and profits, surplus-value nevertheless can be viewed as constraining systematically the range of possible profits.

[23] Two additional points on the question of the implications for research need to be made here. First, Hodgson correctly points out that until the late 1960s and early 1970s Marxists in fact paid very little attention to the labour process as a research problem. If, as I argued, a preoccupation with the labour process flowed 'spontaneously' from the logic of the LTV, this would be hard to explain. In fact, while the categories of the LTV are compatible with a concern over the labour process, I considerably overstated the theoretical linkage when I suggested that they necessitated research on that issue. Second, it is probably not strictly the case that it is the LTV as such which suggests a concern over the labour process, but rather the theoretical commitments which underpin the Marxist concept of class (as discussed above). Those theoretical commitments encourage both the empirical concern with the labour process and the theoretical elaborations of the labour theory of value. While biographically, theorists concerned with the labour process may have passed through the route of the LTV, it is not so obvious that logically this route is necessary.

2. This argument about limits is a purely formal one. None of the traditional Marxist causal defences of the LTV are very satisfactory, since none of them actually explains the causal mechanisms by which value regulates/determines/limits prices.

3. The Sraffian account of profits is also purely formal in character, and thus at this point at least, there is not a coherent causal basis for adjudicating the debate.

4. The positing of surplus labour as a limiting relation, however, does enable us to link the theory of profits to the Marxist concept of class (class based on the decoding of the social relations of appropriation of surplus labour).

5. However, contrary to my earlier conclusions, the Sraffian account of profits does not lead one necessarily to adopt a Weberian, market-based concept of class. The Sraffian approach can also suggest a production-relational conceptualization of class structure.

6. Where a Sraffian-based and a Marxist-based concept of class are likely to differ is on the emphasis on surplus labour, rather than simply production. The Marxist concept of class revolves around the problem of the relations of appropriation of surplus labour; a class concept derived from the Sraffian account of profits and prices is much more likely to focus on the relations of control of labour (the labour process) and the appropriation of surplus products, but not on the appropriation of surplus labour as such.

7. It is not clear, however, that the emphasis on domination within production instead of explicitly exploitation makes a great deal of difference for the theoretical and empirical uses of the concept of class in the analysis of capitalist society. The concept of class derived from the Sraffian treatment of production, like the concept linked to the labour theory of value, would suggest a research programme concerned with transformation of the labour process, degradation of labour, struggles over the control of technology, the mechanisms which facilitate or block the access of different social groups to different kinds of wage-labour positions, etc.

8. The one context where the differences in the two concepts of class may have significant implications is in the conceptualization of socialism. At a minimum, the Marxist concept of exploitation rooted in the appropriation of surplus labour has an important critical function of directing attention directly to the structuring and control of social time.

Where does all this leave us in the Marx vs. Sraffa debate? First of all, the technical debate does not seem to me to be fully resolved. Steedman's argument that the LTV is redundant is not a cogent basis for rejecting the LTV, as I have attempted to show in the original paper and this one as well. And the objections to reconceptualizing value theory as a theory of limits seem to me to be incorrect. If a satisfactory solution to the joint-production problem is developed, then there would be little formal basis for choosing the LTV or the Sraffian approach to profits and prices.

Second, the stakes in the debate are not nearly as high as I suggested in the initial essay, at least for those engaged in empirical/historical research in class analysis. Both the labour theory of value and the Sraffa system imply a conceptualization of class rooted in production, both suggest a relational notion of class, and both direct class analysis towards the investigation of the labour process and its relationship to technology, markets, struggles, etc. While differences in the implied concepts of class remain, particularly concerning the status of the appropriation of surplus labour, it is uncertain that these differences produce substantial consequences for most empirical problems of social analysis.[24]

Finally, there remains, after all is said and done, an important didactic reason for retaining the labour theory of value and using it as the basis for class analysis of capitalism. The labour theory of value brings the relational character of production and exchange into sharp relief; it establishes a compelling way of understanding exploitation and it powerfully reveals the essential structure of capitalism as a

[24] The debate over the status of the labour theory of value probably does have important substantive implications for more narrowly economic analysis, particularly when such analysis takes a particularly abstract-formal character. But even in the case of economic problems it is less clear that the debate bears heavily on concrete empirical investigation, since relatively few empirical investigations dealing with economic problems have attempted to build directly on the categories of the labour theory of value.

regime of domination instead of freedom. Most of this can be read into the formal structure of the Sraffian framework, but the framework itself does not insistently demand such an analysis. The Sraffian framework for the analysis of prices and profits can be used perfectly well as a purely technical apparatus for the formal calculation of economic parameters, and it certainly can be used without any imperative for understanding classes within the system of production. The labour theory of value as developed within Marxism is unintelligible without a production-based class analysis. Thus, while I overstated the ways in which the Sraffian conceptual apparatus impeded class analysis in my initial essay, it remains the case that it does not impel such an analysis as vigorously as the labour theory of value.

To be sure, this is not a scientific basis for defending the labour theory of value. Marxism, however, is not simply a scientific-theoretical programme (although it is that as well). It is also a political and ideological project. The labour theory of value has been so durable in spite of its critics and continues to serve as the point of departure for much Marxist thought precisely because of the ways in which it combines the agendas of Marxism as science, politics, and ideology. And until such time as its scientific-theoretical inadequacies are definitively demonstrated, the labour theory of value can legitimately continue to fulfill this function.

Joint Production:
The Issues After Steedman

Makoto Itoh

Steedman's Critique of Marx

Steedman's *Marx after Sraffa* denounced Marx's labour theory of value in favour of Piero Sraffa's theory of prices. It has renewed the controversy over value and has managed to perplex Marxists to some extent. As was often the case with previous value controversies, this controversy can be a good opportunity to deepen understanding of Marxian value theory.

Steedman claims that Marx's value theory is redundant and inconsistent. In general it is claimed to be redundant. Steedman admits that 'the labour-time required (directly and indirectly) to produce any commodity—and thus the value of any commodity—is determined by the physical data relating to the methods of production' (p. 202). However, he asserts that 'the value magnitudes are, at best, redundant in the determination of the rate of profit (and prices of production)' (ibid.), because the same physical data and the specification of real wages suffice to determine the same results.

In the case in which some production processes produce joint products, values, reckoned as the quantities of embodied labour-time, may be indeterminate. Even when values are determinate, they can be negative, and surplus-value can consequently be negative even when the rate of profit and prices are positive. Let us examine Steedman's example (given on pp. 151–154 of *Marx After Sraffa*).

Suppose there are two different processes of production that produce commodities A and B jointly as follows:

1.   5 units of commodity A + 1 unit of labour
   → 6 units of commodity A and 1 unit of commodity B.

2.   10 units of commodity B + 1 unit of labour
    → 3 units of commodity A and 12 units of commodity B.

The real-wage bundle for a unit of labour is assumed to contain $\frac{1}{2}$ unit of commodity A and $\frac{5}{6}$ unit of commodity B. Let its price be 1, prices of commodities A and B be p_1 and p_2 respectively, and the uniform profit rate be r. Following Sraffa, we assume that the profit rate marks up only the prices of means of production. Then we can formulate the following three simultaneous linear equations:

$$(1+r)\ 5p_1 + 1 = 6p_1 + p_2 \tag{1}$$
$$(1+r)\ 10p_2 + 1 = 3p_1 + 12p_2 \tag{2}$$
$$1 = \tfrac{1}{2}p_1 + \tfrac{5}{6}p_2 \tag{3}$$

The positive solutions to (1), (2), (3) are:
$$r = 20\%,\ p_1 = \tfrac{1}{3},\ p_2 = 1.$$

Let the quantities of labour embodied in a unit of the same commodities A and B be l_1 and l_2. They are determined by the following simultaneous equations:

$$5l_1 + 1 = 6l_1 + l_2 \tag{4}$$
$$10l_2 + 1 = 3l_1 + 12l_2 \tag{5}$$

The solutions to (4) and (5) are:

$$l_1 = -1,\ l_2 = 2.$$

Thus the value of the first commodity, A, the labour embodied in it, must be negative, whereas its price and the rate of profit are positive. If 6 units of labour are employed, 5 operating the first process and 1 operating the second, then the surplus product (5 units of commodity A + 2 units of commodity B) remains after deducting the necessary wage bundle (3 units of commodity A + 5 units of commodity B) from the net product (8 units of commodity A + 7 units of commodity B). The value of labour power V, and the surplus-value S can be calculated in this case as follows:

$$V = 3(-1) + 5(2) = 7$$
$$S = 5(-1) + 2(2) = -1$$
$$V + S = 6$$

Thus surplus-value appears negative, while the rate of profit is positive.

Steedman concludes from this analysis that Marx's labour theory of value is not merely redundant but also inconsistent, and that it should be abandoned and replaced by the Sraffian theory of prices.

Anti-Critiques

Steedman's critique is clearly based on a narrow point of view. He takes the point of Marx's theory of value to be the determination of equilibrium prices just as is the case with the neo-classical or the Sraffian theories of price. From such a standpoint, analysing the quantities of labour appears redundant, since the prices of production can be determined directly from the physical data on production techniques and the real wage. This sort of critique, however, does not correctly understand the essential subject of Marx's value theory.

For Marx, the theory of value is not at all a means by which merely to determine equilibrium prices. It is above all a theory designed to clarify the historical specificity of the capitalist economy. As we see in *Capital*, Marx discovered that the labour process is 'the everlasting Nature imposed condition of human existence' and analysed how this fundamental condition of human societies became the social substance of value-relations under capitalism. In particular, the capitalist social mechanism for obtaining surplus labour, which is the substance of surplus-value, is central for such an analysis. It is thus essential for Marx's theory of value to elucidate the capitalist social relations based on human labour, together with its specific forms and mechanisms. From this standpoint, the observation of the quantities of labour as the substance of value and surplus-value cannot be dispensed with. It is not all redundant, despite Steedman's critique. By assessing Marx's labour theory of value as generally redundant, Steedman shows an inability or reluctance to understand the significance and the task of Marx's value theory as the foundation of historical and social sciences. His total neglect of Marx's theory of value-forms is closely related to this weakness.

Steedman's critique of the inconsistency of Marx's value theory is presented precisely by neglecting the theory of value-forms and by a one-sided technological understanding of the concept of value. The seeming anomalies, as in the case of negative value and negative surplus-value, spring from the Sraffian interpretation, which derives the quantities of embodied labour, or values, of joint products in a mechanical way from a number of different production processes equal to the number of joint products. This interpretation does not care which of the existing techniques is the dominant one supplying social demand. Besides, it cannot define the values or the equilibrium prices in cases in which there is a unique joint-production method or more methods than products.

However, Marxian anti-critiques of Steedman's treatment of joint production have been diversified and not yet very satisfactory, though they have almost unanimously pointed out the significant task of Marx's value theory: to reveal the social substance of surplus-value, in rejecting Steedman's claim that Marx's value concept is redundant.

For instance, Paul Sweezy has criticized Steedman and correctly pointed out that the key concept of the rate of surplus-value has to vanish from an analysis made in terms of prices. (See 'Marxian Value Theory and Crises', in the present volume.) But Sweezy left Steedman's points on the problem of joint production untouched.

N. Okishio treats this problem by assuming a single technique of production for jointly produced commodities, say A and B. Then the value of A can be between zero and the maximum given in the case where the value of B is zero. So the total value of both A and B is determinate, but the value of A or B is not, since Okishio analyses values in a purely technical fashion. As a result, the values of surplus products and of the wage goods become indeterminate when some of them are jointly produced. At the same time, Okishio's fundamental Marxian theorem, that the general rate of profit is positive only when the rate of surplus-value is positive, becomes untenable. Okishio revises it substantially and says: 'The existence of exploitation is determined by whether labourers are forced to produce the surplus products or not; the necessary condition for the existence of profit is that labourers are exploited' in this sense.[1] Sad to say, the essence of Marx's value theory, as an analysis of the capitalist exploitation of

[1] N. Okishio, *Marxian Economics* (in Japanese), Tokyo 1977, p. 169.

the surplus *labour* of wage labourers, is abandoned by Okishio in this context.

Armstrong, Glyn, and Harrison also agree that 'values cannot be attributed to individual commodities' in the case of joint products.[2] However, they attempt to define the value of labour-power as the total labour embodied in a group of production processes that are necessary to produce at least the wage bundle with the smallest possible extra joint products. The rate of exploitation is presented in value terms on the basis of this definition. As they admit, 'the method is not perfect'.[3] It tends systematically to underestimate the rate of exploitation, and cannot be very accurate. The more joint production is interlinked, the more their definition of the rate of exploitation will become meaningless.

Himmelweit and Mohun argue from a different angle. According to them, as a Sraffian Steedman is not concerned with the social logic of commensuration of different sorts of useful concrete labour into abstract labour *through* the exchange of commodities. Consequently, he cannot understand the logic of a second commensuration of labour-time in capitalism *through* the competitive equalization of the rate of profit. The anomalies that cause negative surplus-value with a positive profit 'arise from the contradiction between the fundamental concept of socially necessary labour-time and the development of its full consequences in capitalist competition'.[4] Himmelweit and Mohun attempt to counter Steedman by emphasizing the development of the value concept in Marx from commodity values into prices of production. In their treatment, however, it is unclear why and how the anomalies concerning the joint-production problem arise from the contradiction in the development of the value concept. The anomalies are not solved but rather recognized as a really existing contradiction in a capitalist commodity economy. The first 'commensuration' of Himmelweit and Mohun entails, in my opinion, a basic misunderstanding: that abstract labour, unlike concrete labour, cannot exist without the exchange of commodities.[5] It is also

[2] P. Armstrong, A. Glyn, and J. Harrison, 'In Defence of Value—A Reply to Ian Steedman', in *Capital and Class*, 5, summer 1978, p. 8.
[3] Ibid., p. 9.
[4] See the present volume, pp. 255–59.
[5] M. Itoh, *Value and Crisis*, New York and London 1980, pp. 58–60.

basically dubious whether the logical development from values to prices of production in itself can show the contradiction in a capitalist economy apart from the analysis of crisis.

In sum, in so far as these anti-critiques maintain a common technical approach regarding values as determinable only by physical data of production, they cannot satisfactorily overcome the difficulties with joint production emphasized by Steedman.

An Alternative Solution

In my view, what is missing in this recent controversy is a correct understanding of Marx's concept of form and substance of value. A fundamental defect of the classical school was that it did not analyse the development of forms of value and concentrated merely on the quantitative analysis of values. The presentation of the joint-production problem by Steedman, a neo-Ricardian, and the succeeding controversy have not been immune from this defect. As I have discussed elsewhere,[6] K. Uno has emphasized precisely the significance of Marx's theory of forms of values and distilled it as a basic theory of circulation.[7] He has also clarified the labour process and the dual character of labour as the common economic *rule* for any forms of society. Then he attempted to show the logical necessity of the *law* of value as the law of motion of capitalist production where the common economic rule in the social labour process must be effected completely through value forms. From such a point of view, the commodity market composed of forms of values should not be neglected, but must be treated as an integral part of the working of the law of value. Extending such a view, we can offer an alternative solution to the problem of joint production, as follows.

Steedman deduced negative values and negative surplus-value from an assumption that there were as many different techniques of production as there were different joint products. This assumption was obviously arbitrary. Even when there actually are different techniques of production, one of them must be chosen as representat-

[6] Ibid., chapter 2.
[7] K. Uno, *Principles of Political Economy*, Sussex, 1980.

ive for the standard of social allocation of labour. Let us come back to Steedman's numerical example. If we calculate the net products of a unit of labour in the processes 1 and 2, we get (A1, B1) for 1 and (A3, B2) for 2. As far as circumstances permit, the more effective process 2 must increasingly be selected as a common rule of economic life. However, if process 2 remains in only limited use for a time, while process 1 is an overwhelmingly dominant condition of production, then process 1 must be regarded as the standard condition of production of A and B in the social allocation of labour. In a commodity economy, as long as the dominant condition of supply to meet the fluctuations of demand in the market is process 1, the market-values or the market prices of production of A and B must be regulated by this technical process according to the theory of market prices of production, as I have discussed elsewhere more generally.[8]

Let us suppose, then, that process 1 is the current representative condition of production. Since the net products (A1, B1) are obtained by a unit of labour in this process, the amounts of embodied labour in a unit of A and B together must clearly be $l_1 + l_2 = 1$. Each of l_1 and l_2 can be between zero and one, within the constraint of this equation. There is no common technical rule in various social formations to determine the ratio $l_1/l_2 = \alpha$. In other words, we can recognize a basic freedom or elasticity in the apportionment of labour substance between the joint products, just like the elasticity in the disposal of social surplus labour. For instance, in a communal planned economy without market prices, in so far as the quantity of labour embodied still serves as a regulating factor in the allocation and distribution of social products, the ratio $\alpha = l_1/l_2$ can be lowered when there is a consensus to foster the direct or indirect consumption of A in comparison with B, under a certain social ordering of needs in relation to given technical production processes. The ratio can be adjusted to an appropriate level, by observing the reactions in consumption and production caused by its alteration.

Generally speaking, so far as we can appropriately assume that a representative condition of production is determinable for the time being in each industry, and that the same product is not produced in different industries, the amount of labour substance allotted to

[8] Itoh, *Value and Crisis*, chapter 3.

each unit of joint products can be determined on the basis of social physical conditions of production when the ratios of allotment, such as α, are somehow decided. Moreover, we can use the ratios such as α theoretically to reduce a joint-production industry to separate single production industries with the same technical composition and with sizes differing according to those ratios. These ratios by which the labour substance is allotted between or among jointly produced use-values are not determined merely by the physical system of production. Neither are they deduced from individual subjective-utility functions. As a common economic rule, they are determined in conjunction with both the technical system of production and the system of social needs, always more or less elastically or freely, including political decisions in a socialist economy.

In the basic theory of a capitalist economy, these ratios by which to allot labour substance in joint products are determined anarchically through the form of the measure of commodity values by means of a function of money. The repetitive purchasing of commodities by means of money compels the owners of commodities to revise their arbitrary prices and reveal the gravitational centre of prices as the form of commodity values. This function of money to measure the form of commodity values implies a market mechanism to adjust labour allocation among industries to meet a social system of material needs, simultaneously clarifying the dominant or representative technical condition of supply in each industry. Such a function of money to measure values in a market also serves as a mechanism to determine the ratios by which to allot labour substance between or among the jointly produced commodities, according to the ratios of their equilibrium price levels.

This does not mean that the substance of value in commodity products can be created or increased by their circulation or by degrees of demand. For instance, the substance of value of jointly produced commodities A and B in the above case must each be between zero and one, and their total must be one, as we have seen. This condition substantially constrains the formation of their equilibrium prices in a market. These prices, and therefore their ratio as well, are certainly further conditioned by the prices of production of their substitutes, if available from different industries. Although Steedman's numerical example is simple, in a more general case joint products A and B are interrelated with other industries in the process of reproduction. Inputs into the production of A and B may then require, directly or indirectly, A or B for their production. In this case, the value of inputs and therefore the total value of A and B (l_1 and l_2) will itself depend on how that labour is allocated between A and B (that is on α itself). Therefore, strictly speaking, the ratios for allotting the labour substance among joint products may affect the total amounts of embodied labour. This effect should not be interpreted as a fundamental difficulty for the labour theory of value. In my view, the effect implies that the social estimation of embodied labour-time is to be altered according to a change in the social conditions of reproduction reflected in an alteration of α, just as in the case where the re-estimation of embodied past labour-time is required by the alteration of technical conditions of production.

In any case, the amounts of embodied labour in the necessary means of subsistence for wage labourers and in the social surplus products, and hence the rate of surplus-value, are thus determinable always in a positive range even when some commodities are jointly produced. This holds so long as the ratios by which to allot labour quantities between or among joint products are determined through a function of money in measuring commodity values in a market. This solution of the joint-production problem concerning the rate of exploitation may be meaningless in an extreme case, where a society involves only one industry jointly producing, for instance, commodities A and B. Though the case is conceivable when we follow such a model as Ricardo's corn-rate theory of profit, it is too simplistic to be relevant to the determination of the value substance of joint products. If we exclude the case of fixed capital, in spite of Steedman's claim (since the residual fixed capital is not really jointly produced in the process of its utilization, and so its value substance should be treated differently), then joint production occupies not all but a part of many industries, and is far from forming an exclusive unique industry in a society. Our solution of the values of joint products and the related rate of exploitation can thus be relevant on the basis of a more realistic social position of joint-production industries.

In sum, the joint-production problem presented by Steedman to show the anomalies of Marx's theory of value rather reveals the narrow limitations of the neo-Ricardians' one-sidedly abstract, technological approach to the theory of value. In order to overcome such limitations, together with some confusions among Marxists caused by the problem, a correct understanding of Marx's unique theory of the forms and substance of value is quite essential. From this point of view, the joint-production problem must be solved by clarifying the historically specific forms and mechanisms of the capitalist economy (including the role of the market), which fix the allocation of labour substance among the joint products (even though this allocation is technically indeterminate). This must be done by considering what the problem means in relation to the trans-historical common social economic rule, as we have seen. In my opinion, this solution will not only clear up the issues of the joint-production problem, but can also positively show, in this special case, how capitalism treats social labour anarchically and unconsciously in a historically specific manner.*

* The author is grateful for Andrew Glyn's editing and for useful communications with him, Sue Himmelweit, and Bob Rowthorn, among others.

Value, Production, and Exchange[*]

Michel De Vroey

This article, which synthesizes some of the ideas contained in a forthcoming book,[1] aims at inviting a change in the understanding of the Marxian theory of value that has prevailed in Anglo-American literature until recently.[2] The main characteristic of this interpretation is that it renders the content of the Marxian and Ricardian theories of value identical for all practical purposes. This article, on the other hand, defends an interpretation in which the two theories are radically different.

Three distinctions will be advocated that amount to a narrowing of the scope of relevance of the theory of value. First, I locate the creation of value not in production but at the articulation of production and circulation. Second, I argue that the theory of value simply cannot stand without a theory of money, and that this interconnection has important consequences for the relationship between values and prices. A third and less obvious difference flows from the consideration of the relationship between two dimensions of

[*] The views developed here have been enhanced by discussions with several persons. I particularly want to thank Jacques Gouverneur, Philippe Van Parijs, and Philippe De Ville. Many thanks also to Maryvonne Neyts and to Sue Black for their help in typing and editing the manuscript.

[1] For the moment it exists only in the form of working-papers. M. De Vroey, *Travail abstrait, valeur et marchandise. Une réinterprétation de la théorie de la valeur de Marx, 1ère partie: les concepts de travail abstrait et de marchandise*, Cahiers de l'Université de Montréal, no. 7912; *2ème partie: la valeur dans un système formé exclusivement de marchandises*, Working-Paper de l'Institut des Sciences Economiques de l'Université de Louvain, no. 7915.

[2] See, for example, M. Dobb, *Theories of Value and Distribution Since Adam Smith*, Cambridge 1973; R. Meek, *Studies in the Labour Theory of Value*, London 1974; P. Sweezy, *The Theory of Capitalist Development*, New York 1942.

time, which I call synchronic and diachronic logic (or logical time versus historical time). As I see it, the theory of value provides a space of measurement that enables norms of exchange—prices—to emerge. But these norms derive from instantaneous constraints that pertain only to conditions prevailing at the point of exchange. On the other hand, more than any other system capitalism involves irreversible structural changes that perpetually modify the norms of production and exchange. Therefore, the value regulation is always impeded by the destructuring effects of the diachronic logic. This leads me to argue that although the theory of value is about the definition of a situation of equilibrium in a commodity system, it is nevertheless inherent in this system that this equilibrium can never be reached, not only because of market imperfections but also and mainly because of the effects of this irreversibility of historical time. Awareness of the interrelationship between the two logics has important theoretical consequences. On the one hand, it invites new assumptions and syntheses for the investigation of capitalist regulation. On the other hand, however, it suggests that some paths of research that have been charted by Marxian theoreticians may lead to a dead end.

Taken singly, the ideas presented here are not entirely original. Indeed, this article is influenced by a line of thought fostered mainly by French authors, many of whom have published in the series *Interventions en économie politique*. Although these writers do not necessarily share the same view, they all question the Ricardian interpretation of Marx. In the English-speaking tradition rather similar positions have been taken by authors like Pilling, Gerstein, Fine and Harris, Himmelweit and Mohun, and Weeks. But my main source of inspiration is the work of Michel Aglietta. In fact, this essay could partially be described as an effort to make explicit the theory of value contained in Aglietta's *Theory of Capitalist Regulation* and to present it in a pedagogical way. Such a task is useful because this theory, despite the central role it plays in Aglietta's argument, is introduced in a rather condensed and allusive manner.

It should also be noted that my aim in this article is not to trace the origin of its ideas back to Marx's own writings. I do not claim that my interpretation of his ideas is the only one possible. My feeling is rather that Marx's writings are sometimes contradictory, and that both

Ricardians and 'anti-Ricardians' can thus find passages legitimating their own views. Furthermore, although this article contains an implicit criticism of the way problems are broached by the Ricardian interpretation (indeed, if my problematic is accepted, several of the main questions raised by this interpretation lose their meaning), it does not make this criticism explicit.

The article is composed of five sections. The first argues that commodity production is a specific social form, that the relevance of the theory of value is confined to this social form, and that the creation of value implies an articulation of production and circulation. The second examines the relationship between the two time-structures and its effect on the process of transfer of value. The third advocates the principle that the categories of money and value are indissociably linked. The fourth offers some remarks about the relationship between value and prices. Finally, the fifth section deals with the effects of the lack of attainment of the equilibrium situation. The concept of loss value is introduced to designate the effects of failures in either the creation or transfer of value, while the concept of profits and losses of circulation is developed to designate the effects of the absence of a fully competitive structure or of a discrepancy between supply and demand.

1. The Commodity System

In the English Marxian tradition the labour theory of value is usually defined as a production theory. Value is linked to the difficulty of production—in other words, to the average quantity of labour required to produce a given good. The field of relevance of the labour theory of value is boundless. It aims at universal explanation, being deemed relevant to pre-capitalist, capitalist, and even socialist societies.

The view defended here is different. The pertinence of the concept of value is limited to the capitalist mode of production, seen as a system in which the class structure takes the form of the wage relation and the commodity is the predominant social form assumed by the products of labour. This view implies a definition of the concept of commodity that is narrower than usual (the articulation of a use-value and an exchange-value). Here the notion refers to a specific theoretical space, membership of which depends on the social form in which production is effected, and not on physical criteria.[3] What, then, is a commodity system? It is a particular system of allocation of a society's labour force, or of formation of its *social labour*. The latter concept views the labour of society as a 'collective worker' that must reproduce itself (i.e. the social structure in which it consists) through an allocation of its labour force to several objects of production. Social labour is a generic or universal category. One has thus to distinguish between the specific forms through which it is constituted. In this respect, the main feature of the commodity system is that here social labour is formed in an indirect way. Labour is first performed as *private labour*, initiated by an independent decision. It is transformed into social labour through, and only through, the sale of its product. When social labour is formed in this context, it is called *abstract labour*, the adjective referring to the operation of homogenization or abstraction achieved by exchange on the market.

The notion of abstract labour therefore does not refer to labour in general as a universal category. It simply means: social labour in the context of a commodity system. The specificity of the latter can be approached in another way, by noting that its main feature is the independence of the producers. (This term refers not to the people performing the actual labour but to the agents making the decisions about what to produce: the capitalist class). In this context the creation of value is no longer just a technological process. It depends on social recognition by the market of a privately initiated allocation of the social labour force. *Thus the notion of value, rather than being linked to a mere embodiment of labour, refers to the validation of private labour.* In this system the expenditure of labour (or in the case of services, the mobilization of a labour force at the disposal of customers) and its validation are dissociated. A gymnastic feat is required to re-unite them. This implies that failure is possible. The

[3] To quote Aglietta: 'There are no use-values which are commodities by nature, nor others which are not. The commodity is a social relation of exchange. It can well happen, therefore, that certain use-values that are not commodities under certain types of labour process and certain evolutionary logics of the mode of consumption become so at other periods in capitalist development.' *A Theory of Capitalist Regulation,—The US Experience*, London, NLB, 1979, p. 166.

meaning of private labour is thus as follows. When capitalist units undertake private projects, they are assuming, so to speak, a debt-position toward society. They intervene privately in the allocation of the society's labour force in the expectation that their private choices will receive social recognition through the sale of their commodities.[4] If this expectation is met, the debt is liquidated. Value is created and an income is formed. Capital expenditures are recovered and a profit appropriated. When the project fails, however, the picture is different. Then no creation of value occurs. As Aglietta has pointed out:

'The lack of sale of the production and exploitation deficit signify that the individual producer must himself privately buy something that society has not validated but whose expenditure has for him been inscribed as a cost, since in order to produce these commodities without social utility he has nevertheless withdrawn a part of the productive force from society.'[5]

In this interpretation, the concept of value points to an articulation of production and circulation. It cannot be seen as a production theory, as in the Ricardian interpretation, since in the absence of circulation—that is, of sale—there is no creation of value at all. The transformation of private into social labour occurs only through exchange. On the other hand, however, this is not a pure circulation theory, because once there is a sale and thus a creation of value, the magnitude of value depends on the average conditions of production prevailing at the point of exchange. Exchange creates value but production determines the magnitude of value.[6]

The commodity system thus appears as two-sided. On the one hand, it is anarchic, for there is no explicit and authoritarian

[4] A distinction must be made between the act of validation, which is a yes or no process, and the rate at which it occurs. As will be pointed out later on, it can be the equilibrium rate (when the market price coincides with the equilibrium price) or not (when it does not do so).

[5] Michel Aglietta, *Taux de profit, rotation du capital et obsolescence. Etude des liens entre accumulation et inflation*, working paper of the Centre d'Etudes prospectives et d'informations internationales, 1979.

[6] I dislike the expression 'realization of value' precisely because it suggests that value already exists before being realized and that it is a permanent property of commodities, embodied in them. For me, on the contrary, only a pretence of value (potential) exists before exchange. Furthermore, the existence of value is an instantaneous reality, confined to the moment of exchange.

allocation of the social labour force. On the other hand, however, some social cohesion is required to ensure the reproduction of society. This occurs through a posteriori norms. The theory of value deals precisely with this entire process of indirect regulation.

Logically, the first question this theory must answer is this: If commodity exchange is to be possible, a theoretical space of measurement must exist, so that the heterogeneous products of private labour can be transformed into equivalent categories. This is the *raison d'être* of value. It constitutes a space of commensurability without which no relation of equivalence could be established. Prior to any measurement, an abstraction must be constructed. As Fradin has written: 'In order for the notion of a relation between two goods to make sense, a real measure of goods must be defined (this is either done implicitly or openly admitted). This entirely transforms the notion of economic object, just as the notion of physical object is exploded by the introduction of the mass as a unit of measurement.'[7] Value is therefore a necessary category because it makes possible the transformation of economic objects, which are heterogeneous realities, into commodities, products of abstract labour. All this is realized through exchange. As Gerstein puts it: 'There is no way to reduce observable concrete labour to social abstract labour in advance, outside of the market which actually effects the reduction.'[8]

This reflection on the scope of the theory of value thus leads me to point to two limitations of the theory of value. First, it is valid only for a particular type of system of organization of social labour: the commodity system. The second limitation is more subtle. If value is created at the articulation of production and circulation (in a commodity system), then value refers to a measurement whose validity is limited to the point of exchange. In other words, value is an instantaneous measurement. The social cohesion it sustains is synchronic. The idea of an ever-existing value, an 'embedded' value, makes no sense. This second limitation has important theoretical consequences, which I will now examine.

[7] Jacques Fradin, *Valeur, monnaie et capital*, doctoral thesis, University of Paris 1973, III, p. 7.

[8] Ira Gerstein, 'Production, Circulation and Value', *Economy and Society*, vol. 5, no. 3, p. 250.

2. The Contradiction Between Synchronic and Diachronic Logics

In the conception just stated, the very existence of value can only be fugitive. How, then, are we to relate the different points of exchange? How can an inter-temporal cohesion be established? Several sub-questions are involved. First, there must be a category whose function is to overcome this caesura between the points of the time-sequence. In the next section I will argue that this is precisely one of the two theoretical *raisons d'être* of money. This point will thus be left for future treatment. The second question relates to the way value created in preceding cycles may still intervene in the production of current value. This is the problem of the transfer of value. It arises because there is no overlap between the length of the cycle of production and exchange (if one makes the heroic assumption that a unique cycle could exist) and the length of the process of utilization/destruction of the means of production. This raises a very concrete problem for capitalist units: the amortization of their expenditures on constant capital. The third problem is related to this second one, but, instead of concerning the relation between past and present, it involves that between present and future. Here the problem confronting capitalist units is that by making their decisions, especially on investment, they commit themselves to making definite payments while having only prospects of receipts. This uncertainty (in the sense of Keynes[9]) is the result of two features that are related to the deeper nature of the capitalist system. The first is the separation and independence of the producers, to which I have already referred. The second, to which we shall shortly come, is the irreversibility of time, which capitalism breeds to a far greater extent than any other mode of production.[10]

[9] We have here an important point of agreement between Marx, as I read him, and Keynes, as read by the 'post-Keynesian school'. Cf. H.P. Minsky, *John Maynard Keynes*, New York 1975; P. Davidson, *Money and the Real World*, London 1978; A.S. Eichner, *A Guide to Post-Keynesian Economics*, New York 1978.

[10] Philippe Deville, 'Time and Dynamics in Economics: The Lessons From General Equilibrium Theory', in Bele H. Banathy (ed.), *Systems Science and Science*. Proceedings of the 24th Annual North American Meeting of the Society for General Systems Research with the American Association for the Advancement of Science, San Francisco, January 1980.

The problem of inter-temporal cohesion would not be so crucial if time elapsed without the occurrence of change, or, in other words, if the norms of production and exchange were constantly reproduced. In this case, the principle guiding the integration of past commitments would be rather simple. Let us assume that the means of production retain the same efficiency all through their lifetime and that the latter is a multiple of the duration of the production cycle of final commodities. Then, at each cycle, a part of the total value of the machine will be transferred[11] to the value of the commodity, with the magnitude of the transferred value depending on the multiplying factor. At the end of each cycle, the total value then consists of two components: value created (i.e. the product of present social labour) and value transferred (i.e. the product of past, re-actualized social labour). Likewise, at each cycle the means of production lose a fraction of their initial value, so that in the end they are physically worn out and attain zero value. The transfer of value thus establishes a system of communicating vessels between the means of production and the final commodity. This achieves the inter-temporal cohesion, providing the relations of equivalence are maintained over time. The progressive drop in the value of the means of production, expressing their physical wear and tear, will be called depreciation. Its monetary counterpart is amortization. At the end of the life-cycle of the machine, the amount of money put in the sinking fund should permit the purchase of a new machine.

Let me stress at this point that the transfer of value is not an automatic process but is conditional. As we have seen, the expenditure of private labour is not a sufficient condition for the creation of value. Likewise, a transfer of value does not occur simply because means of production are utilized. The final commodities must be sold. This sale effects two sanctions: on the one hand, it validates private labour; on the other, it re-actualizes social labour, which has already been validated in the past. If these commodities are not sold, the failure also becomes twofold. It is a failure at once to validate and to transfer value. Both the creation of value and its transfer are

---

[11] In my conception, the notion of transfer of value refers to a time-dimension (transfer from one period to another) and not to a synchronic displacement from one agent to another.

instantaneous processes. Means of production may preserve their value either as long as they can be the object of a second-hand sale (this is also the case for other commodities) or as long as they can be productively consumed within an unchanging norm of production. But this preservation is conditional, since it depends on the occurrence of the sale.

However, the notion of time underlying the preceding reasoning, characterized by the absence of change, is untenable. The notion of time as irreversible is more appropriate to capitalism than is any assumption of constant reproduction. The paradox of the capitalist mode of production is that the maintenance of its basic class relation—the wage relation—entails unceasing transformations. These concern the norms of production (and if they change unevenly from one branch to another, they modify the norms of equivalence), including the creation of new products and branches, as well as the mode of consumption, the market structure, and the intervention of the state. The distinguishing feature of these processes is their irreversibility. Once a change has been introduced, it is not possible to return to the previous situation. At the core of this constraint to change, which so uniquely characterizes the capitalist mode of production, I would place neither the 'animal spirits of entrepreneurs', as Keynesians would often say, nor competition, as many Marxists would probably argue. Rather, following Aglietta, we should locate the source of change in the wage relationship itself, in the class antagonism typical of the capitalist mode of production. 'Progress' could thus be seen as the result of class confrontations:

'Technical progress is the essential modality of resolving the conflicts that recur in production. It permits the capitalist management perpetually to assert itself over the wage-earning class. Technical progress is thus indissolubly a material transformation and a change in the social relations established within production. It segments and restructures the wage-earning class, incorporates and defuses wage claims when they tend to become amplified and generalized. It destroys or channels antagonisms by transforming the regulation of labour and the organization of collective labour. Such is the source and orientation of innovation and the reason for its inexhaustible character within the wage relation. Such is the mistake of economists who think that the origin of innovation lies solely in competition between firms, and who have therefore announced the euthanasia of technical progress as a result of the centralization of capital.'[12]

Technical progress makes the norms of production more efficient. This impedes the 'normal' process of transfer of value. Let us assume that the value of a given machine diminishes. This will change the norm of production. A series of changes follows from this: the efficiency rises, the value transferred per unit of product (and thus also the value of the final commodity) drops. In a context of full competition, the endowment to the sinking fund per unit of product is also lowered. This does not present a problem for those capitalist units that bought the machine at the new price, corresponding to the new magnitude of value. But it does for those that bought it at the old price: they cannot fully recover the expense incurred on purchasing it. The same situation occurs when a new machine, which is more efficient, is introduced. As its use becomes generalized, all units must adopt it in order to keep up with the new norm, even if the previous machine is not worn out. In both cases there is a drop in the value of the means of production in addition to its depreciation. I call it a *devalorization*.[13] Its physical counterpart is obsolescence (as distinguished from wear).

The two logics, the inter-temporal one characterized by this unforeseeable irreversibility, and the synchronic one interact in a very specific way. Indeed, the first impedes the full functioning of the second. There is no reason why the relations of equivalence should remain stable over time. Furthermore, since new norms are always emerging, the preceding ones are unable to impose themselves fully.

What is the theoretical consequence of this argument? It does not deprive the theory of value of all significance or consistency, but it undoubtedly indicates its limitations. These can be expressed in two

[12] M. Aglietta, *La dévalorisation du capital. Etude des liens entre accumulation et inflation*, working paper of the Centre d'Etudes prospectives et d'informations internationales, 1980.

[13] The notion of devalorization is of the utmost importance in understanding capitalist regulation. It can, for instance, be argued that the way in which the consequent loss of value is financed and absorbed in a regime of intensive accumulation is precisely the main reason for creeping inflation. See M. Aglietta, *A Theory of Capitalist Regulation*, and my study 'Money and Inflation in Intensive Accumulation', Working Paper, Université de Louvain.

ways. First, the theory of value refers to one dimension of the functioning of the capitalist system and cannot encompass the specificity of physical and structural changes brought about by the development of capitalism. It points only to the invariant elements of capitalism. For example, whatever the regime of accumulation and the structural position, the rate of profit may always be defined as dependent on the interaction between the rate of surplus-value and the value-composition of capital. To express this in another way, one can state that the theory of value is an equilibrium theory, but that the achievement of equilibrium is totally out of reach, not because of market imperfections but because of the importance of the diachronic logic that perpetually mitigates the operation of the instantaneous norms. Although this disruptive logic does not render the theory of value irrelevant, it must not be overlooked. Its presence should influence judgements about the interest of some topics of research, as, for example, simple and expanded reproduction. In the light of the preceding remarks, this becomes a very formal and academic question. Indeed, by assuming the absence of change in the norms of production and exchange, this theory is entirely disconnected from what, in my view, constitutes the core of capitalist development. What is called growth in such theory is the opposite of real capitalist dynamics.

3. Money

Every economic theory admits that money plays an important practical role in market economies, but there is disagreement on its theoretical place. The most common view originated with Adam Smith. It is shared by neo-classical economists and Ricardians, and also by such eminent Marxists as Dobb, Meek, and Sweezy.[14] It claims that in essence market exchange does not differ from barter. Certainly, money facilitates exchange, but its presence is not theoretically required. The system could also function without money. Thus, to use the well-known metaphor, money is a veil that must be lifted if the real world is to be seen. A dichotomy is posited

---

[14] But not by 'post-Keynesians'.

between the field of value (aiming to explain the exchange-ratios) and that of money. This, I would argue, is not at all the case in the abstract-labour interpretation where the two concepts are intrinsically linked.

For me, the theory of value is incomplete without the introduction of money. It simply does not stand up. There are two reasons for this, both linked to the instantaneous character of value. The first results from a paradoxical feature of abstract labour, defined as the form taken by social labour in a commodity system. Abstract labour is considered a theoretical category permitting the commensurability of objects that are heterogeneous in all respects but for the fact that they are products of abstract labour. It is said, as a first approximation that must be amended in the second stage of the reasoning, that the exchange relationships between commodities depend on the amount of abstract labour their production has required. But a problem arises: in fact abstract labour seems not to be able to play its role in the allocation of the social labour force, and this for two reasons. First, it is an invisible category constructed only through reasoning. Second, it bears a real contradiction, which Marx pointed out in his *Contribution to a Critique of Political Economy*.[15] On the one hand, to say that abstract labour serves as the foundation of commensurability and the basic criterion for determining exchange ratios implies that it is logically anterior to exchange. But on the other hand, it is also asserted that abstract labour and value are formed only when exchange actually occurs. This implies that abstract labour is logically posterior to exchange. Thus, to accomplish its function, abstract labour must, first, have a visible and concrete substitute and, second, the latter must be such that it does not betray the paradoxical

[15] 'But the different kinds of individual labour represented in these particular use-values, in fact, become . . . social labour only by actually being exchanged for one another . . . Social labour-time exists in these commodities in a latent state, so to speak, and becomes evident, only in the course of their exchange. The point of departure is not the labour of individuals considered as social labour, but on the contrary the particular kinds of labour of private individuals, i.e. labour which proves that it is universal social labour only by the supersession of its original character in the exchange process. Universal social labour is consequently not a ready-made pre-requisite but an emerging result. Thus a new difficulty arises: on the one hand, commodities must enter the exchange process as materialized universal labour-time, on the other hand, the labour-time of individuals becomes materialized universal labour-time only as a result of the exchange process.' (Karl Marx, *A Contribution to the Critique of Political Economy*, Moscow 1970, p. 45.)

relation of abstract labour to exchange. This is exactly what money fundamentally does. As far as the first aspect is concerned, it is an institutionalized symbol of abstract labour.[16] Money enables private activities to form a social coherence and the products of such activities to exist as commodities. It is through their relationship to money that they are able to gain social recognition. With the introduction of money, the validation process receives a more concrete meaning. Owners of means of production can take whatever production initiative they want, as long as they satisfy one condition, called the *monetary constraint*: their products must be sold, that is, exchanged for money.[17] Payment is the most fundamental rule of the game in a commodity system. Contractual engagements must be fulfilled, under pain of legal punishment. As far as the second aspect is concerned, money contains precisely the paradoxical feature described above. It is a simultaneously autonomous and dependent category. As an autonomous category, it predates exchange and is a locus of new impetus. But it is dependent because, ultimately, the monetary system is subjected to the requirements of commodity exchanges. Any monetary impulse that does not generate a validation leads to correcting effects, whose logic is to re-establish the subjection of money to exchange.[18]

The second reason for the necessity of money flows from the question examined earlier of the contradiction between synchronic and diachronic logic. A diachronic category must exist in order to make possible the transition from one set of norms to another. Again, this is exactly what the reconstitution of the general equivalent permits. On the one hand, money secures the permanence over time of the theoretical categories established in an instantaneous approach. This enables economic agents to make economic calculation over time.[19] On the other hand, the variability of the general equivalence will express the transformation of the social norms. In

[16] This is the reason why its fetishization is not a 'mirage'.

[17] It should be added that, in order to stay in competition, they must sell at a price providing them the average rate of profit of their branch.

[18] This question is examined in depth in my study 'Money and Inflation in Intensive Accumulation'.

[19] This was well perceived by Keynes, who wrote: 'the importance of money essentially flows from it being a link between the present and the future'. *The General Theory*, p. 293.

other words, the inter-temporal instability resulting from technical progress is projected onto money. The following quotation from Aglietta synthesizes the argument:

'Even though the price system assumes a very different sense for each of these schools [classical and neo-classical orthodoxy], it always possesses the characteristic that it can only be defined in relative terms and depends on the exogenous variable of the conditions of production and exchange. Transition from one set of conditions to another is totally unintelligible here. Only the Marshallian school has sought to tackle this problem with a typology of equilibria over time. But for want of any support in an adequate theory of value, this empirical approach cannot analyse the real historical process of irreversible transformations of the conditions of production. Only a theory of value for which the monetary form of price is not a disguise, but rather the exclusive modality of homogenization of production activities and the conditions of existence for exchange relations, can go beyond the notion of a coherent system of relative prices. The permanence over time of monetary prices makes it possible to understand the incoherence over time of the price system as the characteristic of any real dynamic—in other words, one that is irreversible and radically uncertain for the individual economic agents caught up in it.'[20] To sum up, my view (which I admit is as unprovable as the counter-view would be) is that money is not just a practical device designed to facilitate exchange. Rather, its presence expresses a theoretical necessity. It is a category indispensable to the working of value regulation.

Some further comments on the characteristics of money should be made. They may be grouped into three points.

1. The endorsement of a particular use-value in the role of general equivalent occurs through a process of exclusion. This has been well described by Marx. However, it should also be stressed that the operation of attributing monetary status (*monetization*) involves state intervention. This is the minimal economic intervention of the state in a system otherwise characterized by its very absence. It bears mainly on the following objects: the officialization of the choice of

---

[20] Aglietta, *A Theory of Capitalist Regulation – The US Experience*, p. 300.

general equivalent, the definition of the taxonomic system of monetary subdivisions, and in the case where money has a physical support, the definition of the correspondence between the monetary pivotal unit and the physical one.

2. Money must not be confused with its physical support. For example, it is a mistake to say that gold is money. The metal itself never constitutes money. The latter is an institutionalized system of denomination that can, but need not, be affixed on a material basis. In other words, money is a social relationship originating in the process of monetization, and not a physical reality. Although many Marxists will probably agree on the principle, in practice confusions arise quite often. For instance, if money is a sign affixed to an object, then changes affecting the object do not necessarily have any impact on the sign. If the productivity of gold-extraction rises, this *may* affect the exchange-value of the monetary unit, but not necessarily, because the physical modification can be exactly compensated by opposite modifications in the definition of the correspondence between the monetary and the physical units.

3. The notion of value as I understand it is linked to the process of validation of private labour and not to the expenditure of labour. This has one important consequence for the theoretical status of money: we can no longer say, following Marx, that money has a value (and inasmuch as the scopes of relevance of the concepts of value and commodity overlap, that it is a commodity). This assertion is easily defended. I would link the notion of validation to the possibility of non-validation. It cannot be an automatic, guaranteed operation. This, however, is exactly what happens with money. Since it is the institutionalized representation of abstract labour, validation is not a challenge to it. The production of money never faces problems of outlet. Money is always exchanged, albeit at a varying rate.[21] Marx himself demonstrated that money could not have a price. If we now accept that it has no value, then it retains only one of the three features ascribed to commodities: an exchange-value.

[21] This assertion is valid provided we ignore the existence of what we will call 'pseudo-money', privately issued. This is examined in my study 'Money and Inflation. . .'.

188

4. The Articulation of the Concepts of Value and Price

When validation of private labour occurs, only one thing is observable: a given use-value is sold at a certain price, called the market price. But to explain the magnitude of the latter, a series of interconnected concepts, which have no direct observable counterparts, must be constructed. One feature of the Marxian theory of price is that it does indeed develop a conceptual framework far more complex than that of orthodox economics. The concepts of value, exchange-value, and price, which are used as synonyms in other paradigms, are here given very distinct meanings. Furthermore, the notion of price is considered generic, one that must be broken down into several different forms. In this section, these definitions and distinctions are briefly recalled.

First, let us comment on the meaning of the notion of price. In neo-classical and Ricardian paradigms, price is understood to refer to a so-called relative price expressing the equivalence ratio between physical units of different goods. It is a 'real' ratio. Since this is also the definition of exchange-value, the two notions are identical. This amounts to an expulsion of money. To reintroduce it, the adjective 'monetary' or 'nominal' must be added to the term 'price'. In my approach, on the contrary, the notion of price always means monetary price, so the adjective is redundant. 'Price' refers to *one* of all the possible expressions of the exchange-value of a commodity: that in which it is expressed in terms of monetary units. This difference in meaning is not merely a question of convention, but goes back to a radical difference in the role attributed to money. In the conventional view, money is exogenous. Relative equilibrium prices are determined independently of any monetary condition. In my approach, on the contrary, the real economy is first and foremost a monetary economy. Money is what makes prices exist. It is a logical precondition for the construction of the concept of price. As de Brunhoff puts it: 'Money is not added afterwards to a non-monetary economy. It necessarily confronts the commodity, so permitting it to express its value.'[22]

[22] S. de Brunhoff, *The State, Capital, and Economic Policy*, London 1978.

This said, we can now examine the articulation between value and price.[23] These two notions are intrinsically linked, since they refer to the same process, namely the validation of private labour. The creation of value, the establishment of the market price, and the formation of the seller's income must occur at one and the same time. Value is a concept that does not pretend to be observable. It is expressed only through the mediation of price. To speak of a value existing in itself, independent of its expression in a price, makes no sense in my conception.[24] The two concepts can be separated only in intellectual reasoning. It can then be specified that value refers to a foundation aspect, price to a phenomenal one. To borrow from philosophical language, their relation is one of 'dissimulation-manifestation'. On the one hand, the price hides the value, since in the sphere of what is observable, it fills all the space. On the other hand, however, the price indicates the value, since questioning the nature and possibility of the price leads to the construction of the concept of value.

These qualitative considerations, of course, have quantitative consequences. They must be examined at two levels, one referring to the whole of social production, the other dealing with particular commodities. Let us start with the former. Assume a very abstract closed commodity system in which, first, all products of labour take the form of commodities (i.e. there is only productive labour)[25] and second, there is no rent on natural resources. If the velocity of circulation is equal to one, or if the period under examination is confined to one single instant, then the quantity of money in circulation equals the total sales or incomes, i.e. the sum of prices. At this abstract level of a pure commodity system, there is a strict

[23] Little attention will be paid here to the third notion of the triad, that of exchange-value. Let us merely say that it cannot be confused with price (exchange-value is a general concept, meaning that in the formation of an exchange ratio the referent may be any other commodity; the price is *one* exchange-value, in which money plays the role of the referent) or with value (value is an absolute magnitude, while exchange-value is a ratio; value is logically anterior to exchange-value; finally, value and exchange-value need not evolve concomitantly).

[24] Therefore, strictly speaking, there can be no problem of the 'transformation of values into prices', since value is always and immediately transformed into prices. See my article 'On the Obsolescence of the Marxian Theory of Value'.

[25] The distinction between productive and unproductive labour is examined in my article 'On the Obsolescence. . .'.

190

correspondence between the sum of prices and the sum of value. Indeed, in such a situation no income can be formed except by the creation or transfer of value. Thus the total income is the monetary form of the total magnitude of value, and its division among the various agents reflects their claims about the sharing of the total product of social labour. Following Bullock and Yaffe, one can state: 'It is quite impossible for total prices to express anything other than total value.'[26]

This relation must not, however, be misinterpreted. The concepts of value and price belong to different theoretical spaces. As a result, mathematical operations that mix them in the same equations make no sense. Unfortunately, this is rarely noticed, and most people, following Marx in this error, seem to assume that these operations are epistemologically legitimate. They say, for example, that a quantity of value is bigger than a quantity of price, or that the sum of values could be bigger, smaller, or equal to the sum of prices. This cannot be accepted. Only an overall qualitative link can be brought in, through the concept of the *monetary expression of social labour-time* (abbreviated ME):

$$ME = \frac{\text{Sum of prices}}{\text{Sum of values}}$$

This is a pure number indicating how many monetary units the quantum of total value is equivalent to.[27] Empirically, the evolution of the ME is reflected in that of the general level of prices (GLP). An increase of the ME, however, is not necessarily manifested in a similar shift in the general level of prices, because the latter is also inversely proportional to the general evolution of productivity. This is why it is important not to confuse the two concepts.[28] There is insufficient

[26] Paul Bullock and David Yaffe, 'Inflation, the Crisis and the Post-War Boom', in *Revolutionary Communist*, no. 3–4, November 1975, p. 14.

[27] If ME= 1, the same figures apply to the sum of values and the sum of prices. But this numerical equality between non-commensurable magnitudes cannot be considered a meaningful result. It simply follows from a particular assumption about the magnitude of the ME.

[28] In other words: $\frac{\Delta GLP}{GLP} = \frac{\Delta ME}{ME} - \frac{\Delta Productivity}{Productivity}$.

space here to present a full explanation of the factors that determine the evolution of the ME, but it depends, at bottom, on the specific form taken by the general equivalent and the institutional context of the creation of money.[29] But the sum of prices can change in only two ways: through a change in the total magnitude of value or through a shift in the ME.

We can now turn to the relationship between value and price with respect to particular commodities. To begin with, the epistemological remark made above must be reiterated. No arithmetical operations can mix values and prices in the same equations. However, there is one possibility that the same numbers might describe the magnitude of both value and price. This would be the case if the following four conditions were assumed (without forgetting our more general assumptions):

1) $ME = 1$;
2) the different branches have the same organic composition of capital;
3) for all commodities receiving validation, at the supply price the quantities demanded and supplied are equal;
4) absence of market power.

The magnitudes of value and of price would then be designated by the same figures. If the ME was not equal to one[30] but the other three conditions held, a perfect correspondence between the divisions of the two spaces would remain, although different figures would now be affixed for value and price magnitudes. Thus the first condition is not necessary for the correspondence between value and price—it merely adds a numerical identity. When the other three conditions obtain, the price of a commodity is determined exclusively by its value. This magnitude of price is called the *simple price*,[31] because it

[29] The factors explaining changes in the magnitude of the ME are investigated in my study 'Money and Inflation. . .'. Here let us merely note that the quantitative evolution of the ME does not alter the qualitative role of money. For instance, if it doubles, this means that one monetary unit represents only half the fraction of total value that it used to do. But the status of money as the institutionalized symbol of abstract labour does not change as a consequence of this shift.

[30] There is no reason that it would be, except that it facilitates the construction of examples (but at the same time, it may help to bring about the denounced confusion).

[31] The notion of simple price can be found in Bullock and Yaffe's article, 'Inflation, the Crisis and the Post-War Boom', p. 15. It corresponds to Shaikh's 'direct price'.

expresses simply and solely the magnitude of value, without any deviation.

But these three conditions are untenable, and the reasoning must therefore not stop here. If we abandon the first condition and allow inequalities of organic compositions of capital, then the equilibrium price must be modified from the simple price to the price of production. The latter refers to a magnitude of price that deviates from the simple price by an amount such that the same rate of profit would prevail in all branches.[32] The new situation of equilibrium would imply that the market prices coincide with the prices of production. Again, this can be observed only indirectly: if there was equilibrium, all branches would exhibit the same rate of profit. Thus the actual inequalities in profitability indicate how far from equilibrium the economy stands. In my conception, which focuses on the irreversibility of time and on the perpetual remodelling of the norms of production and exchange, as well as of the boundaries of the branches, it is not at all surprising that this state is never achieved— on the contrary, the opposite would be astonishing. Relaxing the other two conditions opens the way for these disruptive effects. The permanent disequilibrium between supply and demand, the shifts towards new products, the market structures, the possible intervention of the state all intervene to create gaps between the market prices and equilibrium magnitudes.[33] There is not sufficient space to discuss these questions fully here. It should, however, be emphasized that these shifts concern an internal re-allocation within the space of prices, but do not imply any change in its overall size, since they are not accompanied by a modification of the ME or of the total production of value. In other words, the sum of simple prices must equal the sum of prices of production, as well as that of market prices. The articulation between value and price and the subdivision of the latter concept into its different logical forms can be illustrated in a simple diagram describing the situation of a commodity system in

Cf. A. Shaikh, 'Marx's Theory of Value and the "Transformation Problem"', in J. Schwartz (ed.), *The Subtle Anatomy of Capitalism*.

[32] In this operation a difference in the rate of profit arises, compared to what it would have been if simple prices were the actual prices of equilibrium. See 'On the Obsolescence. . .'.

[33] All these deviations refer to logical steps, the real process being instantaneous.

which, through an arbitrary choice of ours, there exist four types of commodities, A, B, C, D, having values of 4, 3, 2, 1 respectively. (See figure 1.) The ME is defined as equal to 1. A full validation is assumed, but the organic compositions of capital are assumed to differ, so that the prices of production deviate from the simple prices. Furthermore, it is assumed that some unexplained market situation makes the market prices deviate from the prices of production.

To conclude this section I would like to reassess two more general questions of definition. They relate to the object and objective of the theory of value and to the content of the notion of the law of value. I will consider them in turn. In other paradigms the aim of the theory of value is to explain the level, if not of market prices, at least of long-term equilibrium prices. In the Marxian approach, things are more complex, because the theory develops on two different levels simultaneously. On the one hand, it strives to understand the profound nature of the commodity system. The question raised in this respect is: How can one explain the formation of social cohesion in a system in which all production decisions are private? In other words, what are the conditions of possibility of the functioning of a system in which the products take the form of commodities? To answer these questions, a network of concepts is constructed, which allegedly refer to categories that function in reality, albeit, for some of them, invisibly. Value lies at the core of this network, but it cannot be separated from the other concepts connected to it. On the other hand, however, the theory of value evidently also deals with the narrower question of price determination, as do the other theories. In this respect, though, it is less ambitious than the Ricardian theory. It does not assert that equilibrium prices are explicable only in terms of the socially necessary labour, i.e. excluding circulation factors. Indeed, if they coincide with prices of production, their explanation requires something else than value in the narrow sense. I would therefore argue that, with respect to particular commodities, the theory of value does not aim at fully (or exclusively) explaining their equilibrium prices and exchange-values, but rather it is a theory of the foundation of prices. I therefore uphold the view that value is a logically indispensable feature in the formation of prices, but not that it is the only factor explaining long-term exchange ratios, as Ricardo hoped to demonstrate.

194

THE ARTICULATION BETWEEN VALUE AND PRICES

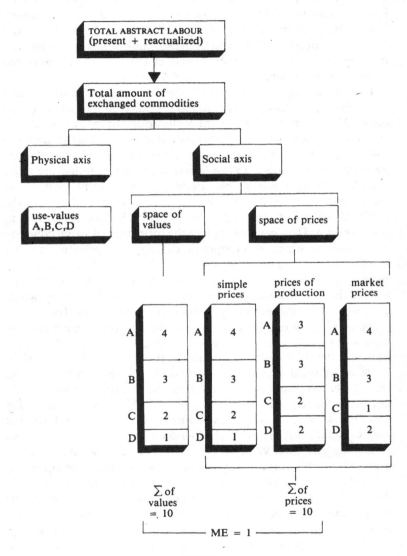

FIGURE 1

On the other hand, the content of the notion of a *law of value* must also be re-examined. It is often taken to refer to the assertion that value is measured in terms of magnitudes of labour. This, however, is a definitional premiss. To call it a law seems misleading, since that term normally refers to a regular linkage between variables, one that ought to be observable, and also potentially refutable. Two other meanings are then possible. First, the law of value could designate the equilibrium norm of exchange: in equilibrium, market price and price of production should coincide. This too, however, could be misleading, because of the risk of confusing the notions of law of value and exchange at value. So understood, the law of value would not be equivalent to exchange at value. I would therefore suggest that another meaning be ascribed the expression 'law of value': it points to the fact that the commodity system, despite its anarchical nature, is governed by a series of norms that impose themselves on the agents. It expresses the submission of commodity producers to a social constraint: they must valorize their advances of capital, or, what amounts to the same thing, they must avoid losses of value. On the one hand, firms may produce whatever commodities they want, provided they can sell them at a price that permits their maintenance in the competitive structure. On the other hand, they must cope with the irreversibility of the time structure and avoid the losses of devalorization. The following section examines the failures to which capitalist firms are exposed.

5. Failures of Private Initiatives

Private initiative intrinsically entails risks. It cannot succeed every time, nor for every decision-maker. Two, qualitatively different types of failure must be distinguished. The first concerns those cases in which there is validation, but at a rate different from the equilibrium one. Their common consequence is to lead to what may be called *circulation profits* and *circulation losses*. The second type of failure refers to cases of *losses of value*, inducing a shrinkage of the spaces of both values and prices. This, in turn, can take two forms: a lack of sale or a devalorization. Let us study them successively.

1. Circulation profits and losses

Profits and losses of circulation result from the lack of full realization of the norms of exchange. They occur when there is a situation of market power or a disequilibrium between supplied and demanded quantities at the supply price (which, at equilibrium, would correspond to the price of production). Both these situations lead to transfers of income from some agents to others. If the sellers are in a position of strength, they will be able to impose a premium on the equilibrium price. If the buyers are in such a position, they will be able to lower the price. The specific nature of these transfers is that globally they are cancelled out, since the circulation profits of some are, by definition, the losses of others: their sum amounts to zero. Moreover, these transfers do not affect the size of the spaces of values and prices (to the extent that the factors causing transfers do not at once lead to losses of value). They simply generate a change in the internal division of the space of prices, by modifying the actual exchange-ratios among commodities (see figure 1).

This compensation, however, occurs only at the global level and not among the several sub-sets of relations into which the total set of exchanges can be divided. This has an important consequence. Let us divide the global set into two categories, the first comprising the exchanges among capitalist units, the second those occurring between capitalist units and the wage-earning class, whether they involve the sale of labour-power or the purchase of commodities by wage-earners. If there is no complete compensation within the sub-set formed by capital/labour exchanges, an *inter-class transfer of income* occurs. It modifies the magnitude of the total mass of profit available for accumulation and consumption by capitalists. If the market power favours the capitalist class, two consequences ensue. On the one hand, the average wage will not allow fulfilment of the norm of consumption; on the other hand, the total mass of profit available for accumulation will consist of two components: profit stemming from surplus-value and inter-class profit of circulation to the benefit of capital. If the market situation is the other way round, then the outcome is also reversed.

2. Losses of value

Losses of value arise from two sources: lack of sale or devalorization of the means of production. The first results from mistaken choices of production. Some private initiative has been taken, the product of which fails to find an outlet (either partially or totally). Thus no validation or creation of value occurs. The effective size of the space of the values (and also, other things being equal, that of the space of prices) is smaller than what it could have been. The notion of loss of value must be understood not in the sense of a subtraction from an existing amount of value, but as a non-actualization of something potential. Besides this lack of validation of private or present labour, the absence of sale brings about another consequence, namely a failure in the transfer of value from the means of production to the final commodity. Both the expense of private labour and the utilization of the machines appear a posteriori to be the wrong choice and a waste.

The loss of value caused by devalorization could theoretically occur even when the product is sold in its entirety and full validation occurs. Again, it involves a mistake, but it appears as such only later. A priori, it was unpredictable. A choice that commits a firm for a certain period, rational at the time it was made, turns out later to be a mistake, because some technical progress has modified the norms of production. The result is a devalorization, a sudden drop in the value of the means of production beyond their depreciation. This causes an incapacity to transfer integrally the amount of value created in preceding periods, and which would have been reactualizable if there had been no technical progress. Figure 2 synthesizes the possible outcomes in terms of failure or success of the transfer process, resulting from the utilization of means of production.

In contrast with the cases of losses of circulation, losses of value are not compensated. Whatever their form, lack of sale or devalorization, they always represent waste in the allocation of the social labour of a commodity society. It is the 'price' paid for the way social cohesion is formed in this type of society.[34] It generates a decline in overall income[35] and social production with respect to the potential

---

[34] In a centralized system of allocation, a waste of resources is also likely to occur, but by definition it could not take the same form.

[35] If there is a drop in the size of the space of values while the ME remains constant, the size of the space of prices also declines. Then we have a drop in the 'nominal income'. If the drop in overall value is accompanied by a rise of the ME, the sum of prices can remain constant or even increase, but there is a decrease in the 'real income'.

198

POSSIBLE OUTCOMES OF THE USES OF MEANS OF PRODUCTION

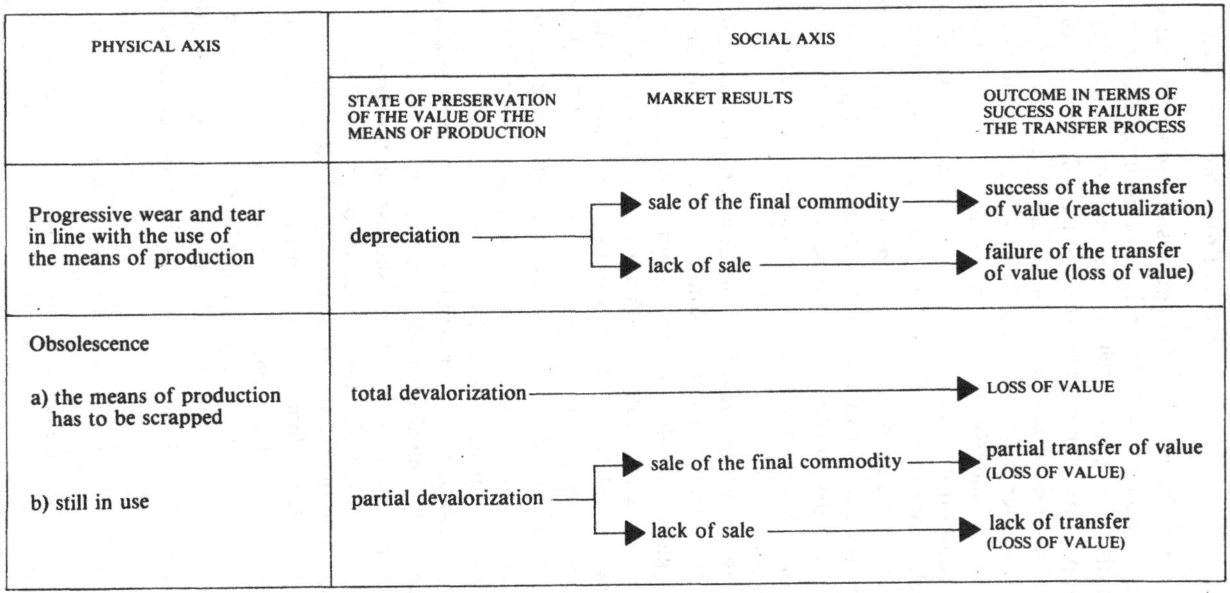

FIGURE 2

amounts that could have been obtained without these errors. The losses of value must be sustained by some agents in the form of a decline in their income. In a social context characterized both by full competition and by a certain stage of development of the monetary system, the sanction of the loss of value falls on the capitalist units that initiated the failed project or are the victims of obsolescence. In another context, however, this sanction can be transferred to other agents. But somebody has to bear the cost. The effects of the different forms of losses of value in the case of a constant ME are illustrated in figure 3.

All these various types of losses can be labelled 'dysfunctionalities' of the system, since they indicate a failure to achieve equilibrium. But they are nevertheless inherent in its functioning. What varies with the business cycle and structural evolution is their relative amount, and the way they are absorbed. I have described them separately, but they are of course intertwined, the one generating the others. For instance, a profit of circulation occurring on one market can diminish the purchasing power that creates effective demand on other markets, so that these would consequently experience either a lack of sale or losses of circulation.

The notions of circulation profits and of loss of value are of central importance in understanding the working of capitalist economies. Unfortunately, they are not given the attention they deserve. This neglect is due to the fact that the Marxian analysis is usually developed in terms of static equilibrium. The mechanism of determination of equilibrium prices is almost always demonstrated in the case of full validation of private labour and the absence of obsolescence. Consequently, the fact that equilibrium is never actually achieved is forgotten by many Marxist analysts. Their apparent concern for pedagogy leads to the loss of two central features of the system they are studying: first, the way social cohesion is formed in a commodity society inevitably leads to market failures; second, the concept of time appropriate to capitalism is that of irreversibility, which means that the norms of production and exchange are perpetually shifting and can never fully impose themselves. The definition of equilibrium is surely a necessary step in theoretical reasoning, but it cannot be the end of the analysis. It is

A DIAGRAMMATIC EXAMPLE OF LOSSES OF VALUE

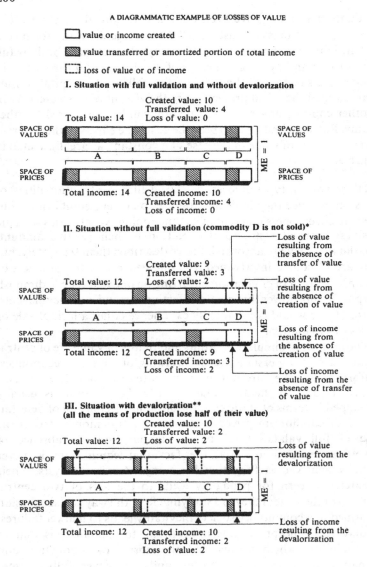

☐ value or income created

▨ value transferred or amortized portion of total income

☐ loss of value or of income

I. Situation with full validation and without devalorization

Created value: 10
Transferred value: 4
Total value: 14   Loss of value: 0

SPACE OF VALUES   SPACE OF VALUES

A   B   C   D   ME = 1

SPACE OF PRICES   SPACE OF PRICES

Total income: 14   Created income: 10
Transferred income: 4
Loss of income: 0

II. Situation without full validation (commodity D is not sold)*

Loss of value resulting from the absence of transfer of value

Created value: 9
Transferred value: 3
Total value: 12   Loss of value: 2

SPACE OF VALUES

Loss of value resulting from the absence of creation of value

A   B   C   D   ME = 1

SPACE OF PRICES

Loss of income resulting from the absence of creation of value

Total income: 12   Created income: 9
Transferred income: 3
Loss of income: 2

Loss of income resulting from the absence of transfer of value

III. Situation with devalorization**
(all the means of production lose half of their value)

Created value: 10
Transferred value: 2
Total value: 12   Loss of value: 2

SPACE OF VALUES

Loss of value resulting from the devalorization

A   B   C   D   ME = 1

SPACE OF PRICES

Total income: 12   Created income: 10
Transferred income: 2
Loss of value: 2

Loss of income resulting from the devalorization

*It is supposed that there is no devalorization.
**It is supposed that there is full validation.

FIGURE 3

also necessary to integrate the elements that act as destructuring forces, and to investigate their effects on the invariant basic ratios that underlie the wage relation: the rate of surplus-value, the value-composition of capital, and the rate of profit.

The Labour Theory of Value and the Concept of Exploitation

G.A. Cohen

> It is we who ploughed the prairies, built the
> cities where they trade,
> Dug the mines and built the workshops,
> endless miles of railroad laid,
> Now we stand outcast and starving, 'mid
> the wonders we have made . . .
>
> *Solidarity*, by RALPH CHAPLIN (to the tune of
> *Battle Hymn of the Republic*)

This essay shows that the relationship between the labour theory of value and the concept of exploitation is one of mutual irrelevance.* The labour theory of value is not a suitable basis for the charge of exploitation laid against capitalism by Marxists, and the real foundation of that charge is something much simpler which, for reasons to be stated, is widely confused with the labour theory of value.

* I am most grateful to Alison Assister, Chris Arthur, David Braybrooke, Daniel Goldstick, Keith Graham, Edward Hyland, David Lloyd-Thomas, Colin McGinn, John McMurtry, Jan Narveson, Edward Nell, Christopher Provis, Stein Rafoss, William Shaw, and Arnold Zuboff, all of whom wrote critical comments on an earlier version of this paper.

I thank the Editors of *Philosophy & Public Affairs* for an excellent set of suggestions, and for tolerating my unwillingness to accept some of them.

'The Labour Theory of Value and the Concept of Exploitation' first appeared in *Philosophy & Public Affairs*, 8, no. 4 (summer 1979). Reprinted by permission of Princeton University Press.

1

I begin with a short exposition of the labour theory of value as we find it in *Capital* Volume 1. (Differences between Volume 1 and later parts of *Capital* will be adverted to later.) I shall first define the term 'value', and then state what the labour theory says about what it denotes. What follows is one way of presenting the first few pages of Volume 1 of *Capital*. Having completed the presentation, I shall describe a different way, which I do not think is right.

It is convenient to define value by reference to exchange-value, with which we therefore begin.

Exchange-value is a property of things which are desired; in Marxian language, then, it is a property of use-values.[1] It is, however, a property, not of all use-values, but of those bought and sold, which undergo market transactions. Such use-values Marxism calls 'commodities'. Exchange-value, then, is a property of commodities.

What property is it? The exchange-value of a commodity is its power of exchanging against quantities of other commodites. It is measured by the number of commodities of any other kind for which it will exchange under equilibrium conditions. Thus the exchange-value of a coat might be eight shirts, and also three hats, and also ten pounds sterling.

Exchange-value is a relative magnitude. Underlying the exchange-value of a commodity is its value, an absolute magnitude. A commodity a has n units of commodity b as its exchange-value just in case the ratio between the values of a and b is $n:1$. The exchange-values relative to one another of two commodities will remain the same when each changes in value if the changes are identical in direction and proportion.

The central claim of the labour theory of value is that magnitude of value is determined by socially necessary labour-time. To be more precise: the exchange-value of a commodity varies directly and uniformly with the quantity of labour-time required to produce it under standard conditions of productivity, and inversely and uniformly with the quantity of labour-time standardly required to

---

[1] Fuller definitions of the technical terms used here will be found in my *Karl Marx's Theory of History* (Oxford and Princeton, 1978), Appendix II.

produce other commodities, and with no further circumstance. The first condition alone states the mode of determination of value *tout court*.

The labour theory of value is not true by the very definition of value, as we defined it. In alternative presentations of the opening pages of Volume 1, value is *defined* as socially necessary labour-time. But a stipulative definition of a technical term is not a theory, and when value is defined as socially necessary labour-time, it cannot also be a central theoretical claim of the labour theory that socially necessary labour-time determines value. Still, those who favour the alternative definition sometimes do advance to a theoretical thesis, namely that value determines equilibrium-price: in equilibrium, price equals value, the latter being defined in terms of socially necessary labour-time.

The size of this dispute can be exaggerated. We have two propositions:

(1) Socially necessary labour-time determines value.
(2) Value determines equilibrium price.

We say that (2) is true by definition. Others say that (1) is.[2] But whoever is right, the conjunction of (1) and (2) entails that:

(3) Socially necessary labour-time determines equilibrium price.

And (3) is not true by definition, on any reckoning. As long as it is agreed that the labour theory of value, Volume 1 version, says (3), and that (3) is not true by definition, I do not wish to insist on my view that the definitional truth is (2) rather than (1). Almost all of what follows could be restated so as to accommodate the other definition. (One bad reason why the other definition finds favour will be presented later.)

We now turn to a supposed[3] corollary of the labour theory of value, the labour theory of surplus-value.

The labour theory of surplus-value is intended to explain the origin of non-wage income under capitalism. Call the energies and faculties

---

[2] For example, Ronald Meek, in *Smith, Ricardo and Marx*, London 1977, p. 95. Meek treats (1) as true by definition and (2) as the substantive thesis. He acknowledges on p. 127 that the issue is contestable.

[3] The labour theory of surplus-value is not, as I shall show elsewhere, validly derived from the labour theory of value.

the worker uses when labouring his *labour-power*. Now note that under capitalism labour-power is a commodity. It is sold in temporal packets by the worker to the capitalist. Being a commodity, it has a value, and like any commodity its value is, according to (1), determined by the amount of time required to produce it. But the amount of time required to produce it is identical with the amount of time required to produce the means of subsistence of the worker, since a man's labour-power is produced if and only if he is produced. Thus 'the value of labour-power is the value of the means of subsistence necessary for the maintenance of its owner'.[4] The origin of non-wage income is, then, the difference between the value of labour-power and the value produced by him in whom it inheres. It is the difference between the amount of time it takes to produce what is needed to keep a producer in being for a certain period and the amount of time he spends producing during that period.

The capital paid out as wages is equal to the value of the producer's labour-power. It is known as *variable capital*. The value produced by the worker over and above that represented by variable capital is called *surplus-value*. The ratio of surplus-value to variable capital is called *the rate of exploitation*:

$$\text{The rate of exploitation} = \frac{\text{surplus-value}}{\text{variable capital}}$$

$$= \frac{\text{surplus-value}}{\text{value of labour-power}}$$

$$= \frac{\text{time worked—time required to produce the worker}}{\text{time required to produce the worker}}$$

---

[4] Karl Marx, *Capital* Volume 1, Penguin Books in association with New Left Review, Harmondsworth 1976, p. 274. Strictly speaking, the value of labour-power is, according to Marx, the value of the means of subsistence needed to reproduce the labour supply, and therefore includes the value of the means of raising children. This complication, which does not benefit the theory, will be ignored here.

2

Why is the term 'exploitation' used for what the rate of exploitation is a rate of? Is it because the term, as used in that phrase, denotes a kind of injustice? It is hard to think of any other good reason for using such a term.

Yet many Marxists say that the Marxian concept of exploitation is a *purely* scientific one, with no moral content. They say that to assert, in the language of Marxism, that *a* exploits *b*, is to offer no condemnation or criticism of *a*, or of the arrangements under which *a* operates. For them, (4) is false:

(4) One reason for overthrowing capitalism is that it is a regime of exploitation (and exploitation is unjust).

Two kinds of Marxist deny (4). The first kind does so because he denies that there is *any* reason for overthrowing capitalism. One just does it, as it were. Or one does it because of one's class situation, or one's morally ungrounded identification with the class situation of other people.

The second kind believes that there are good reasons for overthrowing capitalism, but that injustice is not one of them, since justice, he says, is not a Marxian value. What is wrong with capitalism is not that it is unjust, but that it crushes human potential, destroys fraternity, encourages the inhumane treatment of man by man, and has other grave defects generically different from injustice.

Now I am certain that many Marxists have held (4), among them Karl Marx. But I shall not defend the last sentence. Marxists who deny it will find this essay less challenging, but I hope they will read it anyway. For while my main topic is the relationship between (4) and the labour theory of value, in pursuing it I uncover deep and neglected ambiguities in the labour theory of value itself, and no Marxist will deny that many Marxists do affirm the theory of value.

3

I begin with an argument which is based on the labour theory of value, and whose conclusion is that the worker is exploited, where that is taken to entail an injustice. We can call it the Traditional

Marxian Argument. It may be attributed to those believers in (4) who hold that the labour theory of value supports (4):

    (5) Labour and labour alone creates value.
    (6) The labourer receives the value of his labour-power.
    (7) The value of the product is greater than the value of his labour-power.
∴ (8) The labourer receives less value than he creates.
    (9) The capitalist receives the remaining value.
∴ (10) The labourer is exploited by the capitalist.

Premise (5) comes from the labour theory of value, and the labour theory of surplus-value supplies premises (6), (7), and (9).

This statement of the Traditional Marxian Argument is incomplete in two respects. First, an essential normative premise is not stated. Its content, in very general terms, is that, under certain conditions, it is (unjust) exploitation to obtain something from someone without giving him anything in return. To specify the conditions, and thereby make the premise more precise, is beyond the concern of this essay. A rough idea of exploitation, as a certain kind of lack of reciprocity, is all that we require.

The other incompleteness, also not to be rectified here, is the argument's failure, as stated, to characterize pertinent features of the relationship between capital and labour, such as the fact that the labourer is *forced*, by his propertylessness, to work for the capitalist. This disputed truth will not here receive the refined statement it deserves.[5]

Note, finally, that the Traditional Argument, like the rest of this essay, speaks of '*the* labourer' and '*the* capitalist', thereby individualizing the class relationship, in imitation of *Capital*'s practice. This sidesteps the problem of identifying the working and capitalist classes, which is greater now than it was in Marx's time. I am certain that the problem has a solution which preserves the application of

---

[5] One who disputes this truth is Robert Nozick, in *Anarchy, State, and Utopia*, New York 1974, pp. 262–264. The truth is defended against Nozick in my 'Robert Nozick and Wilt Chamberlain', in J. Arthur and W.H. Shaw (eds.), *Justice and Economic Distribution*, Englewood Cliffs, New Jersey, 1978, pp. 257–259. Some refinements are attempted in my 'Capitalism, Freedom and the Proletariat', in Alan Ryan (ed.), *The Idea of Freedom*, Oxford 1979.

arguments like the Traditional one, but it, too, is not provided in this paper.

4

The Traditional Argument employs the labour theory of surplus-value, which yields premises (6), (7), and (9). But they can be replaced by a truism, which will contribute no less well than they to the conclusion that the labourer is exploited. The result is this simpler Marxian argument (statement (11) is the truism):

(5) Labour and labour alone creates value.

(11) The capitalist receives some of the value of the product.

∴ (8) The labourer receives less value than he creates, and

(12) The capitalist receives some of the value the labourer creates.

∴ (10) The labourer is exploited by the capitalist.

The labour theory of *surplus*-value is, then, unnecessary to the moral claim Marxists make when they say that capitalism is exploitative. It does not matter what *explains* the difference between the value the worker produces and the value he receives.[6] What matters is just that there is that difference. (Note that although the Simpler Marxian Argument drops the labour theory of surplus-value, there is still *a* recognizable concept of surplus-value in it, namely the difference between the value the worker produces and the value he receives; and the value he receives can still be called variable capital.)[7]

5

We began with the labour theory of value, the thesis that the value of a commodity is determined by the socially necessary labour-time

---

[6] It does not matter to the moral claim about exploitation, even if it is interesting from other points of view.

[7] It is the concept of variable capital, not that of the value of labour-power, which is crucial in the key theoretical applications of the labour theory of value, for example, in the reproduction schemas, in the transformation of values into prices, in the doctrine of the tendency of the rate of profit to fall. *Capital* allows at least short-term divergences between the value of labour-power and variable capital per labourer; and wherever there is such a divergence, it is the second, not the first, which must be inscribed in the relevant equations.

required to produce it. We have arrived at an argument whose conclusion is that the labourer is exploited by the capitalist, and which supposedly draws one of its controversial premises from the labour theory of value. That is premise (5), that labour and labour alone creates value. But we shall now show that the labour theory does not entail (5). It entails, moreover, that (5) is false.[8]

Suppose a commodity has a certain value at a time t. Then that value, says the labour theory, is determined by the socially necessary labour-time required to produce a commodity of that kind. Let us now ask: required to produce it *when*? The answer is: at t, the time when it has the value to be explained. The amount of time required to produce it in the past, and, *a fortiori*, the amount of time actually spent producing it are magnitudes strictly irrelevant to its value, if the labour theory is true.

Extreme cases make the point clear. (a) Suppose there is a use-value a, which was produced in the past, when things such as a could come into being only through labour, but that labour is no longer required for things such as a to appear (perhaps a is a quantity of manna, produced by men at a time before God started what we imagine is His now usual practice of dropping it). Then according to the labour theory of value, a is valueless, despite the labour 'embodied' in it. (b) Contrariwise, suppose there is a commodity b now on the market, and that b was not produced by labour, but that a great deal of labour is now required for b-like things to appear. (B might be a quantity of clean air bottled before it became necessary to manufacture clean air.) Then b has a value, even though no labour is 'embodied' in it.[9]

These statements follow from the labour theory of value. The theory entails that past labour is irrelevant to how much value a

---

[8] In the traditional sense of (5), according to which part of what is claimed in saying that labour creates value is that quantity of value is a function of quantity of labour. Other possible senses, such as that dealt with in section X below, are irrelevant here.

[9] It might be objected that b cannot have a value for Marx, since he defines value for products of labour only. The textual point is probably correct (see *Capital* Volume 1, p. 128, for support), but no wise defender of Marx will want to urge in his defence the unfortunate lack of generality of the labour theory. Still, if anyone is impressed by the objection, let him imagine that *very little* labour went into b. The crucial point, which the extreme examples are only meant to dramatize, is that there is, according to the labour theory, 'continuous change of value-relations', since the amount of labour required to produce something of a certain kind is subject to variation. See *Capital* Volume 2, Harmondsworth pp. 152–3.

commodity now has.[10] But past labour would not be irrelevant if it created the value of the commodity. It follows that *labour does not create value, if the labour theory of value is true.*

Let us call the thesis that value is determined by socially necessary labour-time—that is, the labour theory of value—*the strict doctrine,* and let us say that such sentences as (5), or ones which speak of value as embodied or congealed labour, belong to *the popular doctrine.* Strict and popular doctrine are commonly confused with one another, for several reasons. The least interesting reason—more interesting ones will be mentioned later—is that Marx often set formulations from the two doctrines side by side. Examples:

'The value of a commodity is related to the value of any other commodity as the labour-time necessary for the production of the one is related to the labour-time necessary for the production of the other. "As exchange-values, all commodities are merely definite quantities of *congealed labour time.*"'

'. . . so far as the *quantity of value* of a commodity is determined, according to my account, through the *quantity of labour-time contained in it* etc., then [it is determined] through the normal amount of labour which the production of an object costs etc.'[11]

I am not saying that Marx never showed any awareness of the difference between the strict and the popular doctrine. This sentence proves otherwise: 'What determines value is not the amount of labour-time incorporated in products, but rather the amount of labour-time currently necessary.'[12] 'Currently necessary': at the time, that is, when the commodity has the given value. The relevant socially necessary labour-time is that required now, not that required when it was produced: 'The value of every commodity . . . is determined not

[10] Despite the misleading terminology in which it is cast, this is true even of Sraffa's 'dated quantities of labour' analysis. See P. Sraffa, *Production of Commodities by Means of Commodities,* Cambridge 1960, chapter 6; and I. Steedman, *Marx After Sraffa,* London, NLB, 1977, p. 70, n. 3.

[11] For the first example, see *Capital* Volume 1, p. 130. (Marx is quoting from his earlier work, *A Contribution to the Critique of Political Economy.*) For the second, see 'Notes on Adolph Wagner', in T. Carver (ed.), *Karl Marx: Texts on Method,* Oxford 1975, p. 184.

[12] Karl Marx, *Grundrisse,* trans. M. Nicolaus, Penguin Books in association with New Left Review, Harmondsworth 1973, p. 135. I have replaced Nicolaus's 'at a given moment' by 'currently', which gives a more literal translation.

by the necessary labour-time contained in it, but by the social labour-time required for its reproduction.'[13]

So I do not say that Marx was ignorant of the difference between the two doctrines. But I do say that the difference is damaging to key Marxian theses. It has grave implications, which are widely unnoticed and which were not noticed by Marx. Our chief concern is with implications for the idea of exploitation. There are also implications for pure economic theory, some of which will occupy us in a subsequent digression. But first let us look more carefully at the differences between the two formulations.

There are two reasons why the amount of labour which was actually spent on a particular product might differ from the amount now standardly required to produce that kind of product. The first is a non-standard level of efficiency in the actual labour process, which can be more or less efficient than the social norm. The second is technological change, which alters that norm.

Consider the case of inefficient labour. Marxists have always regarded it as a particularly inept criticism of the labour theory of value to object that it entails that an inefficiently produced lamp has more value than one produced efficiently and therefore in less time. And the asserted consequence does indeed fail to follow from the strict doctrine. But why should it not follow from the popular doctrine? If labour creates value by, as it were, congealing in the product, then if more labour is spent, must not more labour congeal, and will there not then be more value in the product?

The case of inefficient labour shows the incompatibility between the strict and the popular doctrines. Marxists know about that case, but they are nevertheless reluctant to reject the popular doctrine. After all, the reason why both doctrines exist in Marxist culture, why neither one is enough, is that each has intellectual or political functions (or both) of its own to fulfil. Accordingly, faced with problems such as that of inefficient labour, many Marxists propose a mixed formulation, the purpose of which is so to modify the popular doctrine as to bring it into line with the strict doctrine. And so it is said, in response to the case of inefficient labour, that

---

[13] *Capital* Volume 3, Moscow 1966, p. 141. (To reproduce a commodity is to produce another just like it.)

212

(13)The worker creates value *if, and only in so far as*, his labour is socially necessary.

To the extent that actual labour-time exceeds what is standardly required, labour is not value-creating. The formulation is obviously intended to preserve the popular idea of creation, without contradicting the strict doctrine. But we shall show that this cannot be done. The strict doctrine allows no such mixed formulations.

The strict doctrine certainly rules out (13), since (13) cites the wrong amount of socially necessary labour-time, namely that which is required when the commodity is being created,[14] rather than that which is required when the commodity is on the market. To have any prospect of being faithful to the strict doctrine, a mixed formulation must say not (13) but some such thing as this:

(14) The worker creates value *if, and only in so far as*, the amount of labour he performs *will be* socially necessary when the product is marketed.

Marxists think (14) follows from the strict doctrine because they mistakenly suppose that (14) follows from something the strict doctrine does entail, but which is of no relevant interest, namely,

(15) Value is determined by (that is, *inferable from*) expended labour-time when the amount expended is what will be socially necessary when the product is marketed.

Statement (15) does follow from the strict doctrine, just as (16) follows from the true doctrine about barometers:

(16) The height of a mercury column on day 2 is determined by (that is, *inferable from*) the atmospheric pressure on day 1 when day 1's atmospheric pressure is what day 2's atmospheric pressure will be.

Statement (16) is entailed by the truth that day 2's atmospheric pressure makes the height of the mercury column on day 2 what it is. But (16) does not entail that day 1's atmospheric pressure makes the height of the mercury column on day 2 what it is. And (15), similarly, gives no support to (14).

The general point is that if a magnitude *m* causally depends upon a magnitude *m'*, and it is given that a magnitude *m"* is equal to *m'*, then whatever *m"* is a magnitude of, magnitude *m will be inferable from*

[14] There may, of course, be no such unique quantity: so much the worse for (13).

magnitude m″. There could then be an illusion that magnitude $m″$ *explains* magnitude m. Just that illusion, I claim, seizes anyone who supposes that (14) is consistent with the strict doctrine.

An additional problem for the mixed formulation is the case of abnormally efficient labour, or of labour which used means of production superior to those now available, where in each instance *less* labour than is now socially necessary was expended. One cannot begin to claim in such a case that value is created by labour subject to the constraint that the amount expended will be socially necessary, since here not enough labour is expended. When there is *inefficiency*, there is a chance of pretending that some of the labour which occurred did not create value. Where there is special *efficiency*, there can be no similar pretense that labour which did not occur did create value.

We conclude that attempts to salvage the popular idea of creation by recourse to mixed formulations will not succeed.

6.

What was required in the past, and still more what happened in the past—these facts are in principle irrelevant to how much value a commodity has, if the labour theory of value is true. But they are not epistemically irrelevant. For since technical conditions change relatively slowly, socially necessary labour-time in the recent past is usually a good guide to socially necessary labour-time now. Typical past actual labour-time is, moreover, the best guide to how much labour-time was necessary in the past. Thereby what did occur becomes a good index of what is now required. It does not follow that it creates the value of the commodity.

Our argument shows that if the labour theory of value is true, labour does not create value. But it would be quixotic to seek a basis *other than* the labour theory of value for the proposition that labour creates value.[15] We may therefore take it that labour does not create value, whether or not the labour theory of value is true.

[15] In, that is, the traditional sense of 'labour creates value', which is the relevant sense here: see n. 8.

Some will ask, if labour does not create value, what does? But it is a prejudice to suppose that value must be *created*. Something must, of course, explain value and its magnitudes, but not all explainers are creators. One putative explanation of value magnitudes is the labour theory of value, the strict doctrine. But it identifies no creator of value, unless we suppose that explaining is creating. *What would now be needed to produce a commodity of a certain kind*—that is not a creator in any literal sense.

Why is the popular doctrine popular? One reason is that it appears more appropriate than the strict doctrine as a basis for a charge of exploitation. We shall see (sections 8 and 9) that neither doctrine supports such a charge, but it is clear that the popular doctrine *seems* better suited to do so, just because it alone says that labour *creates* value. But a partly distinct reason for the popularity of the popular doctrine is that certain arguments against the strict doctrine tend to be met by an illicit shift to popular formulations. This will be explained in the next section, where the theme of exploitation is in abeyance, and where I argue that the strict doctrine is false. The discussion of exploitation is completed in sections 8, 9, and 10, which do not presuppose the next one.

7

An obvious argument against the labour theory of value is that magnitude of value is affected by things other than socially necessary labour-time. One such different thing is the pattern of ownership of means of production, which can affect values, through the distribution of bargaining power which reflects it. Products of means of production on which there is some degree of monopoly are likely for that reason to command a higher price in equilibrium than they otherwise would, and therefore to have a higher value, under the definition of value we have given.

But if value is something the explanation of which must literally create it, then since ownership of means of production literally creates nothing, it would follow that, despite appearances, the pattern of that ownership cannot affect value formation. And that is what a Marxist says. He says that labour alone creates *value*: the pattern of ownership can affect price, and hence how much value various owners *get*. But no part of what they get is created by ownership.

But this line of defence depends essentially on the idea that labour *creates* value. If we stay with the strict doctrine, which rightly does not require that anything *creates* value, it has no motivation whatsoever.

To make this more clear, we return to the three propositions in our initial presentation of the labour theory of value:

(1) Socially necessary labour-time determines value.
(2) Value determines equilibrium price.
(3) Socially necessary labour-time determines equilibrium price.

Recall our view that the definitional statement is (2), and that (1) is the substantive theory. (1) and (2) entail (3). We said we would say why some prefer to see (1) as true by definition. Here is one reason why.

Counterexamples to (3) abound, such as the one we noted about pattern of ownership of means of production, or the cases of divergences in period of production and organic composition of capital. Statement (3) is false, and much of Volumes 2 and 3 of *Capital* is devoted to this fact.

Now if (3) is false, one *at least* of (1) and (2) must be false. If (2) is true by definition, then (1) is false, and the labour theory of value is sunk. What Marxists therefore do is to treat (1) as true by definition—so that counterexamples to (3) cannot touch it—and then simply drop (2). But this deprives the labour theory of all substance. That consequence is, however, concealed by construing (1) in a popular fashion, by thinking of it as saying something like: labour *creates* value, for that does not look like a definition. It is then said that whatever determines market ratios, and thereby who gets what amounts of value, labour alone creates the value there is to get. The popular doctrine supplies an appearance of substance when, under pressure of counterexample, (1) is treated as true by definition, (2) is dropped, and the theory is, in reality, drained of all substance. Volume 1 of *Capital*, because of its simplifying assumptions, can proceed under definition (2) of value. When the assumptions are relaxed, (1) and (2) cannot both be true. Hence, in Volumes 2 and 3, statement (2) is abandoned.

At this point it is instructive to look at a central part of Marx's critique of Ricardo. If I am right, it depends on popular formulations. Ricardo defined value as at (2) above, and provisionally asserted something like (1), and therefore, too, (3). He then acknowledged that variations in period of production falsify (3), and therefore falsify (1) (since (2) is true by definition). So he allowed deviation of value (that is, equilibrium price) from socially necessary labour-time.[16]

According to Marx, Ricardo was here misled by appearances. The true deviation is not of value from socially necessary labour-time, but of equilibrium price from value (that is, socially necessary labour-time).[17]

Now both Ricardo and Marx say that equilibrium price deviates from socially necessary labour-time. What then is the theoretical difference between them? I believe that it can be stated only in popular discourse, to which Marx therefore resorts here. For he says that variations in period of production and organic composition do not affect how much value is *created*, but only how much is *appropriated* at the various sites of its creation. But if one asked, exactly what is it that labour is here said to create?, then, I contend, there would be no answer, once value is no longer, as now it cannot be, defined as at (2).[18]

The labour theory of value comes in two versions, strict and popular. The two contradict one another. But the labour theorist cannot, by way of remedy, simply drop the popular version. For despite their mutual inconsistency, each version can appear true only when it is thought to receive support from the other: 'Labour creates value' seems (but is not) a simple consequence of the thesis that value is determined by socially necessary labour-time, and that thesis appears to survive refutation only when it is treated as interchangeable with the idea that labour creates value.

[16] See chapter 1 of any edition of Ricardo's *Principles of Political Economy*; and see Mark Blaug, *Economic Theory in Retrospect*, London 1968, pp. 96 ff. for a brief, accessible exposition.

[17] See *Theories of Surplus-Value*, vol. 2, Moscow 1968, pp. 106, 174–180, and *Grundrisse*, pp. 562–563.

[18] Hence, if I am right, the transformation problem is a strictly incoherent problem, whether or not it has a mathematical 'solution'.

8

In this section I shall identify the real basis of the Marxian imputation of exploitation to the capitalist production process, the proposition which really animates Marxists, whatever they may think and say. The real basis is not the commonly stated one, sentence (5), but a fairly obvious truth which owes nothing to the labour theory of value, and which is widely confused with (5). And since (5) is itself confused with the labour theory of value, the latter is confused with the fairly obvious truth to be stated.[19]

A by-product of our discussion, then, will be an explanation why the labour theory of value, which ought to be controversial, is considered even by very intelligent Marxists to be a fairly obvious truth. When Marxists think obviously true what others think not obvious at all, one side at least is very wrong, and an explanation of the error in terms of class position or ideological standpoint is not enough, because it does not show how the error is possible, by what intellectual mechanism it can occur. What follows will help to explain how it is possible for very intelligent Marxists to be mistaken.

Recall what has been shown. We have seen that if the labour theory of value is true, then labour does not create value. For if labour creates value, past labour creates value; and if past labour creates value, then past labour determines the value of the product. But the labour theory of value says that value magnitudes are determined by currently necessary labour-time. It follows that past labour does not create value, if the labour theory of value is true. There is, moreover, no plausible alternative basis on which to assert that labour creates value. Hence it is false that labour creates value. And we shall show in section 9 that even if it were true, it would not be a sound basis for a charge of exploitation.

Nor does the labour theory of value itself, strictly formulated, form such a basis. Any such impression disappears once we see that it does not entail that the workers create value. In fact, the labour theory of value does not entail that the workers create anything.

---

[19] 'Is confused with' is not a transitive relation, but the above statement is nonetheless true.

218

Yet the workers manifestly create something. They create the product. They do not create *value*, but they create *what has value*. The small difference of phrasing covers an enormous difference of conception. What raises a charge of exploitation is not that the capitalist gets some of the value the worker produces, but that he gets some of the value *of what* the worker produces. Whether or not workers produce value, they produce the product, that which has value.

And no one else does. Or, to speak with greater care, producers are the only persons who produce what has value: it is true by definition that no human activity other than production produces what has value. This does not answer the difficult question, Who is a producer? But whatever the answer may be, only those whom it identifies can be said to produce what has value. And we know before we have the full answer that owners of capital, considered as such, cannot be said to do so.

Note that I am not saying that whatever has value was produced by labour, for I have not said that whatever has value was produced. I also do not deny that tools and raw materials are usually needed to produce what has value. The assertion is that labourers, in the broadest possible sense, are the only persons who produce anything which has value, and that capitalists are not labourers in that sense. If they were, capital and labour would not be distinct 'factors of production':[20] the capitalist supplies capital, which is not a kind of labour.

Some will question the claim that owners of capital, considered as such, do not produce anything. An owner of capital can, of course, *also* do some producing, for example, by carrying out a task which would otherwise fall to someone in his hire. Then he is a producer, but not *as* an owner of capital. More pertinent is the objection that owners of capital, in their very capacity as such, fulfil significant productive functions, in risking capital, making investment decisions,

[20] I use scare-quotes because there are good Marxian objections to the classification of capital and labour as distinct but comparable factors of production: note that in a sense all that is required for production is capital, since capital buys not only means of production but also labour. That only hints at the objections, which are given in chapter 48 of *Capital* Volume 3, and which do not affect the point made in the text above.

and so forth. But whether or not that is true, it does not entail that they produce anything in the importantly distinct sense in issue here. It does not entail, to put it one way, that they engage in the activity of producing.

To act productively it is enough that one does something which helps to bring it about that a thing is produced, and that does not entail participating in producing it. You cannot cut without a knife, but it does not follow that, if you lack one and I lend you one, thereby making cutting possible, then I am a cutter, or any other sort of producer. The distinction is between productive activities and producing activities. Capitalists arguably engage in the former, but once the distinction is clear, it is evident that they do not (unless they are not only capitalists) engage in the latter.

To be sure, *if*—what I here neither assert nor deny—the capitalist is a *productive* non-producer, that will have a bearing on the thesis that he is an exploiter. It will be a challenge to a charge of exploitation whose premise is that he produces nothing. But it would be wrong to direct the challenge against the *premiss* of that charge, that he produces nothing. As this is generally intended, it cannot be denied.

And it is this fairly obvious truth which, I contend, lies at the heart of the Marxist charge of exploitation. The real basis of that charge is not that the workers produce value, but that they produce what has it. The real Marxian argument for (10) is not the Simpler Marxian Argument (see section 4), but this different one (the Plain Argument):

(17) The labourer is the only person who creates the product, that which has value.

(11) The capitalist receives some of the value of the product.

∴ (18) The labourer receives less value than the value of what he creates, and

(19) The capitalist receives some of the value of what the labourer creates.

∴ (10) The labourer is exploited by the capitalist.

The Plain Argument is constructed in analogy with the Simpler Marxian Argument, under the constraint that premise (17) replaces premise (5). The arguments are totally different, but very easy to confuse with one another.

9

I have said that it is labour's creation of what has value, not its (supposed) creation of value, which founds the charge that capitalism is a system of exploitation. I must now defend this position. We have seen that labour does not create value. I now argue that even if it did, that would have no bearing on the question of exploitation.

The proposition that labour creates value is, to begin with, unnecessary to the thesis that labour is exploited. For if we suppose that something else creates value, the impression that labour is exploited, if it was there before, persists. Thus imagine that the magnitude of value of a commodity is wholly determined by the extent and intensity of desire for it, and that we can therefore say that value is created by desire and not by labour. If it remains true that labour creates all that has value, and that the capitalist appropriates some of the value, does the charge of exploitation lose force? Surely not. Then the assertion that the workers create value cannot be necessary to that charge, since here we suppose that something else creates value, and the charge persists.

But the claim that labour creates value is not only unnecessary to the charge of exploitation. It is no reason whatever for laying such a charge. Once again, we make the point by imagining that desire creates value. If labour's creation of value would give the labourer a claim to value *because* he had created it, then so would the desirer's creation of value give him a claim on that basis. Yet would we say that desirers are exploited because they create the value of the product, and the capitalist receives part of that value? The suggestion is absurd.[21] It must then be equally absurd to think that labourers are exploited *because* they create value which others receive.

[21] Note that I am not saying that a person's desire for something is no reason why he should receive it. Of course it is a reason, albeit one singularly capable of being overriden. But a man's desire for something cannot be a reason for his receiving it *on the ground* that his desire for it enhances its value, even if his desire for it does enhance its value. That ground is surely unintelligible.

One more caveat. I do not suppose in the above paragraphs or anywhere else that the correct principle of reward is according to productive contribution. One can hold that the capitalist exploits the worker by appropriating part of the value of what the worker produces without holding that all of that value should go to the worker. One can affirm a principle of distribution according to need, and add that the capitalist exploits the worker because need is not the basis on which he receives part of the value of what the worker produces.

It is absurd, but it does not seem absurd, and the explanation of the discrepancy is that it is impossible to forget that labour creates what has value. Creating value, when we suppose that workers do that, seems to count, because we naturally think that they could create value only by creating what has it, and the relevance of the latter is mistakenly transmitted to the former. Part of the case for saying that (17) is the real basis of the charge of exploitation is that (5) cannot be yet seems to be, and the relationship between (17) and (5) explains the illusion.

But there is also more direct reason for thinking that the essential thing is labour's creation of what has value. Look at the lines from 'Solidarity', with which this article began. They say nothing about value, and the labour theory is not required to appreciate their point, which is that 'we' are exploited. They do say that 'we' have made all these valuable things.

It is, then, neither the labour theory of value (that socially necessary labour-time determines value), nor its popular surrogate (that labour creates value), but the fairly obvious truth (that labour creates what has value) rehearsed in the song, which is the real basis of the Marxian imputation of exploitation.

We have been discussing the exploitation of the propertyless wage-worker under capitalism. But if anything is the *paradigm* of exploitation in Marxism, it is the exploitation of the feudal serf, who does not, according to Marx, produce value. His exploitation is the most manifest. The proletarian's is more covert, and it is by arguing that his position may in fact be assimilated to the serf's that Marx seeks to show that he too is exploited.

The exploitation of the serf is manifest, because nothing is more clear than that part of what he produces redounds not to him but to his feudal superior. This is not so in the same plain sense under capitalism, where the product itself is not divided between capitalist and worker, but marketed.[22]

Now Marxists allege that the labour theory of value is required to uncover the exploitation of the wage-worker, but I disagree. What is needed is not the false and irrelevant labour theory, but the mere concept of value, as defined, independently of the labour theory, in our sentence (2). It enables us to say that, whatever may be

[22] For further discussion and textual references, see my *Karl Marx's Theory of History*, pp. 333–334.

responsible for magnitudes of value, the worker does not receive all of the value of his product.

Marxists say that

(20) The serf produces the whole product, but the feudal lord appropriates part of the product; and

(21) The proletarian produces all of the value of the product, but the capitalist appropriates part of the value of the product.

I accept (20), but modify the first part of (21) so that it resembles the first part of (20), with this result:

(22) The proletarian produces the whole product, but the capitalist appropriates part of the value of the product.

The exploitation of the proletarian is, on my account, more similar to the exploitation of the serf than traditional Marxism says.

10

In the last two sections I have insisted that labour creates what has value, and I have continued to deny that labour creates value itself. Yet it might be objected that the insistence contradicts the denial, that, in short, (23) is true:

(23) Since labour creates what has value, labour creates value.

But the objection is misguided. For *if* there is a sense of 'labour creates value' in which (23) is true, it is not the relevant traditional sense, that intended by Marxists when they assert (5). 'Labour creates what has value' could not entail 'labour creates value' where the latter is a contribution to explaining the magnitude of the value of commodities, as (5) is supposed to be. How could it follow from the fact that labour creates what has value that the *amount* of value in what it creates varies directly and uniformly with the amount of labour expended?[23]

Is there a sense, distinct from that of (5), in which 'labour creates value' does follow from 'labour creates what has value'? Probably

---

[23] And if it did follow, then the labour theory of value, the strict doctrine, would be false.

there is. If an artist creates a beautiful object out of something which was less beautiful, then we find it natural to say that he creates beauty. And it would be similarly natural to say of a worker who creates a valuable object out of something less valuable that he creates value. But that would not support the popular version of the labour theory of value, though it would help to explain why so many Marxists mistakenly adhere to it.

I have argued that if anything justifies the Marxian charge that the capitalist exploits the worker it is the true proposition (17), that workers alone create the product. It does not follow that (17) is a sound justification, and that the Plain Argument, suitably expanded,[24] is a good argument. Having disposed of the distracting labour theory of value, I hope to provide an evaluation of the Plain Argument elsewhere.

[24] By addition of refined versions of the premisses adverted to in section III above.

Real Abstractions and Anomalous Assumptions

Susan Himmelweit
Simon Mohun

Debate about the fundamental categories of Marxist economics is as old as Marxism itself, but with the collapse of the long post-1945 boom in the world economy, orthodox economics has been shown to be wanting, and interest in such debate revived during the 1970s.* While the debate has touched virtually all areas of Marxian economics, basically it concerns the nature and status of value theory and its relation to the everyday concepts of wages, prices, and profit. Positions on other questions, such as productive and unproductive labour, or whether movements in the rate of profit exhibit tendencies, cannot be taken prior to understanding the fundamental dispute about value. This paper is a contribution to this debate; it addresses the problems central to the modern 'neo-Ricardian' critique of Marx's theory of value. While our discussion of these problems attempts to respond to this critique, it is not thereby concerned to defend the letter of Marx's writings uncritically. Our aim is rather to highlight the issues on which understanding of the concept of value turns, and to examine the theoretical implications of different understandings.

We have had some difficulty with terminology. One of the main points we shall make is that Marx separated certain categories that for others are not different. Thus, for example, Marx distinguishes

* We would like to thank the encouragingly large number of comrades of the Conference of Socialist Economists (CSE), from the UK, USA, and Holland, who took the time and trouble to read earlier drafts of this paper and to send us comments on them. An earlier version was published as 'The Anomalies of Capital' in *Capital and Class*, 6, autumn 1978, and given at the November 1978 conference on 'Value Theory and Contemporary Analysis', sponsored by *New Left Review, Cambridge Journal of Economics*, and the CSE.

'exchange-value' from 'value', while Ricardo tries to make 'value' do for both. In general, we have tried to use the terminology of the author under discussion, but clearly we have had to move into Marx's usage when making specific criticism of the elaboration of the categories themselves. We hope that this will not cause any confusion. In the interests of (at least initial) clarity, we will give our understanding of Marx's usage here. That of other authors, we hope, can be understood from the context.

For Marx, commodities have value because they are produced for exchange in a society in which commodity relations have become generalized. This differentiates them from products of labour in general, and means that the 'value of every commodity . . . is determined not by the necessary labour-time contained in it, but by the *social* labour-time required for its reproduction.'[1] And that social labour-time is validated only by exchange in the market. It is as exchange-values that commodities so exchange. Commodities are bought and sold for money, and the quantity of money for which they exchange is called their price. Money becomes the standard of value, and so the determination of exchange-value is immediately the determination of price; any theory of one is therefore automatically a theory of the other. Accordingly, we use the phrases 'theory of price' and 'theory of exchange-value' interchangeably.

Another pair of categories that Marx distinguished but Ricardo did not are those of abstract and concrete labour. So when we use 'labour' referring to Ricardo, we mean neither abstract nor concrete labour but an undifferentiated category. This is important, for it is easy to slip into viewing Ricardo as merely having failed to make Marx's abstraction, and thinking that what Marx called 'concrete labour' was simply Ricardo's 'labour'. We shall show why we consider this view mistaken.

It is important to note that in general 'abstract' does not mean 'theoretical'; concrete categories are also theoretical and 'facts' themselves are but abstractions. However, a mere consideration of empirical facts (surface phenomena) leads us nowhere. Abstractions are validated as starting-points for analysis if and only if their elaboration produces an understanding of more concrete categories. This seems to us what Marx meant when he wrote: 'The concrete is

[1] Karl Marx, *Capital* Volume 3, London 1972, p. 141.

226

concrete because it is the concentration of many determinations, hence unity of the diverse. It appears in the process of thinking, therefore, as a process of concentration, as a result, not as a point of departure, even though it is the point of departure in reality and hence also the point of departure for observation and conception.'[2]

A final terminological point: we occasionally talk of certain theories and abstractions as unscientific. We mean this in the minimal sense that they hypostasize some category that is historically specific—that is, they take a category that requires explanation as a facet of capitalist production relations and eternalize it, taking it as a given, whether of people, nature, or production in general.

The plan of our paper is this. The first section considers the Ricardian labour theory of value and the fundamental contradiction in which it is enmeshed. The second considers Marx's theory of value, and shows how this theory, while located within a totally different method, incorporates, reformulates, and can thereby resolve Ricardo's dilemma. The next section outlines Marx's critique of Ricardo, making the methodological differences between them more explicit, and concludes with a taxonomy of current positions on the basis of their stance with respect to Ricardo's dilemma. The final two sections examine the current indictment of value on charges of redundancy and inconsistency; the alternative understandings of value are shown to determine what case there is to answer.

1. Ricardo and Embodied Labour

The modern criticisms that have been directed at Marx's theory of value have their origin in Ricardian value theory. The latter must consequently be examined so as to situate subsequent discussion. We must first determine the precise significance of Marx's advance on Ricardo, and we can then show that the epithet 'neo-Ricardian', while often employed as a term of abuse, does have a certain descriptive meaning and validity.

Ricardo developed his theory as an attack upon Adam Smith's cost-determined theory of price. As Ricardo saw it, Smith's view was

[2] Karl Marx, *Grundrisse*, Penguin Books in association with New Left Review, Harmondsworth 1973, p. 101.

that in a society characterized by private property, the price of a commodity was determined by the sum of its three constituent parts: wages, profit, and rent. As Smith put it, 'wages, profit and rent are the three original sources . . . of all exchangeable value'.[3]

Nevertheless, Smith did recognize that 'in that early and rude state of society which precedes both the accumulation of stock and the appropriation of land, the proportion between the quantities of labour necessary for acquiring different objects, seems to be the only circumstance which can afford any rule for exchanging them for one another.'[4]

But he found such a 'labour theory of value' to be insufficient after the emergence of private property and the accumulation of means of production, for it takes no account of rent and profit. Accordingly, Smith abandoned his labour theory in favour of what Marx later dubbed the 'trinity formula'.[5]

In this context, Ricardo's achievement was to generalize Smith's labour theory from the 'early and rude stage of society' to a world in which production involves the use of accumulated stock (capital) and privately owned land. Ricardo rejected any notion that the value of a commodity was determined by the remuneration due to the owners of the labour, capital, and land required to produce it. Instead, he held that the value of a commodity was determined by the quantity of labour necessary for its production—both direct labour and indirect labour embodied in the means of production. Thus Ricardo's labour theory of value is essentially an embodied-labour theory. And Ricardo is quite clear about how he differs with Smith:

'Adam Smith thought, that as in the early stages of society, all the produce of labour belonged to the labourer, and as after stock was accumulated, a part went to profits, that accumulation, necessarily, without any regard to the different degrees of durability of capital, or any other circumstance whatever, *raised* the prices or exchangeable value of commodities, and consequently that their value was no

[3] Adam Smith, *An Inquiry into the Nature and Causes of the Wealth of Nations*, London 1904, p. 57.

[4] Ibid., p. 52.

[5] Smith's discussion is in chapter 6 of *The Wealth of Nations*. Marx's assessment of Smith is in *Theories of Surplus-Value*, vol. 2, London 1969, p. 165, and his discussion of the 'trinity formula' in *Capital* Volume 3, Part VII.

longer regulated by the quantity of labour necessary to their production. In opposition to him, I maintain that it is not because of this division into profits and wages,—it is not because capital accumulates, that exchangeable value varies, but it is in all stages of society, owing only to two causes: one the more or less quantity of labour required, the other the greater or less durability of capital: that the former is never superseded by the latter, but is only modified by it.'[6]

In this letter to James Mill (dated 28 December 1818) Ricardo raises issues germane to current controversies. On the one hand, he had posited a theory of the value of products independent of and prior to their division between classes. In other words, he maintained, commodities have an inherent value, which is *subsequently* allocated according to the claims of each class according to its role in production. This contrasts with Smith's view that the sum of demands for remuneration arising from production relations (i.e. costs) constitutes the value of the commodity itself. But on the other hand, although Ricardo was not always consistent, he generally considered 'exchangeable value' and 'value' synonymous concepts, and whilst he rejected Smith's view of value as *determined* by the sum of costs, he still required their equality. For in any theory of 'equilibrium price'—the term modern vulgar economy (neo-classical economics) gives to 'exchangeable value'—this price, tautologically, must equal the total costs paid, because the money paid for a commodity must be remuneration for someone, and a fully inclusive definition of costs is just total remuneration.[7]

This is why Ricardo was forced to recognize that the durability of

---

[6] David Ricardo, *On the Principles of Political Economy and Taxation*, P. Sraffa (ed.), Cambridge 1951, pp. xxxvi–xxxvii.

[7] The point here is that a tautology is not a theory (though the statement of a tautology may well have ideological content). In formal logic prices are tautologically a sum of costs, but this is not an explanation unless we have some *independent* explanation of costs. There are different ways of evading the need to explain costs. Smith appeared at times not to try at all. Sraffa takes one cost (the wage, or the rate of profit) as given, derives the remaining ones from this, and sums to derive prices. The unexplained part is clearly the initial 'given' cost. Neo-classical economics derives costs from initial endowments, technology, and individual preferences, which are themselves unexplained. Sraffians sometimes use class-struggle in the same way. All such 'theories' do is to draw out by formal logic the implications of their own assumptions; for this

capital modified the determination of value by the quantity of labour embodied. For if commodities do actually exchange in proportion to their embodied labour-times, then the annual rate of profit of a capitalist whose capital has to be tied up for a longer period will be less than that of one whose capital is used faster, even if the total amounts of embodied labour in the two cases are the same. But prices clearly cannot remain in this ratio. The price of the more slowly produced commodity must, in equilibrium, be higher than that of the other—otherwise no capitalist will advance capital for its production. Since it is not the case that all commodities involve that capital be tied up for equal lengths of time, it follows that if value is to be identified with equilibrium price (exchange-value), it cannot be determined by embodied labour-time without modification.

With respect to the durability of capital Ricardo made two very closely related points. He defined capital to be circulating capital if it is turned over at least once in the time period under consideration (i.e., if it is totally consumed during that period), and to be fixed capital if it is turned over in a longer period (i.e., if it is not totally consumed during the period in question). Now, consider two capitals embodying the same total labour. First, they may be very differently divided into fixed and circulating components. Second, they may be identically so divided, but their fixed components may be of different durabilities. Either way, although total embodied labour is the same for each capital, the commodities produced by them must differ in (exchange-)value, because of the different times for which the various components of each capital are tied up. This is necessarily the case in an economy in which competition equalizes the rate of profit on each capital over the time period being considered. Since the distinction between fixed and circulating capital refers merely to the time period chosen, the two cases can be subsumed under a single generic point: since each capital must receive the same rate of profit in equilibrium,

reason they can be classified as vulgar. Within historical materialism, labouring activity provides the basis for explanation. So from this perspective only Ricardo and Marx escape from this classification, because their theories of value have an independent basis in the production process. But it is only Marxian theory that has an ontology of human labour whose dialectical development is both produced by and explains the history of the categories of capitalism. Such a development of the category value is the central concern of this article.

different turnover times must modify the determination of (exchange-) value by labour embodied.

It cannot be stressed too strongly (given their contemporary currency) that these results are not new; they emerge from the first chapter of Ricardo's *Principles,* and indeed gave Ricardo a great deal of trouble. Thus he wrote to McCulloch in June 1820, 'I sometimes think that if I were to write the chapter on value again which is in my book, I should acknowledge that the relative value of commodities was regulated by two causes instead of by one, namely, by the relative quantity of labour necessary to produce the commodities in question, and by the rate of profit for the time that the capital remained dormant, and until the commodities were brought to market.'[8]

But he persisted with his embodied-labour theory of value, writing four months later to Malthus, 'You say that my proposition "that with few exceptions the quantity of labour employed on commodities determines the rate at which they will exchange for each other, is not well founded". I acknowledge that it is not rigidly true, but I say that it is the nearest approximation to truth, as a rule for measuring relative value, of any I have ever heard.'[9] Yet Malthus was correct within this framework. For with the formation of a general rate of profit in the economy, the exchange-values of commodities do vary with both the quantity of embodied labour and the temporal structure of the embodiment of that labour in capitals of different durabilities. If these structures differ, then so do relative (exchange-) values from ratios of embodied labour. Ricardo was reduced to saying that embodied labour was the most important element in the determination of value. But in a theory concerned solely to explain the magnitude of exchange-value, this is an arbitrary assertion.

Thus Ricardo refused to concede that embodied labour-time might not be the predominant determinant of exchange-value; but to justify this refusal he should have set himself the problem of deriving the necessary differences between value and price from the determination of value itself. To pose the problem in this way, however, requires a distinction between the categories of value and exchange-value not consistently present in Ricardo's work. The recognition of the

[8] Ricardo, *On the Principles of Political Economy,* pp. xxxix–xl.
[9] Ibid.

contradiction between an embodied-labour theory of value and a cost-summation account of price marks the limits of Ricardo's scientific achievement.[10]

2. Marx and Abstract Labour

Two resolutions of Ricardo's contradiction are possible. One way out is to abandon the first approximation of the embodied-labour theory of value in favour of some other account of the magnitude of exchange-value. Historically, this path charted the retreat from science to vulgar economy. The other resolution involves the complete reconceptualization of value, a recasting of the theory of value as an abstraction, rather than a hypostatized assumption, wherein its significance and status are such that its apparent inconsistencies can be recreated as the expression of the real contradictions of capitalist society. This was Marx's project, the development of a theory of value as the specific application of his method of historical materialism in analysing the production relations of capitalism.

The method of historical materialism defines the *differentiae specificae* of epochs of history by class relations established between those who produce and those who appropriate the surplus. That is, what 'distinguishes the various economic formations of society . . . is the form in which this surplus labour is in each case extorted from the immediate producer, the worker.[11] More generally: 'The specific economic form, in which unpaid surplus labour is pumped out of direct producers, determines the relationship of rulers and ruled, as it grows directly out of production itself and, in turn, reacts upon it as a determining element. Upon this, however, is founded the entire formation of the economic community which grows up out of the production relations themselves, thereby simultaneously its specific

[10] This formulation of Ricardo's contradiction is to be found in B. Fine, *'Marx's Economics: A Dual Theory of Value and Growth*, by M. Morishima. A Review', in *Bulletin of the Conference of Socialist Economists*, vol. 4, no. 12 (October 1975), and B. Fine, *Economic Theory and Ideology*, London 1980.

[11] Karl Marx, *Capital* Volume 1, Penguin Books in association with New Left Review, Harmondsworth 1976, p. 325.

political form. It is always the direct relationship of the owners of the conditions of production to the direct producers—a relation always naturally corresponding to a definite stage in the development of the methods of labour and thereby its social productivity—which reveals the innermost secret, the hidden basis of the entire social structure.'[12]

The application of this understanding to capitalist societies, then, requires first of all investigation of that which is *specific* to the *form* of production in these societies, namely that it is the production of *commodities*. For without this, the specific form of surplus extraction that defines the capitalist mode of production could not be described. This is because capitalist exploitation is the form of surplus extraction that requires for its definition only relations of commodity production and exchange, including, crucially, the exchange of labour-power as a commodity. For the extraction of surplus-value, which distinguishes capitalism from other class modes of production, is itself a commodity relation. Hence, while Marx had many different starting-points in his analysis, he settled on the commodity to begin his final exposition.

The distinguishing feature of commodities is that they are produced for exchange. In such an exchange process, two commodities are measured against each other in determinate proportions, yielding a relation of equivalence between a certain quantity of one commodity and a certain quantity of the other. There is therefore an *equalization* of the commodities as far as their *exchange-value* is concerned, and a *differentiation* with respect to their *use-values* (the effects to be gained from subsequent consumption of the commodities). Exchange-value is thus merely that which is posed as equal in the pure act of exchange, something manifested by commodities in exchange, *after* their production. But since what is at issue is the production relations of capitalism, the analysis rather than abstracting from the production process itself, has to investigate what it is that differentiates the production of commodities from that of products in general.

Since production of a commodity is the production of both a use-value and an exchange-value, a similar distinction between the labour

[12] *Capital* Volume 3, p. 791.

that produces the one aspect and the labour that produces the other is generated. The labour that produces the individuated useful properties of a commodity is useful or concrete labour; such labour produces products, but it is only in certain sorts of societies that products become commodities. For in these societies, in addition to the aspect of labour that produces use-values, there is another aspect of labour, which produces use-values as *commodities*; this is abstract labour. Marx's 'value' is the product of abstract labour. Accordingly, value is a category of commodity production, whose *form* is exchange-value; what gives commodities exchange-value is the labour that remains upon abstraction from the labour that produces use-value. Since this abstraction is real, produced by the history of capitalist society, the answer to the question of what gives commodities exchange-value is already pre-empted by that very question, for all that Marx has to do is to specify the nature of commodity-producing labour. So to talk of the proof of such a specification is meaningless. But within the framework of historical materialism, that Marx's answer is not arbitrary is ensured by the nature of exchange itself, since it effects, as a real process, the commensuration of the products of labour under commodity production.

There can thus be no a priori determination of abstract labour, for not until commodities are actually exchanged on the market can the products of individual producers satisfy the needs of others. It is the process of exchange on the market that manifests the social character of individual labours, establishes the social connections between independent commodity producers, and thereby determines that the value realized in exchange (exchange-value) is the form of appearance of that labour, and only that labour, which is socially necessary for the production of the commodity in question. Hence value is measured not in units of embodied labour-time, but rather in units of 'socially necessary labour-time'. Thus the reduction of labour to abstract labour can be done only by the market: the value of a commodity has to be expressed, and then only *after* the event, in the use-value of another commodity.

Eventually, one commodity becomes that against which the value of all other commodities is expressed; one commodity becomes the universal equivalent, that is, assumes the money-form. 'Commodities first enter into the process of exchange ungilded and unsweetened, retaining their original home-grown shape. Exchange, however, produces a differentiation of the commodity into two elements, commodity and money, an external opposition which expresses the opposition between use-value and value which is inherent in it. In this opposition, commodities as use-values confront money as exchange-value. On the other hand, both sides of this opposition are commodities, hence themselves unities of use-value and value. . . . These antagonistic forms of the commodities are the real forms of motion of the process of exchange.'[13]

The separation of the expression of the value of a commodity from the commodity itself is now complete. The value of a commodity has no expression except as exchange-value, commensuration of itself against another commodity in the market. But this exchange-value itself has no expression except against one particular commodity, money. Price is this sole expression of value (and exchange-value). There is no manifestation of value in terms of its substance, abstract labour, nor of its measure, socially necessary labour-time. The only form in which value appears, and the only way it *can* appear, is in terms of the money commodity (gold, for example) and its quantitative measure (weight, for example). This is what the *price* of a commodity is, the quantity of the money-commodity for which it will exchange. It is the only form in which exchange-value is expressed, and clearly therefore the only form for the expression of value too.

Marx summarized his method as follows: 'I do not proceed on the basis of "concepts", hence also not from the "value-concept", and I do not have the task of "dividing" it up in any way, for that reason. What I proceed from is the simplest social form in which the product of labour in contemporary society manifests itself, and this as "commodity". That is what I analyse, and first of all, to be sure, in *the form in which it appears.* Now I find at this point that it is, on the one hand, in its natural form a *thing of use-value,* alias *use-value,* and on the other hand that it is *bearer of exchange-value,* and is itself an exchange-value from this point of view. Through further analysis of the latter I discovered that exchange-value is only an "appearance-form", an independent mode of manifestation of the *value* which is contained in the commodity, and then I approach the analysis of this value.'[14]

His starting point, then, is not an arbitrary assumption, but a reality: the commodity, considered as the social, historically specific form of the product. And the abstraction that allows this consideration of the commodity-*form* is a real one. The process of the theoretical discovery of abstract labour is not merely a process of mental generalization, but has a real existence in the reality of the exchange process. The equalization of products of labour on the market occurs every day, standardized by money, the universal equivalent of value. Since individuals alienate their products as commodities in exchange, so too do they alienate the labour producing those commodities. Abstract labour is a real activity, a social reality, whereby individuals alienate their labour-power from themselves.

The analysis of the commodity form thus reveals exchange to be more than the equalization of products. For equality of human labour under capitalism *can only take the form* of equality of commodity values; the measure of abstract labour in terms of socially necessary labour-time *can only take the form* of a quantitative value-relation between the products of labour; and the social relations between the producers *can only take the form* of social relations between their products. This of course is central to Marx's theory of value, for 'the labour of the private individual manifests itself as an element of the total labour of society only through the relations which the act of exchange establishes between the products, and, through their mediation, between the producers. To the producers therefore, the social relations between their private labour appear as what they are, i.e. they do not appear as direct social relations between persons in their work, but rather as material relations between persons and social relations between things.'[15]

From this understanding of commodity fetishism, Marx develops his analysis to reveal the inequality of capitalist production relations that lies behind the equality of the exchange relation. As soon as the direct producers' ability to work (labour-power) assumes the

[14] Karl Marx, 'Marginal Notes on Wagner', in *Value Studies*, London 1976, p. 214.
[15] *Capital* Volume 1, pp. 165–6.

commodity-form, the elaboration of the contradiction immanent in such a form constructs the mode of surplus extraction in capitalism. For once the conditions under which labour-power becomes a commodity are realized, then its unique use-value (realized in its consumption in the labour process) of creating more than its own value is sufficient to explain both the production of the surplus and its extraction as value by the capitalist. Through this understanding of capitalist production relations, the extraction of surplus-value can be understood without recourse to a theory of unequal exchange.

However, this is only the first step. For the formal subsumption of labour to capital on the basis of previous techniques of production gives way to its real subsumption as capitalist relations affect every aspect of the labour-process and 'revolutionize' the mode of production. The laws of motion of capitalist development can then be elaborated. But capital is here still considered as capital in general, 'the incarnation of the qualities which distinguish value as capital from value as value or as money. Value, money, circulation etc., prices etc., are presupposed, as is labour etc. But we are still concerned neither with a *particular* form, nor with an *individual* capital as distinct from other individual capitals etc. We are present at the process of its becoming. This dialectical process of its becoming is only the ideal expression of the real movement through which capital comes into being. The later relations are to be regarded as developments coming out of this germ.'[16]

It is only through the development of these later relations that we can recognize that not only is production under capitalism production for (surplus-) value rather than for use-value, but capital itself is value in process; a process in which a given value takes the form of different use-values in the process of its self-expansion. It is only through this separation of value from use-value, a social and not merely analytic separation, that the exploitative relation that is capital functions. On this basis, capital in general can be individuated into different capitals through the synthesis of production with the circulation of different use-values; but now *commodities can no longer be taken to exchange at the prices corresponding to the level of capital*

*in general: a further development of the form in which value appears is
necessary.*

Marx derives this result by first showing that the logic of his
analysis leads to the presumption of different rates of profit in
different industries, for two reasons. First, only living labour
produces value, but the rate of profit is defined across total capital.
Thus for a given rate of surplus-value, a greater proportion of capital
represented by labour-power (variable capital) than means of
production (constant capital) will produce more surplus-value than
one with a higher ratio, in value terms, of means of production to
labour-power. This ratio, the value composition of capital, determines, for a given value of capital and rate of surplus-value, the
quantity of surplus-value produced. If we could work out the rate of
profit in value terms, it would be the total surplus-value produced per
unit of total capital, and would thus vary, for a given rate of surplus-
value, according to the value composition of capital.

Second, if two capitals—again with the same rate of surplus-value,
and of equal value—have the same value composition but different
turnover times, then the capital that turns over faster (has the shorter
turnover time) has the higher rate of profit, because surplus-value is
produced with each turnover, while the capital advanced remains
unaltered. But having stated the problem with respect to different
turnover times (a statement in which the common basis with that of
Ricardo's stumbling block is most obvious[17]), Marx pro-

[17] Marx's identification of the problem with respect to different turnover times
seems to take us straight back to Ricardo. But Ricardo's capital, as money laid out on
inputs, can vary *only* in the length of time for which it is tied up—hence the distinctions
between fixed and circulating capital, and within fixed capital, purely on the basis of the
time for which such money is tied up. For Ricardo, what is 'involved in both cases is a
transfer of given, previously advanced values to the product, and their replacement
when the product is sold. The sole distinction here is whether the transfer of value, and
therefore the replacement of value, proceeds bit by bit and gradually, or all at once. The
all-important distinction between variable and constant capital is thereby obliterated,
and with it the whole secret of surplus-value formation and of capitalist production,
namely the circumstances that transform certain values and the things in which they
are represented into capital. The components of capital are distinguished from one
another simply by their mode of circulation (and the circulation of commodities of
course has only to do with already, existing given values).' (*Capital* Volume 2, Penguin
Books in association with New Left Review, Harmondsworth 1978, pp. 296–7.) If we
are concerned with market phenomena 'instead of penetrating through to the inner

238

ceeds to concentrate on the problem with respect to different compositions of capital.

The rate of profit under discussion is the 'value rate of profit', or the rate of profit upon each capital in value terms. Algebraically, this is given by

$$r = \frac{s}{c+v} = \frac{s/v}{(c/v)+1}$$

where c, v, and s are, respectively, the constant and variable parts of, and surplus-value produced for, an individual capital. The rate of exploitation is then s/v, while c/v gives the value composition of capital. The effect of competition between capitals is to create a tendency for the rates of profit on different capitals to be equalized, and hence a tendency towards the formation of a general rate of profit. Now, if there is a similar tendency towards the formation of a general rate of exploitation,[18] but no such tendency in the case of value compositions, then the 'value rate of profit' will vary across industries and therefore cannot be this general rate of profit.

Marx therefore implicitly dismissed the 'value rate of profit', at least for an individual capital, when he wrote: 'differences in the average rate of profit in the various branches of industry do not exist in reality, and could not exist without abolishing the entire system of capitalist production. It would seem, therefore, that here the theory of value is incompatible with the real phenomena of production, and that for this reason any attempt to understand these phenomena

mechanism of the capitalist production process' (ibid., p. 294), then different turnover times and different value compositions are equally important. But Marx focuses on the latter, since it is the production of surplus-value that is critical, and not the manner in which particular values are transferred. Emphasis on the transfer of particular values merely brings 'to fulfilment . . . the fetishism peculiar to bourgeois economics, which transforms the social, economic character that things are stamped with in the process of social production into a natural character arising from the material natures of those things'. (Ibid., p. 303.)

[18] Marx justified this tendency by claiming that 'although the equalizing of wages and working-days, and thereby of the rates of surplus-value, among different spheres of production . . . is checked by all kinds of local obstacles, it is nevertheless taking place more and more with the advance of capitalist production and the subordination of all economic conditions to this mode of production. The study of such frictions, while

should be given up.'[19] But of course he does not give up his attempts to understand the real phenomena. Recognition of the incompatibility implies recognition that commodities necessarily cannot exchange at their values, for this is a direct result of the extension of value analysis to its logical conclusions under capitalist competition. For while value analysis is based on the commensuration of socially necessary labour-times through commodity exchange, capitalist competition is based on the 'commensuration' of paid labour-times through the formation of an average rate of profit. These two commensurations have been shown to be contradictory. The latter is a consequence of the former, since it is only as a consequence of the commensuration of commodities in exchange that labour-power can become a commodity and capitalist competition result. Thus, though the commensuration of competition is a consequence of that of socially necessary labour-times, it modifies the operation of the latter.

It is this modification that is supposed to be expressed by the transformation of 'values' into prices of production. The point is to capture the existence of surplus-value in its more concrete individuated form of profit. This capturing of something in a more concrete form could in general be called a process of transformation. The particular transformation at issue here is that which displays surplus-value as profit, and in so doing reveals the contradiction between value and its form, exchange-value (expressed as price).

Now, the method of historical materialism would immediately suggest that this transformation has a historical dimension, but this is not the same as the 'historical transformation problem' as conventionally conceived.[20]

---

important to any special work on wages, may be dispensed with as incidental and irrelevant in a general analysis of capitalist production. In a general analysis of this kind it is usually always assumed that the actual conditions correspond to their conception, or, what is the same, that actual conditions are represented only to the extent that they are typical of their own general case.' (*Capital* Volume 3, pp. 142–3.)

[19] *Capital* Volume 3, p. 153.

[20] In his 'Value and Theory of Rent, Part One' (*Capital and Class*, 3, autumn 1977), R. Murray advocates a historical transformation position and refers to further literature on the subject. There is also an interpretation of the transformation 'problem' as an iteration procedure. (See M. Morishima, *Marx's Economics: A Dual Theory of Value and Growth*, Cambridge 1973, and 'Marx in the Light of Modern Economic Theory', in *Econometrica*, 1974, as well as Anwar Shaikh, 'Marx's Theory of Value and the "Transformation Problem"', in J. Schwartz (ed.), *The Subtle Anatomy*

The buying and selling of labour-power is a later historical development than that of many other commodities. It therefore makes sense to talk of the commensuration of socially necessary labour-times, which takes place through the exchange of commodities, as occurring *before* the other commensuration, which occurs through the equalization of the rate of profit. But—and this is critical—it is only through the development of the wage-labour relation, which simultaneously brings this latter commensuration into play, that socially necessary labour-times are brought into any equivalence with hours of the clock. In the abstraction of simple commodity exchange, there is no reason why the time that a tailor takes to produce that which is exchanged with the produce of one hour's labour of a carpenter should be one hour *measured by the clock*. As socially necessary labour-times these are equivalent. But clock-time is introduced with the wage-labour relation only when labour-power is sold for specified amounts of time. Thus although it is true that before the development of capitalist competition commodities exchange at their values, which are measured in units of socially necessary labour-time, the development of capitalist competition does not introduce a deviation of prices from previously existing socially necessary labour-times, but instead gives those socially necessary labour-times an independent quantitative aspect that they did not previously possess.

Related, but not identical, to the historical transformation procedure is the idea that the transformation is a process of redistribution. This is very much the way Marx alludes to the process, but we feel that such allusions are mistaken. Surplus-value is not *redistributed* between capitals so as to equalize the rate of profit, because there is no state *from* which this *redistribution* occurs. At no stage in the circuit of capital is surplus-value attributed to capitals in proportion to the labour-power they consume. A parable of the sale

of Capitalism, Santa Monica, California 1977.) It could be claimed that such a procedure does involve the necessary mediations we discuss in the text, but this is incorrect, because each step of the iteration is but a redistribution, and such a redistribution, as we shall argue below, has no basis in reality. Morishima and Catephores (*Value, Exploitation and Growth*, Maidenhead 1978) explicitly reject a historical interpretation of the transformation 'problem', while adopting an iterative procedure to solve it.

of the commodity leading to a redistribution until each capital's share of surplus-value is proportional to the total capital advanced[21] is as misleading as parables of a mere redistribution through history. Redistribution is meaningful only if one can specify a state from which it occurs and a state prevailing after the redistribution.

The 'historical transformation problem' and 'transformation as redistribution', then, are both parables misleading in their conceptualization of capitalist history and logic. Just as the movement of capital in general is necessarily expressed in the form of competition between capitals, so surplus-value in money-form is necessarily expressed in the form of profit in money-form. Neither pole of either antinomy can be expressed as a simple quantitative relation of its opposite pole—to attempt such an expression is to misunderstand both the nature of abstraction and the meaning of transformation. The transformation 'problem' is therefore a necessary result of the contradictory nature of capitalist production relations: it is a contradiction in reality, and not at all a problem with Marx's theory, which simply conceptualizes this reality. Indeed, we could rather say that Ricardo's problem is that, having failed to recognize the contradiction between the two commensurations, he did not pose the transformation 'problem'—he just required that it be solved. The contradictory reality that his theory imperfectly recognized thus appeared as a contradiction at the level of formal logic within his theory, rather than one of dialectical reality.

3. Methodological Differences

The previous section situated Marx's theory of value within his problematic of historical materialism. Now, however, we require a more explicit presentation of the methodology of his (abstract) labour theory of value in order to elucidate further both his process of abstraction and his criticisms of Ricardo's (embodied) labour theory of value. Our inclusion of the latter point is justified by the lamentable fact that many today continue to work in the Ricardian framework

---

[21] For a clear exposition of such a parable, see W. Baumol, 'The Transformation Problem: What Marx Really Meant', in *Journal of Economic Literature*, March 1974.

and that indeed much modern 'Marxism' has not only failed to go beyond Ricardo's theory, but has indeed retreated from its very substantial achievements.

Marx's fundamental critique of Ricardo, whom he considered the best exponent of classical political economy, is that he 'never once asked the question . . . why labour is expressed in value, and why the measurement of labour by its duration is expressed in the magnitude of the value of the product'.[22] Thus, for capitalism, he '*does not examine* the form—the peculiar characteristic of labour that creates exchange-value or manifests itself in exchange-values—the *nature* of this labour'.[23] Since the question at issue is why labour and labour-time take these particular forms under capitalism, a failure to resolve this question simultaneously fails to identify the historical specificity of the capitalist mode of production. Thus Marx remarks:

'It is one of the chief failings of classical economy that it has never succeeded, by means of its analysis of commodities, and in particular of their value, in discovering the form of value which in fact turns value into exchange-value. Even its best representatives, Adam Smith and Ricardo, treat the form of value as something of indifference, something external to the nature of the commodity itself. The explanation for this is not simply that their attention is entirely absorbed by the analysis of the magnitude of value. It lies deeper. The value-form of the product of labour is the most abstract but also the most universal form of the bourgeois mode of production; by that fact it stamps the bourgeois mode of production as a particular kind of social production of a historical and transitory character. If then we make the mistake of treating it as the eternal natural form of social production, we necessarily overlook the specificity of the value-form, and consequently of the commodity-form together with its further developments, the money-form, the capital-form, etc.'[24]

Now there are at least two senses in which the analysis could fail to identify the historical specificity of capitalism. In a weak sense, it might just fail to explain what is historically specific. Ricardo's analysis can be judged wanting in this sense, for while he is

[22] *Capital* Volume 1, p. 174.
[23] Karl Marx, *Theories of Surplus-Value*, vol. 2, p. 164.
[24] *Capital* Volume 1, p. 174n.

undoubtedly talking about capitalism, he fails to explain its historical specificity. Because of this failure, Ricardo's analysis is enmeshed in a contradiction that cannot be resolved within his framework. Its resolution in the direction of vulgar economy leads to the strong sense of the lack of historical specificity: historically specific categories are rendered universal and hence natural. It follows that any analysis that employs these categories uncritically will always tend to ascribe asocial, natural, even eternal qualities to what is socially specific to capitalism.[25] For economic categories are but thought-constructs that are determinate abstractions of the prevailing relations of production. That is: 'The categories of bourgeois economics . . . are forms of thought which are socially valid, and therefore objective, for the relations of production belonging to this historically determined mode of social production, i.e. commodity production.'[26]

Without this recognition, Marx held, no analysis can be scientific. Ricardo's 'great historical significance for science' was to show that the 'basis, the starting-point for the physiology of the bourgeois system—for the understanding of its internal organic coherence and life process—is the determination of value by *labour-time*. Ricardo starts with this and forces science to get out of the rut, to render an account of the extent to which the other categories—the relations of production and commerce—evolved and described by it, correspond to or contradict this basis, this starting-point; to elucidate how far a science which in fact only reflects and reproduces the manifest forms of the process, and therefore also how far those manifestations themselves, correspond to the basis on which the inner coherence, the actual physiology of bourgeois society rests on the basis which forms its starting-point; and in general, *to examine how matters stand with*

[25] As long as these categories define the frame of reference of the analysis, then in so far as political conclusions can be deduced from the employment of these categories, such conclusions will tend away from the advocacy of revolutionary change. Thus there resulted, in the early stages of capitalism, an imperative to generalize what was already implicit in the status quo (hence Ricardo's advocacy of the interests of industrial capitalism against the interests of the landlords), and, in the period of capitalism's maturity, a tautological justification of the status quo (hence the concentration of neo-classical economics on equilibrium analysis). Alternatively, critical theories that remain within this framework can reject the status quo only on the basis of an arbitrary ethical principle (hence petty-bourgeois or utopian socialism).

[26] *Capital* Volume 1, p. 169.

244

the contradiction between the apparent and the actual movement of the system.[27]

But his procedure was misguided: 'Ricardo's method is as follows: he begins with the determination of the magnitude of the value of the commodity by labour-time and then *examines* whether the other economic relations and categories *contradict* this determination of value or to what extent they modify it. The historical justification of this method of procedure, its scientific necessity in the history of economics, are evident at first sight, but so is, at the same time, its scientific inadequacy. This inadequacy not only shows itself in the method of presentation (in a formal sense), but leads to erroneous results because it omits some essential links and *directly* seeks to prove the congruity of the economic categories with one another.'[28]

But there can be no proof of 'the congruity of the economic categories with one another' in the way Ricardo attempts. For Ricardo *begins* with the existence of commodities, wages, capital, profit, the general rate of profit, the various forms of capital in circulation (fixed and circulating), and so on. In other words, he begins with the whole of capitalist production and a complete theorization of the relation between wage and profit rates. Far from postulating the existence of a general rate of profit, 'Ricardo should rather have examined how far its *existence* is in fact consistent with the determination of value by labour-time, and he would have found that instead of being consistent with it, *prima facie*, it *contradicts* it, and that its existence would therefore have to be explained through a number of intermediary stages, a procedure which is very different from merely including it under the law of value.'[29]

The lack of mediation of categories in Ricardo's work proves to be an insuperable barrier within his frame of reference. Given the logical contradiction between a labour-embodied theory of value and a cost-summation account of price, Ricardo's scientificity consisted in his obstinacy in maintaining the former in the face of the latter, rather than dissolving it in the vulgarity of passive reflection on appearances. Yet consider the category embodied labour. A sort of

---

[27] *Theories of Surplus-Value*, vol. 2, p. 166; first emphasis in the original, second added.
[28] Ibid., pp. 164–5.
[29] Ibid., p. 174.

abstraction is certainly being made, for in so valuing a commodity, various aspects of the labour performed in its production are ignored, such as who did it, where it was done, and what it produced. But the content of this abstraction is purely that of rendering physically heterogeneous objects commensurable. Embodied labour is thus a means of aggregation, and there is nothing to restrict its application to any particular sort of society.[30] The mere recognition of commensurability is insufficient to make the concept historically specific to capitalism, which is to say that embodied labour is not abstract labour. The point is not that no abstraction is involved in the concept of embodied labour; rather it is not a *social* abstraction corresponding to a particular social process, but it is *arbitrary*, a mental convenience: an assumption that labour is homogeneous *when plainly it is not*. Ricardo's concept of labour has no historical specificity, because it is not the product of a social process of abstraction; for this reason his theory as a whole fails to explain what is historically specific.

Ricardo's theory, then, is a model built upon assumptions rather than the theorization of a real-world process by means of abstraction. Assumptions are thought-constructs that have no real existence but are invented in order to simplify and structure the complexity of the analysis (consider, for example, the assumptions of neo-classical perfect competition). Assumptions, of course, are designed to be able to say something about the world, but to the extent that they do this, they do so purely by virtue of being imposed upon empirical 'facts' in order to render appearances coherent and plausible. Hence they are expressions of surface phenomena that see in such *immediate* forms the *whole* nature of the phenomena in question. But descriptions of surface phenomena exclude the possibility of necessary contradic-

---

[30] It might be claimed that a restriction is imposed, since the existence of a general rate of profit ensures that it is capitalism that is being theorized. While that is true for Ricardo's theory of price, it says nothing that restricts the use of embodied-labour to capitalism. It might further be claimed that a restriction to certain societies is implied by the commensurability of labour times: that this commensurability applies only to those societies in which labour is mobile. This clearly does not restrict the use of the concept of embodied labour to capitalism, for slave or communist societies would satisfy this condition too.

tions as the determinants of the motion of these immediate forms. For at the level of the particularity of phenomena, appearances either are or are not contradictory with each other, and *contingently* so. The recognition of any determinate contradictory reality is thus ruled out. And it further follows that nothing can be deduced from assumptions that is not already entailed by those assumptions; hence theory becomes tautology, the deduction of conclusions from assumptions.

By contrast, Marx's method of abstraction, his dialectical method, is precisely concerned to show that the forms of appearance of capitalism are just that: forms of appearance. Through his critique of these forms and their reflection in bourgeois thought Marx shows first, that these reflections fail to identify the social forms they express but instead treat them as natural phenomena (commodity fetishism); and second, that the forms of appearance of capitalism are always transitory, in that they constitute barriers to their further development. This is no mystical idealism, but a materialist recognition of the process of motion through contradiction, which constitutes the process of human history. Such a dialectic is 'in its essence critical and revolutionary'; it 'includes in its positive understanding of what exists a simultaneous recognition of its negation, its inevitable destruction; because it regards every historically developed form as being in a fluid state, in motion, and therefore grasps its transient aspect as well;'.[31]

Since the process of history can be captured only by this method, it follows that the real social abstractions so produced account for that history only by a dialectical analysis. Abstract labour is thus derived by an abstraction inherent in the exchange process in order to capture the moment of the social fabric of capitalist society in its simplest form. The immanent development of the pure value-form into its specific capital-form is immediately posited (just as, historically, commodity production preceded and evolved into capitalist production), and the contradictions constituting the most abstract moment are elaborated through mediation, suspension, and their reappearance in successively more concrete moments.

Now, it is true that Marx distinguishes the method of inquiry from the method of presentation. As regards the former, his years in the British Museum enabled him 'to appropriate the material in detail, to

[31] *Capital* Volume 1, p. 103.

analyse its different forms of development and to trace out their inner connection. Only after this work has been done can the real movement be appropriately presented'.[32] But he further argues that if this method of inquiry is successful, if 'the life of the subject matter is now reflected back in the ideas, then *it may appear as if we have before us an a priori construction*'.[33] Nevertheless, this 'a priori construction' is a construction of materialist reality, for value is the real constitutive form of the social relations of capitalism, from which the analysis proceeds through a hierarchy of abstractions in order to comprehend the real world. Only once the basic capital/labour relation has been grasped can 'the various forms of capital . . . approach step by step the form which they assume on the surface of society, in the action of different capitals upon one another, in competition, and in the ordinary consciousness of the agents of production themselves.'[34]

Considerable mediation thus is required before competition can be explained on the basis of abstract labour. Of course, 'Competition merely expresses as *real*, posits as an external necessity that which lies within the nature of capital; competition is nothing more than the way in which the many capitals force the inherent determinants of capital upon one another and upon themselves.'[35] Nevertheless, such mediation is essential in order to explain the forms of appearance necessarily adopted by social relations in the capitalist mode of production. For all the various phenomena arising from the process of competition '*seem* to contradict the determination of value by labour-time as much as the nature of surplus-value consisting of unpaid surplus labour. *Thus everything appears reversed in competition.* The final pattern of economic relations as seen on the surface, in their real existence and consequently in the conceptions by which the bearers and agents of these relations seek to understand them, is very much different from, and indeed quite the reverse of their inner but concealed essential pattern and the conception corresponding to it.'[36]

[32] Ibid., p. 102.
[33] Ibid. Emphasis added.
[34] *Capital* Volume 3, p. 26.
[35] *Grundrisse*, p. 647.
[36] *Capital* Volume 3, p. 209.

Marx's account of the formation of a general rate of profit in competition, his transformation procedure, is precisely the transition from the 'inner but concealed essential pattern' to the 'pattern of economic relations as seen on the surface'. It is a movement, a procedure of transformation, required between abstractions of different orders of conception. What it is not, as has already been argued, is a process of redistribution of aggregate surplus-value. Of course, competition distributes aggregate surplus-value according to total capital advanced, but there is no *re*distribution. Rather, the process is one of conceiving the value produced by production first in abstraction from competition, and second while allowing for the effects of competition. This transformation between abstractions of different orders of conception is perhaps rendered more comprehensible without resort to parables of redistribution.

We can now bring together the threads of the discussion in order to draw some conclusions about Ricardian and Marxian value theory, and the different methodologies employed. First, a Ricardian concept of value as embodied labour leads to irreconcilable contradictions. Prices are, and must equal, costs, and cost-determined 'theories' of price are therefore correct (and lacking in content). But it follows that embodied-labour values cannot be assigned to commodities in general in any way that preserves a meaningful functional correspondence between embodied-labour values and equilibrium prices, or between their rates of change. This, however, has long been known—it is one of the reasons why neo-classical economics is not Ricardian. What is needed is a transformation procedure that deduces the forms of appearance of values, based on a full elaboration of the contradictions inherent in the real abstraction that is value itself. The capital-relation is a value-relation, but values as quantities of abstract labour can exist only in commodity-form, and commodities are purchased and sold on markets for prices. In this way the fundamental contradiction between value and use-value finds its most complete expression in the fact that it is through competition that the laws of motion of capitalist development are expressed. For quantities of value are expressions of social relations, the fact that there is a necessary connection between a certain article and that fraction of aggregate social labour-time required to produce it. It is the market that makes this connection, and necessarily only in a distorted form. Only market processes realize the quantitative expression of the abstract labour, and this quantitative expression has only a price-form. As we have seen, the abstraction that is value yields the price-form directly, but as soon as *competition* is taken into account, abstract labour cannot directly be assigned to commodities. In this sense, all Marx's numerical examples are potentially misleading in their assignment of numerical values to commodities, and his formal solution to the transformation 'problem' fails on the same grounds. To assert otherwise is to fail to escape from Ricardo's problematic.

It was Ricardo's failure to recognize the historical specificity of capitalist production, and thus of the value-form, that led him to insist that his (embodied) labour theory of value had to have a direct bearing on the determination of price, a connection that neither his theory nor the contradictions of capitalism could support. The reason we have included this digression into the history of political economy and Marx's critique of it is that much modern work that claims to employ a Marxist understanding of value has not, in fact, advanced upon Ricardo's. Indeed, the contradiction between a labour-embodied theory of value and a cost-summation account of price, which beset Ricardo, can serve to classify such work in modern political economy.[37] Under the heading of 'Ricardian' come those analyses that remain enmeshed in Ricardo's problem and do not advance beyond it.[38] 'Sraffian' is a term that applies to those that 'solve' the problem by clinging to one horn of the dilemma,

[37] Subsequent footnotes classify the more prominent advocates of each tendency we identify. But there is so much confusion in the literature that many writers adopt vacillating and obscure positions; we have omitted these. Fine and Harris (*Rereading Capital*, London 1979) and Gerstein ('Production, Circulation and Value: The Significance of the "Transformation Problem" in Marx's Critique of Political Economy', *Economy and Society*, vol. 3, 1976) recognize that Ricardo's problem is insoluble at the level of formal logic and that reconceptualization is required, but the way in which they pose the necessary mediations tends to force an *absolute* separation between value and price. This is because of their tendency to construct a priori concepts into which to fit reality, rather than real abstractions that are both produced by and capture it. Nevertheless, these are the recent authors who have brought the problem most clearly to light.

[38] Examples are Glyn and Sutcliffe, *British Capitalism, Workers and the Profit Squeeze*, Harmondsworth 1972, and Armstrong, Glyn, and Harrison, 'In Defence of Value', in *Capital and Class*, 5, summer 1976.

abandoning the category of value altogether, thus repeating, more than a century later, the post-Ricardian retreat from political to vulgar economy.[39] In spite of this difference (that Sraffian analysis forms a part of vulgar economy, while Ricardian does not), the two together have generically been called 'neo-Ricardian'. Indeed, they do have certain common features. For in both, labour is neither abstract nor concrete, value (whether consequently rejected or not) is embodied-labour, capitalism is not rendered historically specific, and occasionally a sociological theory of class struggle is appended as a guarantee of 'Marxist' authenticity and rectitude (as if the class struggle were discovered by Marx, when it is plainly present in the work of Ricardo and many others).[40] As we shall see, such work is enmeshed in all the contradictions that beset Ricardo, which is not really surprising.

Another school, called by some 'fundamentalist', does not recognize Ricardo's problem and its consequences.[41] While the term 'fundamentalism' may be appropriate to their apparent desire to show every word of Marx's to be correct, more importantly they miss

[39] Examples are Samuelson, 'Understanding the Marxian Notion of Exploitation: A Summary of the So-Called Transformation Problem Between Marxian Values and Competitive Prices', *Journal of Economic Literature*, vol. 9, no. 2, 1971; Hodgson, 'Marxist Epistemology and the Transformation Problem', in *Bulletin of the Conference of Socialist Economists*, II, no. 6, autumn 1975; Hodgson, 'Exploitation and Embodied Labour Time', *Bulletin of the Conference of Socialist Economists*, V, 13, February 1976; Steedman, 'Value, Price and Profit', *New Left Review*, no. 90, 1975; and Steedman, *Marx After Sraffa*, London, NLB, 1977.

[40] Capitalist competition, introduced simultaneously with rather than derived from an analysis of commodity exchange, becomes logically as fundamental as the relations of exploitation, which do derive from the latter. Even if the proponents of such theory recognize the more fundamental significance of the exchange between capital and labour, that recognition is a purely arbitrary choice, following not from their theory but from a superimposed ethical position. When all parts of the whole are analysed simultaneously, there is no way in which the exchange between a worker and a capitalist is necessarily exploitative, unless that between one capitalist and another is potentially so as well.

[41] The term is used by Fine and Harris ('Controversial Issues in Marxist Economic Theory', in Miliband and Saville (eds.), *Socialist Register 1976*, London 1976). Examples are Yaffe, 'The Crisis of Profitability: A Critique of the Glyn-Sutcliffe Thesis', *New Left Review*, no. 80, 1973; Yaffe, 'Value and Price in Marx's *Capital*', *Revolutionary Communist*, 1, January 1975; Williams, 'An Analysis of South African Capitalism—Neo-Ricardianism or Marxism?', *Bulletin of the Conference of Socialist Economists*, IV, 10, February 1975; and Murray, 'Value and Theory of Rent: Part One', *Capital and Class*, 3, autumn 1977.

the fundamental issue. While adopting a basically Marxist understanding of value, and recognizing the necessity of accounting, on this basis, for the appearances of the real world, their insistence on interpreting the transformation 'problem' as a redistribution parable implicitly assumes, despite their explicit methodological promises to the contrary, that value is a category of direct applicability as an analytic tool at successively lower levels of abstraction. Thus they want appearances and reality, if not to coincide (like Ricardo), at least to be immediately accessible to the same tools of analysis without transformation. The issues of this paper, then, are of considerable relevance to a critique of 'fundamentalism'. But rather than continue to criticize a school whose tendency is to dissolve the real world into an epiphenomenon of capital in general, we shall continue to focus on these issues directly.

On the basis of this understanding, we now turn to an examination of certain modern 'puzzles' in value theory, to demonstrate how analysis of them within an embodied-labour framework provides no escape from Ricardo's problematic save that of vulgar economy. The reason is simple: these puzzles are of the same genus as the transformation 'problem' itself. By contrast, a Marxist analysis of them will serve to develop the understanding of abstract labour and price that we have established above.

4. The Modern Assault on Value

An interpretation of Marx's transformation procedure as a 'problem' provides the starting-point for much of the modern criticism of Marx's value theory. Such modern criticism, whose ancestry goes back at least as far as von Bortkiewicz and Böhm-Bawerk, is now based largely on the work of Sraffa. As such, it is precisely subject to the strictures that Marx considered applicable to Ricardo's work. For the introduction of competition at the outset of the analysis leads to the same problems, which have devastating consequences for what is interpreted to be Marx's value analysis. Indeed many have gone so far as to say that 'the project of providing a materialist account of capitalist societies is dependent on Marx's value magnitude analysis *only* in the negative sense that continued adherence to the latter is a major fetter on the development of the former.'[42]

In its strongest statement, this claim has two foundations, each apparently equally damaging to value analysis, together invincible. The first is that value as a concept is internally inconsistent, the second that it is redundant: 'it has been proved that Marx's value reasoning is often internally inconsistent, completely failing to provide the explanations which Marx sought for certain central features of the capitalist economy. By contrast, these same features can be given a coherent explanation in terms which make no reference whatsoever to any value magnitude.'[43]

1. The redundancy of values

We will take the charge of redundancy first. To avoid any misunderstanding, we will read the charge from a work of one of the least circumspect of the accusers, Steedman:

'If there is only one available method for the production of each commodity, each method using only circulating capital and producing only one product then:

'i) the physical quantities of commodities and of labour specifying the methods of production, together with the physical quantities of commodities specifying the given real wage rate, suffice to determine the rate of profit (and the associated prices of production);

ii) the labour-time required (directly and indirectly) to produce any commodity—and thus the value of any commodity—is determined by the physical data relating to methods of production: it follows that value magnitudes are, at best, redundant in the determination of the rate of profit (and prices of production);

iii) ... The traditional value schema, in which all the constant capital and all the variable capital elements in a productive activity are summed and represented by a single "c" and a single "v" figure, is

[42] Steedman, *Marx After Sraffa*, p. 207.
[43] Ibid., pp. 206–7.

not adequate to the determination of the rate of profit (and prices of production.)'[44]

To summarize, the rate of profit, prices, and values can all be calculated once the methods of production and the wage are specified; on the other hand, none of these other variables can be calculated from a knowledge of values alone. Thus values are but statistics derived from the methods of production, a compression of the full data, and a compression that loses much that is of importance.

Now, in their own terms the Sraffians are clearly correct. A full specification of physical input-output requirements *does* give sufficient information to calculate exchange ratios and a rate of profit.[45] But further, such a full specification also gives sufficient information to calculate amounts of labour embodied, were such information required. But in no sense is it, since knowledge of the amounts of labour embodied is *not* sufficient to calculate exchange ratios and rates of profit. For them, this clinches the argument that 'values' are redundant: they are derived from the physical input-output specification, not vice versa. They cannot be used by themselves to derive exchange ratios and rates of profit, while the physical input-output specification can do that directly.

It should, of course, be clear that the 'value' being talked about here is total labour embodied, the Ricardian concept. For how else could (as in (ii) above) the value of a commodity be determined by the physical data relating to methods of production rather than vice versa? Why else would one elaborate the determination *of* value

---

[44] Ibid., pp. 202–3. The point of these provisos at the beginning of the charge is to look at the simplest and most unproblematic cases. If there is only one available method for the production of each commodity, each method using only circulating capital and producing only one product, the cases that give rise to the puzzles that lead to the charge of inconsistency cannot arise.

[45] Formally, their equations can be shown to be equivalent to Seton's simultaneous equation system. (See Seton, 'The Transformation Problem', *Review of Economic Studies*, vol. 24, 1957.) Gerstein ('Production, Circulation and Value . . .') has an interesting discussion of the mathematics. Strictly speaking, it should be noted that Sraffa actually specified the composition of output, so that he worked with the total amounts of inputs necessary to produce the specified outputs rather than with input-output coefficients. As a result, he did not need to make any assumption about returns to scale, since he had precluded variation in outputs.

rather than the determination *by* value? The former means the mere functional determination of one quantity (values) by other quantities (input coefficients and labour input vectors). The latter encapsulates the method whereby the relations of commodity production are such that input coefficients and labour input vectors can be specified. For it is only through the exchange of products that individual labours are commensurated and socially necessary labour-times established. And this is critical. For what is being counterposed here is on the one hand an understanding of values as mere derivates of physical quantities required for production, and on the other hand an understanding of the social quantification of production requirements posited on the value abstraction.

How, then, has Steedman advanced on Ricardo? As we have seen, Ricardo recognized the lack of functional dependence of prices and the rate of profit on embodied labour-times. The point is that Steedman, following Sraffa, has solved this problem of Ricardo's by showing us upon which variables prices and the rate of profit *do* functionally depend. In doing so, however, Sraffa and Steedman are treading a well-worn path—the path that leads to vulgar economy and a cost 'theory' of price. In solving Ricardo's problem, they have simply stated a series of tautologies—for that, after all, is all a proof of functional dependence can be. Halted by the contradiction between a labour-embodied theory of value and a cost-summation account of price, Sraffians are thus led to jettison the former as redundant.

While Steedman emphasizes the logical purity of his conclusions, it is in fact in Sraffa's own work that the argument is clearest. For Sraffa never saw his task as specifically one of criticism of Marx, and thus he found it unnecessary either to introduce a concept of value as distinct from price or even to consider value as labour-embodied. What Sraffia did was to show that with a full specification of the input-output requirements of each commodity (that is, a list of the amounts of all commodities, including labour-power, required to produce a given commodity), the price of each commodity can be calculated as a sum of its costs of production together with the profit accruing to the capitalist on whose account the production of the commodity is taking place. It is important to recognize, then, that Sraffa's famous dated-labour analysis, in which the price of a commodity is broken down into the sum of labour-input costs incurred in all periods from the present backwards, is just precisely that: an expression of price in terms of costs. Sraffa therefore implicitly rejects any theory of value as a property of the labour employed in the production of a commodity (whether 'embodied' or 'abstract') in favour of an account of price as determined by costs of production. That the coefficients involved in the dated-labour equation are quantities of labour embodied in no sense relates to Ricardo's labour-embodied theory of value, and in no sense removes Sraffa from the school of vulgar economy. For Sraffa, and for vulgar economy, prices are made up of costs—and costs, of course, are but prices.[46]

Sraffian economics is thus clearly different from Ricardian. It is talking about the physical product and its division between classes, instead of the total labour of society and its division. Nevertheless, both Sraffians and Ricardians work on the assumption that the specification of input requirements (whether in terms of physical inputs of particular use-values or in terms of quantities of labour required) is a given. But Marxists recognize the very process by which input requirements are specified as social. This does not mean, as neo-Ricardians would claim, that the specification of input requirements is simply determined by the class struggle and by profit maximization. What it rather means is that specification of what is produced (the composition of output) and how (the technical coefficients of production) is meaningless in abstraction from the way in which the labour process is organized and from the way in which production, as a social activity through the market's universal commensuration of what is produced, determines both what is produced and how it is produced. Hence neither of the latter can be considered as given.

2. The inconsistency of values

The other criticism the Sraffians level against Marx's value theory is that there are internal inconsistencies in the concept of value itself. The argument can be dressed in more or less technical clothing. Here we shall give it in the most uncomplicated way we can, and will show why the sheep's clothing hides nothing but a sheep after all.

---

[46] The limited nature of Sraffa's results impels Sraffians to turn, sooner or later, to the general linear production model of von Neumann. For a very clear exposition of what it is possible to do with such a model, see C.J. Bliss, *Capital Theory and the Distribution of Income*, Amsterdam 1975.

The claimed inconsistency arises when established methods of calculating values give either indeterminate or negative results. The former can arise when there is a choice between two equally profitable techniques of producing the same commodity, the latter when two different commodities are the simultaneous result of the same production process and a question arises as to how to allocate the total embodied labour-time between them. Basically, both problems arise from the same source: capitalists, who control what is produced and how, make their decisions on the basis of maximizing their rate of profit, which for the production of a given commodity means minimizing their costs. But costs are prices, not values, and the minimization of one may not, and in general will not, be the minimization of the other. Anomalies may thus arise.

Let us take the two cases in turn. The first occurs when there are two methods of production of the same commodity that are (in price terms) equally cheap and cheaper than all the others. Clearly, these methods are the only ones that will be used by efficient capitalists, but because there is no difference between them on the criterion of profit maximization, some capitalists will use one method, some the other. Now, there is no reason why these two methods should use the same quantities of total embodied labour. Where such a choice of techniques exists, which method of production determines the value of this commodity?

The second anomaly arises when there is joint production of two commodities. Joint production is considered an important problem because this is the standard way to incorporate fixed capital into Sraffian analysis. The inputs to such a production process are a machine of a certain age (and thus productive capacity), other means of production, and labour; the result is a commodity that will be sold, plus a slightly more used machine, which will be employed in the production process during the next period. The machine will continue to be used during each period until it is scrapped, because it is no longer profitable to use it. This way of looking at production processes involving fixed capital, together with the existence of clear real cases of joint production, point to the problem of how to allocate the embodied labour between the two commodities produced in order to determine the values of each commodity.[47]

[47] Cases of joint production proper are not at all uncommon, particularly in the chemicals industries. Consider, for example, the cracking of oil in refining processes.

If some other process exists and is in use for producing one of the commodities alone, we could determine the labour embodied in that commodity from this non-joint process and determine the labour embodied in the other commodity by subtracting from the total quantity of labour embodied in the joint process. But the total labour embodied in the joint process may be less than that in the non-joint one, leaving a negative 'value' for the second commodity after subtraction. It is possible that a process that used more labour to produce only one product than another used to produce two would remain in use, because, as we have seen, capitalists decide which production method to use on the basis of profit calculations based on prices, not on the basis of embodied-labour calculations, and the former process might be as profitable as the latter, though clearly more 'wasteful' of embodied labour. This anomaly thus arises for the same fundamental reason as the other: capitalists make their decisions on the basis of prices rather than on the basis of embodied-labour values. The problem, however, appears in a different form; now 'values' may be not merely indeterminate, but even negative.

Various solutions to these problems have been suggested, primarily by those who want to rescue the Ricardian concept of value, but all solutions proposed involve some modification of the concept.

One approach to the problem of the indeterminacy of the 'value' of a commodity for the production of which two methods are currently in use is to take the value of the commodity to be the average 'actual labour-time' embodied in it.[48] By 'actual labour-time' is meant the total labour-time spent on production of that commodity divided by the quantity of the commodity produced. This certainly provides an answer, given the required information, but the required information is much greater and more concrete than that previously required. It begs the question of why 'labour embodied' is a

---

The joint products thereby produced include tar, bitumen, high-octane fuels such as kerosene, petroleum, lubricating oils, most precursors to plastics, such as PVC, synthetic food materials, and industrial alcohol. The latter is also produced in other joint production processes. Joint production is therefore a significant phenomenon, sufficient to problematize the quantification of embodied labour, and, considering that most of the products just mentioned are themselves used as inputs in further production processes, to problematize the calculation of ratios such as value compositions based on quantities of embodied labour.

[48] Armstrong, Glyn, and Harrison, 'In Defence of Value', p. 78.

worthwhile quantity to calculate even more strongly than before, if to calculate it requires a full specification not only of methods of production but also of the extent of their use. It is now a purely descriptive statistic, stripped of any analytic content; and in any case such an approach is forced to concede the indeterminacy of embodied labour values of individual commodities in the case of joint production, the other anomaly. Thus the cost of such a rescue attempt is the reduction of Ricardo's analytic procedure to the empirical inspection of actual labour-times in cases in which it is hoped that joint production is not significant.

A considerably more robust approach is that of Michio Mori-shima.[49] Following von Neumann, he formulates his theory of value in terms of inequalities rather than equations. This means that the value of a commodity is the minimum total labour-time required to produce a net output that includes one unit of the commodity. So in the case of two equally profitable methods of producing the same commodity, its value is given by the method that uses least total labour-time. Joint production does not affect this; if x units of total labour-time are needed to produce commodities A and B jointly and there is no other way of producing commodity A, then x is the minimum total labour needed to produce A and is thus the value of A. If there are other methods of producing A, each will require a certain amount of labour, and then the value of commodity A will be the smallest of these requirements. This way clearly avoids the problem of indeterminate or negative values, for every process uses a determinate, positive amount of labour. The value of the commodity is just the smallest of these determinate, positive amounts. On the other hand, a different problem arises, that of non-additivity of values. The value of two commodities jointly produced, such as A and B above, will not in general equal the sum of their individual values. Indeed, in the case above, if commodity B also cannot be produced by any alternative method, the values of commodity A alone, of commodity B alone, and of a bundle consisting of A and B together will all be the same. This non-additivity poses problems in calculating such variables as the rate of exploitation, since the sum of necessary

[49] See Morishima, *Marx's Economics: A Dual Theory of Value and Growth* and 'Marx in the Light of Modern Economic Theory'.

and surplus labours may not equal total labour performed. Nevertheless, it does capture the labour-embodied concept of value and does not lead to nonsensical results. In so far as this is Morishima's purpose, he has clearly and elegantly succeeded.

To summarize then, the attack on value as a redundant and inconsistent concept is well-founded within the Ricardian framework. Attempts to salvage the concept of embodied labour from the attacks on its consistency by some modification of the concept must fail, on the same count as Ricardo, to provide a basis for a theory of price. Yet within this framework, the calculation of embodied labour-times, in whatever form, has no other justification. The problem of redundancy—already present in Ricardo's own work—is thereby rendered even more acute.

5. Redundancy, Inconsistency, and Marx's Theory of Value

In this section we return to Marx's theory of value in order to examine, whether the charges of redundancy and inconsistency have any validity when directed against the category abstract labour. As a preliminary, we note that the charge of redundancy has already been answered: value theory is not redundant in Marxism because it is necessary to the very specification of the production relations of capitalism. The redundancy of values cannot therefore be 'proved' by showing that values can be derived from a specification of production conditions, by input-output data. For the law of value itself is the process by which those production conditions are such that they can be technologically represented by an input-output specification at all. It is value analysis that reveals what is historically specific to the capitalist mode of production, and the burden of our argument has been to show that values have a real, social existence. To render them an arbitrary piece of theoretical baggage, to be taken on board or jettisoned at will, is precisely to think of values as a mental construct, an assumption from which to make deductions to be compared with the facts, rather than the necessary result of a real process of abstraction. The reality of values stands or falls with the reality of commodity exchange, whose generalization is capitalism. Abstract labour is necessarily always being performed in such a society; since it is not a purely theoretical construction, its redundancy is not a purely theoretical question. Occam's razor cannot therefore be used to excise the category of abstract labour; the charge of redundancy must be rejected.

The second charge is that of inconsistency. We have seen that the calculation of quantities of embodied labour involves insuperable difficulties unless the concept is redefined in a programming framework, in the manner of Morishima. The question is whether any of the same difficulties are involved in the calculation of quantities of abstract labour, in the calculation, that is, of socially necessary labour-times.

To answer this question we must re-examine the separation of abstract from concrete labour as it applies to the anomalous cases described in the last section. In these, the problem arose either because one commodity was being produced by two different production processes or because two different commodities were being produced by one production process. Now, two commodities can differ qualitatively only in their use-values. Therefore the identity of the commodities produced by two production processes or the difference of two commodities produced by one is at first just a question of use-value.

Marx used the differences between use-values to differentiate concrete labours. Provided we consider only use-values that are produced singly with only one technique in use at any time, this allows a one-to-one correspondence between use-values and concrete labours. The problem with the anomalous cases is that this one-to-one correspondence breaks down. For joint production involves one type of concrete labour to produce more than one use-value, and different techniques are different concrete labours producing the same use-value.

These peculiarities arising from the use-value aspect of the commodity would be of no significance for the value aspect were it not that the difference or identity of use-values is manifested in their exchange. For the different use-values produced by a joint production process will be sold at their own, in general different, prices. Conversely, if two different production processes produce identical use-values, they must be sold at the same price. In the anomalous cases, the one-to-one correspondence between production processes and the process of exchange of their products breaks down. However, the specification of that correspondence is *always* a contradictory one, counterposing value as an attribute of what is produced with its manifestation in the commodity-form upon exchange.

This relates back to the necessity to derive the contradiction between value and its form, exchange-value, from the unfolding of the value abstraction itself. For until this unfolding leads to the level of abstraction at which capitalist competition is introduced, there is no need for the distinction between values and prices of production, and the anomalous cases disappear. At this level, the market allocation of labour to different production processes is not in conflict with the law of value; cost minimization is value minimization. Therefore any individual commodity produced will have a determinate, positive value. For at no level would commodities be produced unless their *exchange-values* were each positive, and at this level this occurs if and only if their *values* are each positive.[50]

But the development of the commodity-form through exchange entails capitalist competition. As soon as this is taken into explicit account, prices of production must in general differ from values. So we can retain values as attributes of production processes, but we cannot allocate values to individual commodities produced in joint production processes, nor a unique value to the indistinguishable product of two different production processes. Prices of production remain but the expression of value. However, and this is the crucial point, they are the *only* expression of value. Thus the uniqueness and separability of the former is essential, while that of the latter is not.

Marx himself, of course, did not consider these problems specifically. But our treatment here is quite consistent with Marx's own elaboration of his categories, albeit in different contexts. Thus when he considers the results of the production process as a mass of commodities whereby the total capital advanced reproduces itself together with a surplus-value, he remarks: 'The labour expended on each commodity can no longer be calculated—except as an average, i.e. an ideal estimate. The calculation begins with that portion of the constant capital which only enters into the value of the total product

[50] This point comes from Fine and Harris, *Rereading Capital*, chapter 2.

262

in so far as it is used up; it continues with the conditions of production that are consumed communally, and ends with the direct social contribution of many co-operating individuals whose labour is averaged out. This labour, then, is reckoned *ideally* as an aliquot part of the total labour expended on it. When *determining the price* of an individual article it appears as a merely ideal fraction of the total product in which the capital reproduces itself.'[51]

Individual values become 'ideal estimates', fractions of the total, which may or may not be realized in the price-form depending on the quantities of the commodities actually sold. And in his discussion of the time-chitters, he writes: 'Every moment, in calculating, accounting etc., that we transform commodities into value symbols, we fix them as mere exchange-values, making abstraction from the matter they are composed of and all their natural qualities. On paper, in the head, this metamorphosis proceeds by means of mere abstraction; but in the real exchange process a real *mediation* is required, a means to accomplish this abstraction.'[52]

Such a real mediation accounts for the real contradiction underlying all the problems discussed in this paper. The anomalous cases discussed are no more anomalous than the solution of the transformation 'problem', for in each case the anomaly arises from the contradiction between the fundamental concept of socially necessary labour-time and the development of its full consequences in capitalist competition. For the former has implicit within it the operation of the law of value, the minimization of values, while the latter is expressed through the formation of the general rate of profit, and the minimization of costs, that is, prices. It is this contradiction itself that renders the assignment of numerical values to commodities impossible as soon as explicit account is taken of competition. It is this contradiction itself that renders an understanding of the transformation problem as a real-world procedure of the redistribution of surplus-value mistaken; what is required is the dialectical development of categories in order to appropriate a real contradictory world in thought.

It follows that because the law of value operates through the

[51] *Capital* Volume 1, p. 954.
[52] *Grundrisse*, p. 142.

distorted form of capitalist competition, the capital that sets in motion some production processes which are 'wasteful' of total social labour may still be validated by that competition, and hence produce a portion of the total surplus-value. Such 'wasteful' processes are those in which the time spent in the production of a given use-value is longer than that spent in the production of that same use-value by another process (one anomalous case); or those which produce one use-value where another can produce the same use-value plus something extra for the same or less expenditure of human labour-power (the other anomalous case); or those whose continued use is validated by the market in competitive capitalist conditions rather than by the 'pure' operation of the law of value. The last, of course, is the general case of capitalist production, which is itself the ultimate anomaly.

Conclusion

We have attempted in this paper to explain and extend Marx's value theory. In order to provide a framework in which much of the debate on the nature and significance of value theory can be situated, we made a distinction between a Ricardian embodied-labour theory of value and the Marxian theory of value based on the category of abstract labour. While the former is intended immediately to be a theory of price, the latter is so only after several mediations. These mediations are critical to the fundamental differences in method between the two theories.

Ricardo made no distinction between value and exchange-value, demanding unsuccessfully of his theory that it be an immediate explanation of surface phenomena. He failed because capitalist relations are inherently contradictory, and the forms they take constitute a set of appearances that do contradict their fundamental determinations. Two responses to Ricardo's failure were possible. One, that of vulgar economy, was to abandon the search for explanation, seeing in appearances the whole matter in question, and limiting the scope of any particular theory to the requirements of internal consistency. The other, that of Marx, was to recognize capitalist reality as contradictory, and to attempt to structure theory in such a way as to elaborate within it the contradictions of the capitalist world. Therefore his method has to be one that adequately càptures the movement of reality, the historical specificity of the capitalist mode of production, and hence its transience. We have shown how this method of abstraction differs from a method of building theory on assumptions, a method common to the defeated Ricardo and vulgar economy. And by this method of abstracting value as that which is specific to capitalist products, Marx not only had a justification for the distinction between value and exchange-value, but could derive the very necessity for that distinction from the category of value itself.

Hence Marx's transformation procedure is not, as it would be for Ricardo, an attempt to correct an unfortunate disjuncture between an embodied-labour theory of value and the requirements that the equalization of the rate of profit makes of prices. Rather, that disjuncture is recognized as the necessarily contradictory link between value, as the explanation of capitalist production relations, and its expression as exchange-value in prices. Hence it is not surprising that, when competition is accounted for, the one-to-one relationship of values to exchange-value disappears.

We then considered certain modern objections to values, and showed that when brought against Ricardo (often addressed under the pseudonym of Marx) they have validity. But the substance of the objections is not new, in the sense that they are objections to the results of the distinction between exchange-value and value. For this reason, the same objections have no relevance to Marx's theory of value, for the contradictions between value and price, and the anomalies that thereby arise, are explained within the theory itself as consequences of the recognition of value as an attribute of the production of commodities that is validated only by their exchange. Again, it should not be surprising that, when capitalist competition is accounted for, the one-to-one relationship of values to exchange-values disappears.

The anomalies are therefore all of the same sort. They arise out of the elaboration of the contradiction between value and use-value in order to account for the phenomena of capitalist competition. We have shown how this contradiction is contained in the distinction between abstract labour (which produces value) and concrete labour (which produces use-value). The former is commensurated through the exchange of commodities. But there is a second commensuration in capitalism: the equalization of the rate of profit consequent on the purchase and consumption of labour-power in definite amounts of time. The commensuration of these quantities of time through the equalization of the rate of profit contradicts the commensuration of socially necessary labour-times through commodity exchange. The burden of this paper has thus been to show that both commensurations are fundamental to an account of capitalism which reproduces the contradictions of capitalist reality.

For fundamentalists, values are sacred; the commensuration of paid labour-time, while recognized, is allowed no effect on socially necessary labour-times. For Sraffians, values are irrelevant; the only commensuration is that of capitalist competition, and production is a black box technology of input-output coefficients. For Ricardians, there is no realization of Ricardo's contradiction; commensuration is a muddled one of actual labour-times, and analysis cannot be developed since contradiction cannot be contained within Ricardo's framework.

What this paper has attempted is an approach that develops the contradiction between use-value and value such that the contradictory commensurations of capitalism *are* integrated within a methodology of historical materialism. But this is only a beginning in the understanding of the complex reality of the capitalist mode of production.

The Poverty of Algebra

Anwar Shaikh

1. Introduction

Not long ago, it was fashionable in orthodox social science to proclaim that the millennium had begun: the end of poverty; the end of alienation; the end of ideology.

But this was all in theory, of course. Capitalist reality, on the other hand, has continued to develop in its own brutal and crisis-prone manner, in blatant disregard of the tender sensibilities of its ideologues. Nowhere has this had a more devastating effect than in orthodox economics, whose standing has plunged as it has suffered from what Marx once called the 'practical criticism' of the real. At the same time, this justly deserved decline in the status of orthodox economics has been attended by a correspondingly rapid revival of interest in Marx and Marxian economics. We are all Marxists now, after a fashion.

But the trouble is that there is quite a difference between Marx and Marxian economics. Marx laboured over the great body of work in *Capital* for more than twenty-five years, and he never quite finished even this core of his planned greater work.[1] Moreover, the systematic completion of this plan, which he had hoped would be carried out by his successors, was never really undertaken. Instead, in the more than 100 years since his death, Marxian economics has developed erratically and unevenly, with only sporadic connection to Marx's own work:[2] an equation here, a scheme of reproduction there, and a

[1] On the place of *Capital* in Marx's overall planned work, see R. Rosdolsky, *The Making of Marx's Capital*, London 1977, chapter 2.

[2] David McLellan's *Marxism After Marx* (New York 1979) makes abundantly clear

dialectical class struggle everywhere—with the intervening holes filled in with whatever material was álready at hand. *And this material, by and large, has been appropriated from orthodox economics.* As a consequence, the original relationship between Marxist theory and capitalist reality has been 'subtly but steadily substituted by a new relationship between Marxist and bourgeois theory'.[3] We are all Keynesians now, after a fashion.

Given this history, it was inevitable that the revival of interest in Marx, especially in *Capital*, would pose a tremendous difficulty for Marxian economics: how to absorb Marx's conceptual structure, and particularly his theory of value, into a pre-existing 'Marxian' economics in which the great bulk of the analysis is founded precisely on the *absence* of such concepts. How does one absorb the concept of value, for instance, into the dominant analyses of the labour process, price theory, effective demand, accumulation, imperialism, etc., when as currently constructed none of these really 'use' this concept in the first place?

The predicament is unavoidable. If the structure of *Capital* is indeed scientific, then it is based on a *system* of concepts, interlocked and interdependent, and one cannot simply sample individual concepts as one might recipes in a cookbook. Moreover, each concept not only has its place in relation to others, but also has its own particular effects: it influences the facts one uncovers and the conclusions one draws. *It makes its presence felt.* From which it follows that its absence will be felt just as much. It is not possible, for instance, simply to absorb the concept of value into pre-existing analyses that are in fact predicated on its absence: *one or the other must give way.*

There are really only two basic ways out of this quandry. Either

that very little of the history of Marxist thought depends on the specific analysis developed in *Capital*. Economics plays only a small role in all this, and even here a good part of the history is one of a series of struggles to justify the need to set aside the analysis in Marx, or at least 'modernize' it by ridding it of unnecessary and outmoded concepts (such as value). Colletti's essay 'On Bernstein and the Economics of the Second International' brilliantly analyses this process of revision and its conceptual roots (L. Colletti, *From Rousseau to Lenin*, New York 1972). See also Perry Anderson's stimulating book *Considerations on Western Marxism*, London, NLB, 1976.
[3] Anderson, p. 55.

one must demonstrate that the system of concepts in *Capital* can indeed be extended and concretized to deal with existing arguments and historical evidence, or one must show that the dominant formulations in what is currently defined as Marxian economics are in fact based on a superior structure, and Marx's concepts, where 'appropriate', must be reformulated to fit this. In the former case, it is Marxian economics that will inevitably be altered, perhaps decisively, as it is critically appropriated into Marx's conceptual structure. In the latter case, this conceptual structure itself will be modified, and perhaps even rejected in good part, as being inconsistent with currently accepted theories.

The neo-Ricardians, of course, adopt the latter position. Their framework, they argue, is vastly more rigorous than that of Marx, and within it they are easily able to treat a host of issues involving prices of production without any reference whatsoever to value analysis. It follows from this, they insist, that the very notion of value is redundant. What is worse, it is inconsistent with price analysis, since magnitudes in terms of values generally differ from those in terms of price. Operating on this basis, they then conclude that the concept of value must be abandoned, as must a panoply of other arguments of Marx, such as those involving productive and unproductive labour, the falling rate of profit, etc. The remainder, that portion which fits into their framework, is then defined to be the 'essence' of Marx's analysis, and this of course can easily be integrated into a modern framework in the Ricardo-Marx-Sraffa-Keynes-Kalecki tradition.[4]

I wish to argue exactly the opposite position. The analysis of Marx is, 1 claim, vastly superior in its overall structure to anything imaginable within the flat conceptual space of the neo-Ricardians. Indeed, it is their vaunted algebra, on which they base so many of their claims to rigour, that is in fact their greatest weakness. This is so, as we shall see, precisely because their algebra goes hand in hand with a series of concepts taken directly from what Marx calls vulgar economy: equilibrium, profit as a *cost*, and worst of all, perfect competition and all that it entails. It is not the algebra but rather these concepts, whose apologetic and ideological roots are well known,

[4] Ian Steedman, *Marx After Sraffa*, London, NLB, 1977, chapter 14, pp. 205–207.

that generate their basic conclusions. This will become immediately apparent when it is shown that exactly the same algebra generates very different answers and hence very different conclusions, once it is 'asked' different questions. And these questions, in turn, are different exactly because the method and the system of concepts in Marx, his scientific analysis of the law of value, is so unlike that of vulgar economy.

It should be emphasized that I am *not* claiming that neo-Ricardian analysis should be dismissed. On the contrary, I wish to argue that its real contributions can be fully utilized only when they are divested of the vulgar concepts smuggled in with them. This is what the term critique always means: a critical appropriation of knowledge.

In what follows I will therefore briefly outline the structure of Marx's argument in order to highlight the reason why labour-time appears as the regulating principle of exchange relations and the way this regulation occurs. This will be done in section 2.

In section 3 I will present and critically examine the principle arguments of the neo-Ricardians, as represented by the work of Ian Steedman. Here, the argument will proceed along the lines outlined earlier. Section 4 will then contain concluding remarks directed not only at the neo-Ricardians but also at some of their Marxist critics who, having capitulated to the neo-Ricardian algebra, are then forced to revise the concept of the magnitude of value out of existence altogether—in order to 'save' Marx from their misunderstanding of him.

2. The Basic Structure of Marx's Argument

1. The Role of Labour in the Reproduction of Society

In all societies, the objects required to satisfy human needs and wants imply a certain allocation of society's productive activities, of its labour-time, in specific proportions and quantities. Otherwise reproduction of the society itself is impossible: the relation of people to nature must be reproduced if society is to be reproduced. Moreover, the relation of people to nature exists only in and through definite relations of people to people; these are therefore two aspects of the same set of relations that define the mode of (re)production of social life. The production of material wealth goes hand in hand with the reproduction of social relations.

None of this suggests that labour acts unaided. On the contrary, labour is a relation between people and nature, in which people actively and consciously utilize nature to their own ends. The important point here is that *the production process is a labour process, a basic human activity, without which the reproduction of society would be impossible.* By the same token, while it is true that use-values may occasionally arise as the spontaneous fruits of nature (wild grapes, for example), it is obvious that no society could long exist without the *production* of use-values, that is, without labour itself.

In all class societies, labour acquires yet another aspect, since under these circumstances it is the extraction of surplus labour and the creation of the resulting surplus product that forms the material basis for the reproduction of the class relation.

It is therefore Marx's contention that *labour-time is fundamental to the regulation of the reproduction of society:* the performance of labour produces both use-values and social relations; the performance of surplus labour reproduces both the surplus product and the class relation; and a particular distribution of the 'social labour in definite proportions' results in the production of 'the (specific) masses of products corresponding to the different needs' of society.[5]

2. The Role of Labour in the Regulation of Capitalist Society

Capitalist production, like that in every other class society, is also subject to the same fundamental regulation through labour-time. But capitalist production has the peculiarity that is based on generalized commodity production, in which the vast bulk of the products that constitute the material basis of social reproduction are produced without any direct connection to social needs. They are produced instead by private independent labour processes, each one dominated by the profit motive. Neither the connection of a given labour process to the social division of labour, nor indeed the actual usefulness of the

[5] Marx to Kugelmann, 11 July 1868, in *Marx-Engels Selected Correspondence*, third edition, Moscow 1975, p. 196.

product itself, is of any immediate interest to the capitalist involved: only profit matters, in the final analysis.

And so Marx points to the fundamental contradiction that exists here. On the one hand, each labour process is privately undertaken *as if* it was independent of all others, with exchange-for-profit as the goal. On the other hand, this undertaking assumes in advance that other similar labour processes will also intervene at the right time and in the right proportions. Buyers of this product, sellers of the means of production for this process, and sellers of the means of consumption for these capitalists and workers, must all be presupposed if this endeavour is to succeed, and even more important, if it is to be repeated (reproduced).

Each apparently private and independent labour must therefore *presuppose* a social division of labour. Moreover, in order for this presupposition to be realized in practice, the private and apparently anarchic labours must somehow in fact end up being integrated into a social division of labour.

It is in exchange that the apparent independence of each private labour process *collides* with the true inter-dependence inherent in a social division of labour. Exchange is the sphere, as Marx puts it, where the contradictions of commodity production are 'both exposed and resolved'.[6] It is the sphere where the private independent labours are *forcibly articulated into a social division of labour.*[7]

Notice what is being said here. Exchange is the sphere in which the contradiction *internal to production itself*, the contradiction between private labour and the social division of labour, is made visible. It is here that each capitalist first gets the good or bad news, through the medium of prices and profits. But at the same time, because this contradiction is internal to the social division of labour itself, its resolution implies the *domination* of the outcome of exchange, of prices and profits, by social labour-time. The outcomes of exchange are 'the form in which this proportional distribution of labour asserts itself'.[8]

And so we have a double relation: prices and profits as the

[6] K. Marx, *Capital* Volume 3, New York 1967, p. 880.
[7] Colletti, p. 83
[8] Marx to Kugelmann, p. 196.

immediate regulators of reproduction, and social labour-time as the intrinsic regulator of prices and profits and hence of reproduction. The operation of this double relation is what Marx calls the law of value, and it is precisely because of his analysis of the role of labour-time in social reproduction that the law of value rests on a labour theory of value: 'in the midst of the accidental and ever fluctuating exchange relations between the products, the labour-time socially necessary to produce them asserts itself as a regulative law of nature.'

3. Abstract Labour and Value

We have seen why labour-time enters in a fundamental way into the regulation of exchange-value. Now we need to specify exactly how this regulation takes place.

In all form of societies, concrete (i.e. specific) types of labours produce specific types of products: a weaver produces cloth, a baker produces bread. The concrete qualities of their labours result in the concrete forms of their use-values.

However, commodity production is production for exchange, and in exchange the distinct qualities that give various commodities their concreteness are abstracted from by the process of exchange itself. When cloth is exchanged for bread, a certain quantity of the former is socially equated with a certain quantity of the latter. Their concrete differences are therefore subordinated to a common social property, that of having 'quantitative worth'—what Marx calls exchange-value. So, by becoming a commodity, a use-value acquires an additional aspect, that of possessing exchange-value.

As a product, a use-value is the result of concrete labour. This means that the social process of equating different use-values and hence abstracting from their concrete qualities is at the same time a social process of abstracting from the concrete qualities of the labours whose results are these use-values. It follows that the very same set of social relations that endows use-values with the common quantitative property of exchange-value also endows the labour that produces this concrete use-value with the capacity to produce a common abstract quantity. Thus labour too acquires an additional aspect when it is aimed at producing commodities: it acquires the aspect of abstract labour, and from this point of view all commodity-producing labour becomes qualitatively alike and quantitatively comparable.

Because it is only labour actually engaged in the production of commodities that acquires the property of abstract labour, it is only the labour-time of this commodity-producing labour that regulates the exchange-values of commodities. Moreover, since from a social point of view the total labour-time required for the production of a commodity consists of direct and indirect labour-time, it is this total that Marx calls the *intrinsic measure of* a commodity's exchange-value, the labour value of the commodity.[9]

It is important to stress here that the abstraction process described above is a real social process. Abstract labour is the property acquired by human labour when it is directed towards the production of commodities, and as such, it exists *only* in commodity production. The concept of abstract labour is not a mental generalization that we somehow choose to make, but rather the reflection in thought of a real social process. This in turn means that *abstract labour, and hence value, are also real*:[10] commodity-producing labour creates value, which is objectified (materialized) in the form of a commodity. We will see shortly how important this point is in relation to the neo-Ricardians.

There is one further issue here. We have seen that abstract labour has its origin in the process whereby a use-value becomes a commodity. But this process in turn has two possible forms, with quite different implications for abstract labour.

Consider the case of a type of product produced not for exchange but for direct use, say by pre-capitalist peasant labour. Suppose now that a portion of this product happens to find its way into exchange. Then, in this case these use-values become commodities only in the *act* of exchange—which in turn means that the concrete labour that produced them is abstracted from, also acquiring the additional property of abstract labour, only in the moment of exchange itself. Non-commodity *production* therefore involves concrete labour and use-values only, and a portion of these are *realized* as abstract labour and commodities, respectively, only in exchange itself.

[9] Marx, *Theories of Surplus-Value: Volume IV of Capital*, Part II, Moscow 1968, p. 403.
[10] Colletti, p. 87.

274

The matter is very different in the case of *commodity production*. Here the use-value is produced as a commodity, and indeed the whole nature of the production process is dominated by the fact that it is the exchange-value of this commodity that is central to the producer. In this case the use-value acquires its character as a commodity by virtue of the fact that this labour process exists within and through commodity relations, and not merely at the moment of exchange. This use-value is a commodity from its very conception, and the labour is both concrete and abstract from the very outset. *Thus labour involved in the production of commodities produces value, while exchange merely realizes it in money-form.* It is only because of this that Marx can distinguish between the amounts of value and surplus-value created in commodity production, and the generally different amounts realized through exchange. I will return to this point later on, for it is the defenders of Marx themselves who stumble over this issue.

4. *Money and Price*

The preceding analysis also implies that money is an absolutely necessary aspect of developed commodity production. Exchange is the process in which people equate different use-values to another, and money is the necessary medium in which this equation is expressed, and through which the articulation of the private labours is accomplished. Money is the medium of abstraction, and the means of forcible articulation.

The price of each commodity is therefore always a money-price, the golden measure of its quantitative worth. It is what Marx calls the *external measure* of exchange-value, and hence the *form* taken by value in exchange.[11]

Because price is the monetary expression of value in the sphere of exchange, it is always more complexly determined than value. Even in the simplest case, when prices are proportional to values, the money price of a commodity is still a quantity of money (say gold) determined by the value of the commodity *relative* to the standard of price (say one ounce of gold), *and is therefore already a (trans)formation of*

[11] Marx, *Capital*, Volume 1, Penguin Books in association with New Left Review, Harmondsworth 1976, p. 139.

the commodity's value. As such, the movement of prices need not parallel those of commodity values. For instance, prices may rise even when commodity values are falling, if the value of gold falls even faster.[12]

We know, of course, that as Marx develops his argument in *Capital*, the relative complexity of the price-form becomes greater. In Volume 1 price is generally treated as a simple money-form of value, but wages, as time-wages and piece-wages, are already more complex forms of the value of labour-power. In Volume 2 costs of circulation and turnover add fresh determination to the price-form. Lastly, in Volume 3, the development of prices of production and of the division of surplus-value into profits, rents, and interest further concretizes the price-form, while the distinction between individual and average value concretizes the determination of value magnitudes, and through them, those of price magnitudes (individual, average, and regulating prices of production; differential profitability; and rent, absolute and differential). It must be noted here that the increasing complexity of the price-value relationship is no defect. Since price magnitudes are the immediate regulators of reproduction, the law of value must contain within it a theory of the structure of price phenomena—right down to their most concrete determination. Otherwise the law remains abstract, unable to grasp the real movements of the system.

On the other hand, because the price magnitudes are themselves regulated by the socially necessary distribution of labour, the various forms of price categories must be developed in relation to the quantities of socially necessary labour-time whose magnitudes and movements dominate and regulate these price phenomena. We must be able to conceive not only of the relative autonomy of price magnitudes, as expressed in their variability (complexity) relative to values, *but also of the limits to these variations, and of the connection of these limits to social labour-time.* It is significant that in his own development of the increasingly complex categories of price phenomena, Marx never loses sight of the domination of these phenomena by the law of value. 'No matter how the prices are regulated, we arrive at the following:

[12] Ibid., p. 193.

276

'1)   The law of value dominates price movements with reduction or increases in required labour-time making prices of production fall or rise. . . .

'2)   The average profit determining the prices of production must always be approximately equal to that quantity of surplus-value which falls to the share of individual capital in its capacity of an aliquot part of the total social capital. . . . Since the total value of the commodities regulates the total surplus-value, and this in turn regulates the level of average profit and thereby the general rate of profit—as a general law or a law governing fluctuations—it follows that the law of value regulates prices of production.'[13]

In a highly modern vein, Marx goes on to note how meaningless—but how very convenient—it is to treat the difference between price and value (i.e. the *relation* between the two) as a mere separation: 'The price of production includes the average profit. . . . It is really what Adam Smith calls *natural price*, Ricardo calls *price of production*, or *cost of production* . . . because in the long run it is a prerequisite of supply, of the reproduction of commodities in every individual sphere. But none of them has revealed the difference between price of production and value. We can well understand why the same economists who oppose determining the value of commodities by labour-time, i.e. by the quantity of labour contained in them, why they always speak of prices of production as centres around which market-prices fluctuate. They can afford to do it because the price of production is an utterly external and *prima facie* meaningless form of the value of commodities, a form as it appears in competition, therefore in the mind of the vulgar capitalist, and consequently in that of the vulgar economist.'[14]

I remind the reader that Marx is speaking here of economists of his time who claim to ground themselves in 'classical' economics—minus the labour theory of value, of course!

5. Two Aspects of Socially Necessary Labour-Time

In any society, the necessary distribution of social labour-time has two distinct aspects, and these in turn give rise to two different senses of socially necessary labour-time.

[13] K. Marx, *Capital* Volume 3, pp. 179–80.
[14] Ibid., p. 198.

On the one hand, under given conditions of production a certain type of use-value will require a definite quantity of social labour-time for its production. Let us suppose, for instance, that 100,000 hours of social labour-time are required (directly and indirectly) for the production of 50,000 yards of linen. Then 2 hours of labour-time are socially necessary on average to produce *one* yard of linen.

But suppose the expressed social need for linen is actually 40,000 yards. Then the total amount of social labour-time that needs to be directly and indirectly allocated towards the production of linen would be 80,000 hours, other things being equal.

We can thus see that these are two senses of socially necessary labour-time. The first sense represents the actual total labour-time (100,000 hours) expended under given conditions of production. In conjunction with the actual total product (50,000 yards), this defines the average labour-time required per *unit* of product (2 hours per yard).

The second sense, however, refers to the total labour-time that would be required in this branch in order to satisfy expressed social need (80,000 hours).

In commodity production, these two aspects of socially necessary labour-time have further implications.

To begin with, the first aspect defines the total value of the product (100,000 hours) and the unit *social* value of the commodity. The latter is the average amount of abstract labour-time socially necessary for the production of one unit of the commodity.

This unit social value is in turn the basis of the regulating price, a term by which Marx means that price which acts as the centre of gravity of the commodity's market price. In Volumes 1 and 2 this regulating price is supposed to be the commodity's *direct price* (price proportional to unit social value). In Volume 3, after the form of value has been further developed, the price of production takes the place of the direct price as the centre of gravity of market price. For ease in exposition, let us stick to direct price as the regulating price, and let us further assume that $1 represents 1 hour of abstract labour-time. Then since the unit social value of a yard of linen is 2 hours, its direct price will be $2.

The second aspect of socially necessary labour-time then specifies the relation between the regulating price and the market.

The actual production of linen is 50,000 yards, which represents

278

100,000 hours of value created in production. The regulating price of this, which is by assumption the direct price, is $2 per yard. Suppose now that at this regulating price, the expressed social need, i.e. the effective demand, for this product is only 40,000 yards of linen, which represents only 80,000 hours of labour-time. Then the fact that the actual amount of total labour-time devoted to linen production is greater than the amount socially necessary to meet effective demand means that the market price of the commodity will fall below its direct price of $2—to say $1.50 per yard of linen. The 50,000 yards actually produced will therefore sell for $75,000 in the market, and since $1 represents one hour of abstract labour, this means that the value realized in exchange, in the form of money, is 75,000 hours. And so we see that because the actual labour-time devoted to this branch is greater than the labour-time socially necessary to meet effective demand, a product representing a value of 100,000 hours is sold in the market for the monetary equivalent of only 75,000 hours. The 'violation of this (necessary) proportion makes it impossible to realize the value of the commodity and thus the surplus-value contained in it.'[15]

To summarize: Socially necessary labour-time in the first sense defines the total value and unit social value of the commodity, and through the latter, the commodity's regulating price. Socially necessary labour-time in the second sense, on the other hand, defines the relation between regulating price and market price. Both senses must be kept in mind if one is to understand exactly how social labour-time dominates and regulates the exchange-process. We will see later that a failure to distinguish between these two real aspects of socially necessary labour-time, and hence a failure to recognize Marx's own distinction between these two aspects, so confuses some Marxists that they end up abandoning the concept of the magnitude of value (as distinct from price) altogether.

3. Critique of the Neo-Ricardians

In what follows I will divide the main points of the neo-Ricardian

[15] Ibid., p. 636.

position, as summarized by Steedman, into four major groups and then address each in turn.

1. The Redundancy Argument

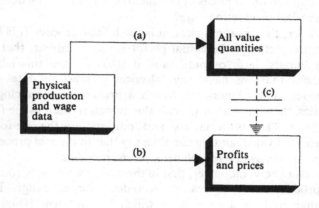

FIGURE 1

Figure 1 above illustrates the first major argument marshalled by the neo-Ricardians, which as Steedman notes, has been made 'in various forms, by many different writers over the last 80 years', and in which he claims 'no logical flaw has ever been found'.[16] Such brave words clearly deserve a closer examination.

Steedman explains the argument as follows. The box on the left represents the physical production data and the real wage, and these 'suffice to *determine* the rate of profit ... and all prices of production', as illustrated by the path marked '(b)'. At the same time, 'the quantities of labour embodied in the various commodities ... can themselves only be *determined* once the conditions of production are known', as illustrated by path (a). From this it follows at once that

---

[16] Steedman, *Marx After Sraffa*. The diagram is from p. 48, the quotes from p. 49, note 15.

labour values therefore '*play no essential role* in the *determination* of the rate of profit (or of the prices of production)'.[17] In other words, values are redundant in the analysis of exchange relationships.

Notice how often the word 'determine' crops up: the physical production data *determine* values, and in conjunction with the real wage also *determine* prices of production. But what then determines this physical production data?

In Marx, the answer is clear: it is the labour process. It is human productive activity, the actual performance of labour, that transforms 'inputs' into 'outputs', and it is only when this labour is successful that we have any 'physical production data' at all. Moreover, if the labour process is a process of producing commodities, then it is one in which value is materialized in the form of use-values. Thus both 'inputs' and 'outputs' are the use-forms of materialized value, and we can then say that in the *real* process, it is *values that determine the 'physical production data'.*

We also know, moreover, that in the *real* process of reproduction, the production of use-values *precedes* their exchange. Indeed, exchange itself is a process in which the different labour-times involved in producing these use-values actually confront each other, and are eventually articulated into a social division of labour— through the medium of money prices. Thus it is *values that also determine prices*, in a double sense: prices are the forms taken by values in exchange, and the magnitudes of these values dominate and regulate the movements of their price forms. The latter point must of course be developed further, since we need to show not merely that prices of production and profits rest on the expression in circulation of value and surplus-value, but also that the former magnitudes are regulated by the latter. This we take up in the next section. Nonetheless, we may summarize the above argument in a diagram, figure 2, that serves as a contrast to figure 1.

How do neo-Ricardians manage to miss so elementary a point? It is, I think, because of two fundamental weaknesses characteristic of their analysis. First, in spite of their protestations to the contrary,[18]

---

[17] Ibid., p. 14. In all these quotes, the emphasis on the word 'determine' is mine.

[18] Steedman states that 'all production is assumed to be carried out by workers, in a socialized labour process . . .'. (Ibid, p. 17). Nonetheless, he remains quite oblivious to the elementary implications of this assumption, and continues to speak of 'physical

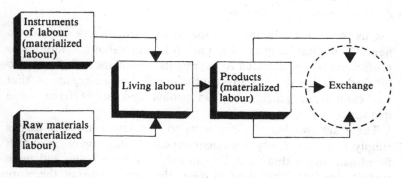

FIGURE 2

they tend to view production as a technical process, as physical data, instead of a labour process in which human labour is objectified in use-values. Hence the characteristic emphasis of the neo-Ricardians on distribution: once the labour process is seen as a technical process, only 'distribution' appears truly social.

Second, they typically confuse the real process with its appropriation in thought. In the real process, as we have seen, social labour-time *really* regulates exchange. The physical *data* are then a conceptual summary of the real determination, and if we then use the data to conceptually *calculate* values, we only capture in thought their real magnitudes. Such a calculation no more determines these values than does the calculation of the mass of the earth determine either the earth or its mass. It merely recognizes what already exists. This is a fundamental point in a materialist view of the world, and the eighty-year failure of the neo-Ricardians to distinguish real and conceptual determination reveals their long attachment to an idealist method.

---

conditions of production' *determining* 'the quantities of labour embodied in the various commodities' (ibid., p. 14).

282

2. *The Inconsistency Argument*

Let us return for a moment to the neo-Ricardian fork diagram in figure 1. In that diagram, the path (c) from value magnitudes to profits and prices is dotted to express its redundancy. But it is also blocked off, in order to represent the neo-Ricardian argument 'that one cannot, in general, explain profits and prices from value quantities . . .'.[19]

There are two basic components to this argument. The first is simply the redundancy argument repeated once again, in which Steedman insists that since he can *calculate* both value and price magnitudes from the physical data, the former cannot therefore determine the latter. For him, only algebra 'explains' anything. We have already dealt with the superficiality of this type of reasoning.

The second element is more substantive, though it, like the first, is hardly new. In essence, this point has to do with the 'transformation problem'. In what follows I will therefore present both the problem and its treatment, though the main results I will utilize are developed by me elsewhere, and will merely be outlined here.

The basic issues are well known. Following Steedman's own analysis, we abstract from fixed capital and joint production,[20] and consider a given mass of use-values representing a given sum of values and sum of surplus-values. Then, with prices proportional to values (for simplicity in exposition, let $1 represent 1 hour of value), this mass of use-values will be expressed in exchange as a sum of direct prices and direct profits. Under these circumstances all money magnitudes are directly proportional to the corresponding value magnitudes, and therefore all money ratios are equal to the corresponding value ratios. In this case, the relationship between production and circulation is specially transparent.

Now consider the same mass of use-values, hence the same sum of values and surplus-values, exchanged at prices of production. We are considering, in other words, a change in the form of value alone, from

[19] Ibid, p. 49.
[20] Ibid, p. 50. Steedman notes that these general conclusions hold even when we abstract from fixed capital and joint production. We will therefore similarly restrict our analysis here, all the more so since a proper treatment of these two questions cannot be undertaken until the simpler ones have been addressed. The 'choice of technique', on the other hand, will be treated in the next subsection.

direct prices to prices of production. Prices of production are therefore transformed direct prices, and since the latter are themselves the monetary (trans-)forms of value, prices of production are doubly transformed values.

The relation between the sum of prices and the sum of values defines the value of money. If we then keep the value of money constant in order to simplify the analysis, the sum of prices of production will equal the sum of direct prices. The sum of money prices will, in other words, be constant across the transformation. Nonetheless, individual prices of production (transformed direct prices) will differ from individual direct prices. Strictly speaking, one should refer to these differences as 'price of production – direct price deviations'. This is a very awkward term, however, and it is much simpler to follow Marx's usage and speak of 'price-value' and 'profit-surplus-value' deviations. I will therefore stick to this traditional usage, but with the clear understanding that the deviations we speak of are between money magnitudes.

It is evident that no change in the mere exchange ratios through which a given total product is distributed can alter the total mass of use-values so distributed. It follows immediately, as Marx points out, that no change in exchange ratios can alter either the sum of values or the sum of surplus-values; it can only result in a different kind of division of these totals.[21]

It does *not* follow that the *monetary* expression of these sums is invariant: even with the value of money constant, so that the sum of prices is constant, the sum of transformed profits (corresponding to prices of production) will in general differ from direct profits. The question is, given that circulation neither creates nor destroys values (assuming the whole product is sold), how is it that profits can differ from surplus-value?

When a commodity is sold at its direct price, the seller and buyer exchange equal values in commodity-form and money-form, respectively. But when prices deviate from values, a transfer of value takes place during the exchange process. For instance, when a commodity sells at a price below its value (i.e. below direct price), the capitalist who sells the commodity receives a value in money-form that is less

[21] Marx, *Capital* Volume 3, p. 43.

than the value he hands over in the form of a commodity, and vice versa for the buyer. Surplus-value is therefore transferred from seller to buyer.

To understand the general implications of this, let us first divide the total social production into three great branches (means of production, workers' articles of consumption, and capitalists' articles of consumption), and then, on this basis, analyse the effects of price-value deviations on the transfers of value in simple reproduction. To do this we will consider the effect of price-value deviations in each branch *taken singly*, holding the prices of the remaining two branches exactly equal to values. We are therefore momentarily allowing the sum of prices to deviate from the sum of values, though we will soon return to this equality. It is important to note that this is an analytical device only, not a description of an actual process.

Suppose the first branch raises its total price above its total value, with the other two keeping their prices equal to values. Then the gain in profits of the first branch is exactly equal to the rise in the sum of prices. This branch, however, sells means of production, which in simple reproduction are equal in magnitude to those used up as constant capital in all three branches. Therefore the price rise of the first branch, *which is the same thing as the rise in the sum of prices*, produces an exactly equal rise in the total cost-price of all three branches. But if the sum of cost-price rises as much as the sum of prices, the difference between the two, which is the *sum of profits*, is not changed at all. It follows therefore that though the first branch can alter its own profits by altering its price, other things being equal, this cannot in any way give rise to any change in the sum of profits. What is gained by one capitalist as *capital-value*, in the *form of profits*, is exactly offset by what is lost by the capitalist class as a whole as *capital-value*, in the form of constant capital. *The transfers of value therefore remain within the circuit of capital, so that within this circuit the net transfer of value is zero.*

A similar analysis can be conducted for the second branch, which sells workers' articles of consumption. Here, any rise in this total price is initially at the expense of the immediate buyers, who are the workers as a whole. But since we are considering a change in the form of value alone, the value of labour-power and hence the real wage are held constant, so that any rise in the price of workers' means of subsistence is also a rise in the variable capital advanced by capitalists in all three branches for the purchase of labour-power. Consequently, here too the sum of cost prices will rise exactly as much as the sum of prices, so that total profits remain unchanged. The second branch can alter its own profits, but only at the expense of the profits of the remaining two branches, because what it gains as capital-value in the form of profits is also lost by the capitalist class as a whole as capital-value in the form of variable capital. Once again, the transfers of value remain internal to the circuit of capital, with the consequence that the net transfer is always zero.

We come finally to the sale of capitalist articles of consumption, the third branch. A change in total price here, say a fall in total price below value, holding all other prices constant, means an equivalent fall in its profit below surplus-value, and of course an equal fall in the overall sum of prices. Thus far, this is similar to the previous two cases. But from here on the analysis differs, because the loss in *capital-value* due to profits being below surplus-value in the third branch appears as a gain in *revenue-value* to the capitalists who buy these articles of consumption. Though this loss in capital-value is indeed compensated by a corresponding gain elsewhere in social reproduction, this compensating effect disappears from the purview of the circuit of capital and is therefore not 'charged', so to speak, against the fall in profit. It is this transfer of value between the circuit of capital and the circuit of revenue, through the process of exchange, that explains why price-value deviations can give rise to deviations between the sum of profits and the sum of surplus-values, *without violating the law of the conservation of value through exchange*.

The above results were explicitly derived for the case of simple reproduction only. However, as I show elsewhere, they can be extended to cover expanded reproduction also. Moreover, in this general form they hold true for any price-value deviations at all, not merely those arising from the formation of prices of production.

In most analyses of social reproduction, the circuit of capitalist revenue is not explicitly accounted for. Of course, under these circumstances it appears completely mysterious that as prices deviate from values, a given surplus-product and hence a given mass of surplus-value can manifest itself as a variable mass of profit.

However, once the *whole* of social circulation is analysed, the mystery disappears. To the extent that price-value deviations give rise to transfers between the circuit of capital and the circuit of capitalist revenue, these transfers will manifest themselves as differences between actual profit and direct profits. Ironically, though this phenomenon is evidently a mystery to most Marxist discussions of this issue, it was no mystery to Marx himself: 'This phenomena of the conversion of capital into revenue should be noted, because it creates the *illusion* that the amount of profit grows (or in the opposite case decreases) independently of the amount of surplus-value.'[22]

None of this should come as any surprise once the difference between value and form-of-value has been grasped. Value and surplus-value are created in production, and expressed as money magnitudes in circulation. Since the circulation magnitudes are more concrete, they are necessarily more complexely determined than value magnitudes, for they express not only the conditions of production of value but also the conditions of its circulation. As such, the relative autonomy of the sphere of circulation necessarily expresses itself as the relative autonomy of price magnitudes from value magnitudes. Profits, in other words, depends not only on the mass of surplus-value but also on its specific mode of circulation.

The concept of the relative autonomy of circulation from production implies not only that profit can vary independently of surplus-value, *but also that this independence is strictly limited.* It is necessary, therefore, to show how value categories themselves provide the limits to the variations in their money-expressions.

Intuitively, it is evident from the preceding discussion that the overall deviation of actual profits from direct profits is the combined result of two factors. First, it depends on the extent to which the prices of capitalists' articles of consumption deviate from the values of these articles—that is, it depends on the manner in which surplus-

[22] Marx, *Theories of Surplus-Value*, Part III, Moscow 1971, p. 347. It is interesting to note that Marx discovers this phenomenon in connection with his analysis of differential rent, and not that of price of production. It is often forgotten by Marxists that differential rent also implies price-value deviations, since it is the marginal conditions of production that regulate the market price while it is the average conditions of production that always determine (social) value. Thus even when the regulating price is equal to value, it is in this case equal to the unit value in the marginal land, which is necessarily different (higher) than the average unit value. Thus the regulating price deviates from (average) value.

value is distributed among capitalists, and on the resultant pattern of individual price-value deviations. And second, it depends on the extent to which this surplus-value is consumed by capitalists as revenue—that is, on the distribution of this surplus-value between capital and revenue. Even when prices deviate from values, the size of any transfer from the circuit of capital to the circuit of revenue will also depend on the relative size of the circuit of revenue. Where all surplus-value is consumed, as in simple reproduction, the deviation of actual profits from direct profits will be at its maximum. When, on the other hand, all surplus-value is re-invested, in maximum expanded reproduction, then there is no circuit of capitalist revenue and consequently no transfer at all: total actual profits must, in this case, equal total direct profits, regardless of the size and nature of individual price-value deviations.[23]

With only a little more effort, one can extend the preceding results on the sum of profits to the case of the rate of profit. It will be recalled that when all capital turns over in one period, as is assumed here, the rate of profit is equal in magnitude to the mass of profit divided by the cost-price. The sum of prices, on the other hand, is the sum of cost-prices and the sum of profits. Then, if with a constant sum of prices, individual price-value deviations cause the sum of profits to be larger than surplus-value, the sum of cost-prices will be correspondingly smaller than $C+V$. Then the average money rate of profit will be larger than the value rate of profit $\left(\dfrac{S}{C+V}\right)$ on account of both a larger numerator and a smaller denominator. Nonetheless, the general relation between the two is merely another expression of the total profit-surplus deviations analysed above, and is therefore subject to the same fundamental determination.[24]

All this was based on arbitrary market prices. If we now confine

[23] This result has been mathematically known for some time, *though not conceptually grasped*, as the equality of profits and surplus-value along the Von-Neumann ray. See A. Shaikh, *Theories of Value and Theories of Distribution*, unpublished Ph.D. dissertation, Columbia University, 1973, chapter 4, section 4, and M. Morishima, *Marx's Economics*, Cambridge 1973, p. 142.

[24] For further details, see my unpublished paper 'The Transformation From Marx to Sraffa (Prelude to a Critique of the Neo-Ricardians)', March 1980.

288

ourselves to prices of production, we can be even more precise. Since the mass of profit and the rate of profit are so closely connected as far as these issues are concerned, it is sufficient to illustrate the argument for the latter.

We begin by noting that for given conditions of the labour process, the value rate of profit r° can always be expressed as a steadily (i.e. monotonic) increasing function of the rate of surplus-value.

$$1. \qquad r^\circ = \frac{S}{C+V}$$

where S = surplus-value, V = value of labour power. Let $L = V + S$ = value-added by living labour (if N = the number of workers employed, and h = the length of the working day in hours, then $L = Nh$). Let $k = \dfrac{C}{L}$ = the ratio of dead to living labour. Then

$$2. \qquad r^\circ = \frac{\dfrac{S}{V}}{\left(\dfrac{C}{L}\right)\left(\dfrac{L}{V}\right)+1} = \frac{\dfrac{S}{V}}{k\left(1+\dfrac{S}{V}\right)+1}$$

Since k depends only on the technology and the length of the working day h, when these conditions of the labour process are given, r° will vary directly with the rate of surplus-value. Thus the value rate of profit is a monotonic increasing function of the rate of surplus-value.[25]

In recent years, several authors have shown that when direct prices are transformed into prices of production, though the transformed money rate of profit r will in general deviate from the value rate (we have already seen how and why), nonetheless this transformed rate also is a monotonic increasing function of the rate of surplus-value.[26] But once it is recognized that the value rate of profit r° and the transformed rate r both increase as $\dfrac{S}{V}$ increases, it follows at once that

[25] A. Shaikh, 'The Transformation From Marx to Sraffa', section III. 3.
[26] A. Shaikh, *Theories of Value* . . ., chapter 4, section 4, and M. Morishima, *Marx's Economics*, p. 64.

they must move together: *when the value rate of profit rises (falls) its reflection in the sphere of circulation, the transformed rate of profit, also rises (falls)*.

Figure 3 depicts this intrinsic relationship. For the sake of illustration, it is assumed here that $r°$ is larger than r, though of course it could equally well be the other way around.[27]

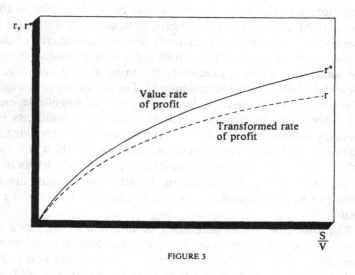

FIGURE 3

It is interesting to note that although Marx insists that the equalization of the rate of profit and the formation of individual prices of production are of great importance for individual capitals or subsets of capitals, he also insists that for the system as a whole the previously derived laws are basically unaltered. In a letter to Engels, after presenting the basic phenomena arising from the transformation process, Marx goes on to summarize what remains to be

[27] The general shape of the functional relationship of r to S/V can be derived graphically from M. Morishima, *Marx's Economics*, p. 64, figure 2. The relationship between $r°$ and S/V, on the other hand, follows simply from equation 2 in this paper. A much more detailed treatment of the theoretical and empirical relationship between the value rate of profit $r°$ and the transformed rate of profit r is provided in my paper 'The Transformation from Marx to Sraffa . . .', sections III and IV. In the aggregate, these two ratios turn out to be virtually indistinguishable.

developed. 'Further: the *changed outward form* of the law of value and surplus-value—which were previously set forth and which are still valid—*after the transformation of value into price of production.*'[28]

At all times and in all places, price is the outward form of value, the reflection of value in the sphere of circulation. What the transformation does, Marx argues, is to transform this outward form, to introduce into it certain fresh determination and new sources of variation, but to do so in such a way as to leave the intrinsic connections unchanged. Look again at figure 3. It illustrates this conception perfectly: in the relatively autonomous mirror of circulation, the transformed rate of profit appears *as a displaced image of the value rate of profit*, essentially the same in determination but somewhat different in exact magnitude. The autonomy of the sphere of circulation is expressed in this displacement of magnitude; on the other hand, the limited nature of this autonomy manifests itself precisely through the fact that it is the structure of value categories (the pattern of organic compositions, and the proportion of surplus-value that is converted into revenue) that provides the limits to this displacement effect. The variations in the form of value are thus shown to be conditioned and limited by the very structure of value itself.

The notion of relative autonomy, of variation within limits, is of course entirely absent from the neo-Ricardian discussion. Given their own deep debt to orthodox economics, this should come as no surprise. Consequently, they have always insisted that the difference between value and its expression in circulation implies an inconsistency, a complete divorce of inner connection, between the two.

The money rate of profit, Steedman notes, is generally different from the value rate. From this he concludes that 'the latter ratio provides no adequate measure of either the rate of profit in a capitalist economy or the potential for accumulation in such an economy. . . .'[29] This is the ventriloquist voice of his method speaking, not the algebra. It is, moreover, an obscurantist voice, precisely because it takes refuge in algebra in order to obscure the profound silence on the question of method.

[28] Marx to Engels, 20 April 1868, in *Marx–Engels Selected Correspondence*, p. 194.
[29] Steedman, p. 205.

Three further points should be made on this subject. First of all, even though we can establish that individual price-value deviations do not alter the fact that aggregate value magnitudes clearly regulate aggregate price magnitudes, it is not sufficient to stop here. Once we move to a more concrete analysis, then the individual price-value deviations and the transfers of value to which they give rise become quite important in their own right. For the analysis of the phenomena of competition, of regional and international differences, of development and underdevelopment, the relation of the parts to the whole is itself of paramount concern.[30] Once we consider these issues, then it becomes important to address the theoretical determinants of individual price-value deviations, in terms of both their directions (which dictate the directions of the transfers of value) and their magnitudes (which indicate how large such transfers are likely to be).

In addition, we also need to look at the empirical magnitudes involved. Indeed, this second issue is implicit in the issue of the theoretical determinants, since in Marx's method the purpose of theory is to grasp the structure of the real relations—which can be done only through the study of these real relations themselves.[31]

This in turn leads to the third point. Given that theory must be developed in conjunction with the '"material of observation" which, precisely because it is *material*, can "weed out . . . hypotheses, doing away with some and correcting others until finally the law is established in a pure form" . . .',[32] it follows that scientific abstraction must be what Marx calls a 'determinate abstraction'. Abstraction must be typification, the extraction from some aspect of the real of its 'simplest characterization'.[33]

In bourgeois social science, however, abstractions tend to be idealizations, not typifications. When Marx speaks of the reproduc-

[30] See, for instance, my paper 'Foreign Trade and the Law of Value', *Science and Society*, fall 1979 (Part I) and spring 1980 (Part II), in which I discuss the role of trade, capital flows, and transfer of value between capitalist regions.

[31] In my paper 'The Transformation From Marx to Sraffa' I establish on both theoretical and empirical grounds that the typical price-value deviation is $\pm 20\%$ for both market prices and prices of production, with typical correlation coefficients (adjusted for heteroskedasticity) of about 93%. As I note in my paper, Ricardo seemed to have a vastly superior grasp of these relations than do the neo-Ricardians!

[32] Colletti, p. 42.

[33] Ibid, p. 43.

tion of the moving contradiction that is capitalist commodity-production, a reproduction process that necessarily must occur by trial-*through*-error, he always speaks of a process of tendential regulation in which discrepancies and errors of one sort constantly produce those of an opposite sort. 'The total movement of this disorder is its order.'[34] Similarly, when he speaks of capitalist competition, he speaks of it as a *war* in which 'each individual capital strives to capture the largest possible share of the market and supplant its competitors and exclude them from the market—*competition of capitals*'.[35]

The neo-Ricardians, on the other hand, are safely ensconced within equilibrium analysis, conducted on the assumption of 'something like perfect competition'.[36] These concepts do not merely idealize capitalist reality, they systematically and ideologically obscure it. Their pride of place in neo-Ricardian analysis therefore highlights once again the profound limitations of this school of thought. It has been so successful in its struggle against neo-classical theory not merely because it is better than its adversary, but also because it is so similar to it. With this in mind, we turn to the third major type of argument made by the neo-Ricardians against the theory of value in Marx.

3. The Primacy Argument

In the previous section I argued that the quantitative difference between, say, the value and money rates of profit did not and should not obscure the more fundamental qualitative *and* quantitative relation between the two. Steedman does not see this, naturally, because his method does not afford him the concept of relative autonomy. But to this Steedman would reply: 'Now if these profit rates differ, which is the significant one? Which will affect capitalists' decisions and actions? And which will tend to be made uniform, as between industries, in a competitive economy? The answer is self-

[34] K. Marx, *Wage-Labour and Capital*, reprinted in the *Marx-Engels Reader*, edited by Robert C. Tucker, New York 1972, p. 175.

[35] Marx, *Theories of Surplus-Value*, Part II, p. 484.

[36] Armstrong and A. Glyn, 'The Law of the Falling Rate of Profit and Oligopoly: a Comment on Shaikh', *Cambridge Journal of Economics*, 1979, 3, p. 69.

evident; it is the money rate of profit which affects decisions and tends to be equalized. The "value rate of profit", used by Marx, is of no concern to the capitalists, it is unknown to the capitalists. . . . The implication is clear; $S/(C+V)$ is not a significant rate of profit in a capitalist economy, and it does *not* equal the actual, money, rate of profit.'[37]

There are three levels of argument here. At the first, Steedman notes that all actual decisions are made in terms of money magnitudes. This is, of course, the point of departure for Marx also. Money prices and profits are the immediate regulators of reproduction, and the very object of the law of value is to discover their inner laws.

At the next level, Steedman goes on to say that because the value rate of profit is 'unknown to the capitalists', 'of no concern' to them, it is '*not* a significant rate of profit in a capitalist economy'. How extraordinary it is to claim that only what 'the capitalists know' is significant, in other words, that appearances are significant but essences are not! In one stroke Steedman throws out all science.

But there is a third level here, with an even deeper problem. Let us stop for a minute and ask what it is that these capitalists in fact 'know'.

Well, capitalists know that capitalism is an unplanned society, in which they are free to take their chances producing commodities in the hope of making a profit. And they certainly know that there is no guarantee they will receive this profit, *or any profit at all*, and even if they do, that they will be able to repeat it. They therefore know that prices and profits fluctuate constantly, and that there is never at any moment a *uniform* rate of profit, *so that prices of production never exist as such*. It follows from this that the prices, the individual profit rates, and even the average rate of profit, on which capitalists base their actual decisions, are never equal to prices of production and the uniform profit rate on which Steedman apparently bases *his* decisions.[38] The uniform rate of profit is of course 'unknown to the

[37] Steedman, p. 30.

[38] Steedman makes much of the fact that since direct prices differ from prices of production, the average profit rate in terms of direct prices (which is the value rate of profit) will differ from the average profit rate in terms of prices of production (which is, of course, the uniform rate of profit). But he does not seem to notice that this would

capitalists', hence of 'no concern to them', and therefore by his own argument it is '*not* a significant rate of profit in a capitalist economy'.

Fortunately for him, the last proposition is not true. And that is simply because it is his argument itself that is not significant. But then if one argues instead that prices of production and the uniform rate of profit are important even though they never exist as such in circulation—precisely because they dominate and regulate the constantly fluctuating constellation of market prices and profit rates—then it is equally true that values and the value rate of profit are even more important because they in turn dominate and regulate prices of production and the uniform rate of profit. And this is just what Marx argues all along.

One might ask: how could Steedman make so egregious an error? Quite simply because he operates entirely within the concept of equilibrium. If one assumes that there is no contradiction between private independently undertaken labours and the social division of labour, so that the articulation of labour is *immediate*, then one can equally well assume that prices of production and the uniform rate of profit obtain directly in circulation. *But then the characteristic contradiction of capitalism has been spirited away altogether.* Once you replace the concept of tendential regulation with that of equilibrium, you have switched from abstraction as typification to abstraction as idealization. This is, of course, characteristic of vulgar economy, and is built into the basic mathematical formulations on which Steedman relies so heavily.

4. The Choice of Technique Argument

The neo-Ricardian pattern of confusing tendential regulation with equilibrium, and of competitive battle with perfect competition, shows up even more forcefully in their analysis of the so-called choice of technique. Since I have discussed this issue elsewhere, I will only mention the central points here.[39]

---

also hold for any two sets of differing prices, so that in general the average profit rate in terms of market prices will *never* be equal to the uniform rate of profit.

[39] A. Shaikh, 'Political Economy and Capitalism: Notes on Dobb's Theory of Crisis', *Cambridge Journal of Economics*, 1978, 2, pp. 233–251. See also the debate surrounding the above article, and my rejoinder on 'Marxian Competition Versus

Steedman begins by noting that capitalists in a particular industry often have the possibility of more than one method of production. The method chosen, he argues, is then the one that yields the highest rate of profit,[40] as estimated in terms of existing wages and prices. As always, these existing prices are exactly equal to prices of production, all rates of profit are exactly equal to the uniform rate, and equilibrium rules everywhere. Because capitalists choose the method with the highest rate of profit, no method will be adopted unless it is higher than their own existing rate of profit, and since this rate is identically equal to the uniform rate of profit, they will adopt a new method only if it yields a rate of profit higher than the uniform rate. It follows from this that the adoption of a new method in effect adds a new higher rate of profit to the existing rates (which by assumption are all equal to the uniform rate), and therefore ends up eventually raising the uniform rate of profit itself.

From a neo-Ricardian point of view, this means that if we had knowledge of all the possible methods in all the different industries, we could assemble them into different combinations of one method per industry, and then argue that the particular combination that in practice would be adopted at a given real wage would be the one that yields 'the highest possible uniform rate of profit'.[41] So, the knowledge of the real wage and possible combinations of methods enables Steedman to identify the combination that would yield the highest uniform rate. He therefore concludes that it is the real wage and the spectrum of possible combinations that 'determine' the uniform rate of profit and the actual combination (physical data). And only when the actual combination is given, according to him, are values 'determined'. The 'determination of the profit rate is thus *logically prior* to any determination of value magnitudes', so that when 'there is a choice of technique, any attempt to ground the theory of the rate of profit on any value magnitudes must be ill-conceived'.[42]

This whole analysis is a résumé of the characteristic confusions of

---

Perfect Competition: Further Comments on the So-called Choice of Technique', *Cambridge Journal of Economics*, 1980, 4, pp. 75–83.

[40] Steedman, p. 64.

[41] Ibid, p. 64.

[42] Ibid, p. 65.

296

the neo-Ricardian school. To begin with, once it is recognized that market prices and profit rates can never exactly equal prices of production and the uniform rate of profit, then the whole process of reducing the question to one of selecting the combination that yields the highest uniform rate of profit falls apart. Suppose, for instance, that market prices differ from prices of production, so that industry profit rates differ from the uniform rate of the neo-Ricardians. Then, precisely because calculations are being made in terms of prices that do not directly embody the uniform rate of profit, a new method in a particular industry can raise the industry's profit rate *and at the same time lower the uniform rate.* A production method that yields a higher than average rate of profit at one set of prices need not do so at some other set. Steedman himself emphasizes this possibility vis-a-vis the 'inconsistency' between prices of production and direct prices, without noting that it applies with the same force to the 'inconsistency' between market prices and prices of production.[43] Had he done so, however, he would have been forced to conclude on the basis of his own logic that prices of production and the uniform rate of profit are not significant on two counts: not only are they 'unknown to the capitalists', etc., but their very use in analysis can lead us to false conclusions.

However, there is an even more basic error in Steedman's logic. Consider the fact that when capitalists evaluate methods of production, they do so not only on the basis of anticipated prices of the plant, equipment, materials, and labour-power, but also on the anticipated performance of the labour process associated with this method (which will determine the anticipated relation between 'inputs' and 'outputs'), and finally on the estimated conditions of sale. Therefore, the profits they evaluate are themselves potential profits based on the potential creation of value and surplus-value in production, and on their estimated realization in circulation. So we may say that, *even in thought,* surplus-value regulates profit. Moreover, for this potential itself to be made real, actual value and

---

[43] It is only in some recent unpublished papers that Steedman has begun to notice that the difference between actual market prices and theoretical prices of production 'raises important questions for contemporary analysis'. (Ian Steedman, 'Natural Price, Market Price, and the Mobility of Money Capital', unpublished paper, 1978, p. 5).

surplus-value will have to be produced and then realized, so that *in practice also*, surplus-value regulates profit.

Lastly, I would argue that even the neo-Ricardian description of the process whereby methods are evaluated is false. Steedman tells us that 'each industry will seek to adopt that production method which minimizes costs'.[44] On the surface, this is similar to Marx's argument that competition drives capitalists to increase the productivity of labour in order to lower cost-prices. But when Steedman speaks of 'costs', he means *prices*, i.e. cost-prices *plus* profit. The neo-Ricardian analysis, in other words, *is predicated on the treatment of profit as a 'cost' of production*. Once profit is treated as what it truly is, an excess over all costs, then on top of everything else, the neo-Ricardian claim that the profit rate cannot fall due to a rising organic composition is also falsified.[45] In the end, rather than being their strongest case, their treatment of the so-called choice of technique turns out to be the weakest of all.

4. Concluding Remarks

Recent events have led to a tremendous revival of interest in Marxian economic analysis. But this process has also produced its own specific problems, because as Marxian economics gains in respectability, the temptation to represent itself in 'respectable' terms grows accordingly. And these terms, in the end, are almost always the wrong ones.

There is no question that Marxism must appropriate all modern developments. But to appropriate them involves much more than merely adopting them: it involves tearing them out of the bourgeois framework in which they appear, examining their hidden premises, and re-situating them (when and if possible) on a Marxist terrain—a terrain that cannot be derived merely by algebraic variation or sociological transformation of the premises of orthodox economics. We must, and indeed we do, have our own ground to stand upon.

It is my contention that the neo-Ricardian (Sraffa-based) tradi-

[44] Steedman, *Marx After Sraffa*, p. 64.
[45] For a more detailed presentation of this argument, see the papers cited in footnote 39.

298

tion is by far too 'respectable'. Its roots in (left) Keynesianism are easy to establish, and its refuge in mathematical economics is quite revealing. Nonetheless, the claims made by this school must be addressed, and its real contributions must be separated out from what is merely part of its cloak of respectability. In this paper I attempt to do just that, by focusing on the central arguments involved. Secondary matters involving questions of fixed capital and joint-production are not treated here, in part because of their greater difficulty, and in part because of the astonishing weakness of the neo-Ricardian formulation of these issues. An adequate treatment of these issues would require confronting these formulations themselves, in terms of both their internal consistency and their (external) adequacy to the relations they pretend to represent. Such an investigation is well beyond the scope of the present paper.

The neo-Ricardians tell us that the concept of value in Marx is not only unnecessary in the analysis of capitalism, but also irreconcilable with the actual relations involved.

In order to address these claims, I have first attempted to set out how and why *labour* appears inextricably bound up with Marx's notion of value, why the magnitude of value is measured by abstract labour-time, and why Marx argues that this magnitude *regulates and dominates* what he calls the 'ever fluctuating exchange-relations between the products'.

With this in mind, I then address the specific arguments made by the neo-Ricardians, as summarized by Ian Steedman, concerning the redundancy of values, their inconsistency with respect to prices, and the primacy of the latter over the former. In all cases I utilize the same algebraic formulations as they do, and within this framework I demonstrate that there are a host of issues and results that the neo-Ricardians remain unable to discover precisely because they remain so closely tied to the structure of orthodox economics. The concept of value, including the magnitude of value, illuminates the whole qualitative *and* quantitative analysis of price relations, uncovering relationships and causalities where the neo-Ricardians see merely discrepancies. It informs and orders the analysis, thereby demonstrating precisely its scientific power.

By the same token, the logical contradictions and inconsistencies in the neo-Ricardian analysis are thrown into sharp relief. For instance,

Steedman's own logic, if correct, would lead one to conclude that not only values and the value of rate of profit, *but also* prices of production and the uniform rate of profit, are *not* 'significant . . . in a capitalist economy'. But of course his logic is not correct, and its correction reinstates both the latter and the former. It only goes to show that algebra is no substitute for logic.

I wish to end on a different note, however. It seems to me that whatever their shortcomings, the neo-Ricardians squarely face the question of the relation between the magnitude and form of value. The complexity of the relation, as well as the weakness of their own conceptual structure, misleads them into concluding that the two magnitudes are irreconcilable. Nevertheless, at least they face the issue and conclude openly that the magnitude of value must be excised from Marxist analysis.

How much easier it is to 'save' Marx by simply denying that the problem exists at all! This has the great virtue of being able to criticize the evident conceptual weaknesses of the neo-Ricardians without the difficulty of having to address the problems they raise. Nonetheless, the effect is the same in the end, because here too the magnitude of value is excised from Marx, only by denying its existence altogether.

The paper 'Real Abstractions and Anomalous Assumptions', by Himmelweit and Mohun, provides a good illustration of this approach. First and foremost, they fully accept the neo-Ricardian argument on the redundancy and inconsistency of the concept of value, an argument they concede is 'well-founded' as long as value is conceived of as 'embodied labour'. *Thus they completely capitulate to the neo-Ricardian onslaught.*

Well, if one comes this far and yet wishes to retain the concept of value, then only one avenue is left open: to redefine value itself. And this forms the second principal axis of their argument. Value, they claim, is abstract *socially* necessary labour-time, and '*social* labour-time is validated only in exchange in the market'. Since that is so, value can have no magnitude other than price itself, because it comes into existence only when 'commodities are actually exchanged in the market'.

Naturally, if value *is* price, surplus-value *is* profit, and there can be no question of any discrepancy between the two realms. Marx, they note, does not seem to fully understand this implication of his theory of value (!), and continues to make mistaken 'allusions' to value and surplus-value as if they exist independently of their form.

Aside from their evident haste to escape the conclusions of the neo-Ricardians, their denial of the powerful distinction between value and realized value rests, it seems to me, on their failure to recognize two crucial points of Marx, concerning abstract labour and socially necessary labour.

First, there is Marx's distinction between use-values produced for direct use and converted into commodities only when exchanged, and use-values produced for exchange and hence produced as commodities. Their argument applies only to the first case, and hence to non-commodity production only! We discussed the significance of this point in section 2 above.

Allied with this is the second point: the distinction between the two types of socially necessary labour-time. In conjunction with the first point, this gives rise to precisely the issue that Himmelweit and Mohun evade: the difference between value and realized value, and the question of their inter-relationship.

For instance, suppose we consider a given product produced under given conditions but nonetheless sold under varying sets of relative prices (this is basically the problem of the effects of price-value deviations, which we analysed earlier). We are therefore holding all production conditions, the real wage, etc., constant, and varying only the conditions of circulation. Then, as we know, the magnitude of the money profit will vary even when the sum of prices is held constant. Are we now to say that the mass of surplus-value gets bigger or smaller as relative prices, and *nothing else*, vary? If surplus-value *is* profit, then we cannot speak of any transfers of value to account for this, and must conclude that relative price variations alone can create or destroy surplus-value.

Worse yet, consider a crisis in which so little of the social product is sold that profit is actually negative (this is a recurrent real phenomenon in capitalism). Are we then to say that even though workers were exploited and a surplus product produced, surplus-value is itself negative? If we are not allowed recourse to the distinction between value produced and value realized, then of course surplus-value is no longer connected to any rate of exploitation at all. It is merely an epiphenomenon of circulation. And so what begins as a tactical capitulation to the neo-Ricardians turns into a rout.

Printed in the United States
By Bookmasters

Printed in the United States
by Baker & Taylor Publisher Services